Father Nugent

SPIRITUAL REFLECTIONS IN HONOR OF GOD THE FATHER

May the Holy Spirit
Inspire you!
Annette Darling

SPIRITUAL REFLECTIONS IN HONOR OF GOD THE FATHER

By
Rev. Msgr. Richard T. Nugent

Illustrated by
Annette T. Darling

St. Bernadette R.C. Church
Orchard Park, New York

Published in the United States by St. Bernadette R.C. Church.

ISBN # 1-932433-10-4

Cover painting: "Eternal Father" created in 1741 at the request of Mother d'Youville, foundress of the Sisters of Charity aka the Grey Nuns. The painting was saved from a fire in 1765. Formerly kept at the Mother House of the Grey Nuns at 1150 Guy St., Montreal, it was recently moved back to its original location at Maison de Mère d'Youville, 138 St. Pierre Street, Montreal.

Inquiries may be directed to:

St. Bernadette R.C. Church
5930 S. Abbott Rd.
Orchard Park, NY 14127 USA
Phone (716) 649-3090
Fax (716) 649-0211
www.stbernadetteopny.org

ACKNOWLEDGEMENTS

The author would like to thank the following people, without whom this book would not have been possible: Anne Downey and Dawn Curazzato, who assisted with editing the book; Annette Darling, who gave generously of her time and talents in creating the drawings for the book; Lynda Rzeszutek, Phil Huber, Kathy Wabick, Matthew Tremblay and all the others at St. Bernadette who helped to prepare and promote the book; the Sisters of Charity of Montreal aka the Grey Nuns, who gave permission to use the painting of God the Father on the book cover; and Phil Nanzetta at Signature Book Printing, who made the self-publishing experience a joyful process.

DEDICATION

I dedicate this collection to my parents, John and Dorette Nugent, who brought me into this world, and I consecrate it to our Heavenly Father, who allowed them – and who allows all of us – to become the persons He desires and loves.

Father Nugent

"And I will ask the Father, and he will give you another Advocate to be with you always, the Spirit of truth…." (John 14:16-17)

"Whoever loves me will keep my word, and my Father will love him, and we will come to him and make our dwelling with him." (John 14:23)

Table of Contents

PREFACE

As I dedicate all my thoughts and words to God, Our Father, I reflect on the unusual and prophetic way that Our Father uses to reach our minds, our understanding and eventually our hearts. He begins with His Son, Jesus, the center of His universe, who is God's eternal Word and then, with His Holy Spirit, communicates His Word to a receptive human mind and heart. With God's grace, His Word is then translated in various forms and languages to God's human family. Although God could communicate directly with us, He chooses to use us – and that is the miracle of God's grace.

Father Nugent

FOREWORD

What is a pastor? He is a spiritual advisor, a father figure, a leader in the community and in the church, and a man who walks in the footsteps of Christ. Matthew 18:12 says "If a man has a hundred sheep and one of them goes astray, will he not leave the ninety-nine in the hills and go in search of the stray?" It is the duty of a pastor to be a good shepherd to his flock. This challenging position is fueled by the two greatest commandments, love of God and neighbor. It is this love that is the driving force behind all the duties and requirements of his vocation.

In Monsignor Richard Nugent, we find a man who is a pastor among pastors. Ordained in 1949, he has faithfully served at St. Bernadette's Parish in Orchard Park, New York since 1974. Throughout the years, Msgr. Nugent has been actively involved in all the dynamics of parish life. In recognition of his outstanding dedication, humility, wisdom and love, Msgr. Nugent was the recipient of the Curé of Ars award bestowed by Christ the King Seminary in 2000.

This book, Spiritual Reflections in Honor of God the Father, is a compilation of Msgr. Nugent's columns – entitled 'Pastor's Corner' – that appeared in the St. Bernadette weekly bulletin over a number of years. The columns touch on a wide array of Catholic topics. They are the gentle call of a shepherd to his sheep. We are reminded of what it means to be Catholic. There are reflections on the Sacraments, Church Tradition, Jesus and Mary, the mother of God. Interwoven in each commentary is the enlightenment and guidance of the Holy Spirit. Msgr. Nugent leads us down the narrow path with strength and simplicity, bringing clarity to topics that are sometimes shrouded with confusion in today's world. If it is truth you seek, you will find it in these pages!

Greatness is not defined by a title, or by how many friends we have, or even by how much we are loved by others. It is defined by our ability to love others as Jesus loves us. It is a call to action, reaching out to others in need and persevering in all the trials put on our path. It is conforming – not to the ways of the world – but to the will of God. It is trusting in Jesus and saying "I believe and I try!" That is what matters to

God - not that we succeed, but that we try. We must always strive to achieve perfection, knowing full well we will never attain it, but we do it anyway for love of Him. That is the life of a saint, one we are all called to live. A saint does God's work while still here on earth. A pastor does this with compassion, humility, and obedience, only seeking the divine promise of eternal life. He will leave the flock to help the sick, dying, poor, and suffering. As Christians we are called to console the suffering, but many clergy and lay people run from it because they are too busy. Being too busy is the greatest cancer of our times and the greatest cause of the sins of omission. Sadly, many people leave the church when they are ignored or poorly treated during their sufferings. Many do not know what they are walking away from.

Several years ago my grandchild was born with multiple handicaps and I was led to Msgr. Nugent, who became my comforter, consoler, confessor and spiritual advisor. I was lost and teetering. I was suffering and felt abandoned. He pulled me out of the throes of suffering and put me into the light of Christ. His words were warm and simple and I will never forget them because I felt my burden lighten immediately when he said, "You are always welcome here, and I will pray for your grandchild and your family." He was sincere, always returned calls and made time for me. He led not only with words but by his good example, which brought me into a greater fullness of my faith. Perhaps the reward of this faith was the miraculous healing of little Katelin through the 'Good Shepherd,' Jesus Christ.

Who will God say is the greater priest if not the one who ministers to the least of his brothers and sisters? The Church is in crisis and the responsibilities of a pastor are many. Sometimes this takes him away from the very people who need him most. With prayer and patience this problem will find resolution. The best place to take our petitions is adoration before the Blessed Sacrament. Prayers are answered when said with faith and trust in Jesus.

May these Spiritual Reflections of Msgr. Nugent help you to learn your faith, love your faith and live your faith!

Dawn Curazzato
Author of Memoir of a Miracle

THE APOSTLES' CREED

I believe in God, the Father Almighty, Creator of heaven and earth; and in Jesus Christ, His only Son, our Lord; Who was conceived by the Holy Spirit, born of the Virgin Mary, suffered under Pontius Pilate, was crucified, died, and was buried. He descended into hell; the third day He arose again from the dead. He ascended into heaven, and sits at the right hand of God, the Father Almighty; from thence He shall come to judge the living and the dead. I believe in the Holy Spirit, the Holy Catholic Church, the communion of Saints, the forgiveness of sins, the resurrection of the body and life everlasting. Amen.

I believe in God

God Is Everywhere

In the movie *Oh, God!* John Denver played the role of an employee in the produce department of a supermarket. When "God," played by George Burns, sent him a note in a head of lettuce to meet Him, John believed that someone was playing a joke on him. Yet the real God does reach out to us in normal happenings. Most of us ignore God's approach to us because we think that God is too busy and important to approach in an ordinary way.

Most of us have not the faith to believe that God sends His angels and saints to us in all kinds of normal circumstances. Occasionally God sends His Son and His Mother to assist us – even though we fail to recognize them. Only when we begin to develop a habit and pattern of prayer to God will we begin to recognize His presence.

Brother Lawrence, a baker in his religious community, developed the "practice of the Presence of God," so that at any time of his waking hours, Brother Lawrence consciously spoke to God and listened to His response. There was no place in or outside the monastery that Brother Lawrence did not communicate with God. We should try it in our homes and at our workplace.

God is everywhere. If we listen and observe with the ears and eyes of faith, we might be surprised how God approaches us – even in a supermarket. You never know.

Luncheon with Jesus

The bread came from the fields of wheat; the fish came from the sea. Together it was the perfect menu for a luncheon on the hillside with Jesus. Jesus took the five loaves and the two fish, and looking up to heaven, said the blessing, broke them, and gave the food to the disciples to set before the multitude. All ate and were filled. (Luke 9:16-17)

Jesus multiplied the bread and fish and fed 5,000 families to satisfy their physical hunger and also to prepare them for the Eucharistic bread and wine of the Last Supper, by which He would also feed their souls one year later.

When Cardinal Karol Woytyla was visiting Buffalo in 1976, many of the priests were invited to a lunch in his honor. Those who did not go missed the opportunity of having lunch with the future Pope. He was elected Pope in 1978.

But each day we are all invited to the Eucharistic meal with Jesus at daily Mass. What a great privilege our Catholic people have – to be in the presence of Jesus every day and to receive Him into our body and into our hearts. Even the angels envy us, since we eat His Body and drink His Blood – something they cannot do.

In the United States we are free to participate in daily Mass – an event not available to others as in China, Cuba and many African and South American countries where freedom of religion is not observed. Yet most American Catholics do not appreciate and take advantage of their freedom to attend daily Mass. In most Catholic parishes, daily Mass is the practice of a very few faithful.

With the growing decline of our priests through death and retirement, the advantage of daily Mass will also decline. It is already happening in many parishes that have lost their pastors. People depend on Eucharistic ministers for their administration and for a short prayer service in the morning. Maybe it is God's way of responding to our own lack of faith or interest in the Eucharist. We need to respond better to the Lord.

Teach Us to Pray

Before we can pray, we have to believe that we are talking to someone outside of ourselves. We have to believe in God; otherwise we are talking to ourselves. Perhaps people do not pray because they do not really believe in God.

If we truly believe and still do not pray daily, then we are rude and offensive and do not deserve to know of God's existence. We deserve to be ignored and punished by God. We are like children who are blessed with wonderful parents and who choose to ignore them and even deny them attention and care.

Yet many Catholics choose to ignore and even deny God's presence by their disregard for prayer and absence from His sacrificial Eucharist. They fail to know the history of God's relationship with His people through the ages. They visit the Dead Sea in the Holy Land and fail to appreciate that this was once the site of the vibrant cities of Sodom and Gomorrah – cities that chose, by their actions, to ignore God and His commandments. In time God destroyed them through fire and salt. He had sent His angels as a last resort, but they were ignored.

Again, later, after God saved His people from the slavery of Egypt and fed them with quail and manna in the desert, they chose to turn away from Him. In response, God turned them back from the Promised Land and they wandered forty years in the desert. Not one ever entered the land promised by God to Moses.

We are living in the presence of the same God, but now we have His Son, Jesus, to help us attain our heavenly reward. But unless we learn to pray and communicate daily and live in harmony with His Gospel, we will be no better than the people of Sodom and Gomorrah or the people led by Moses in the desert.

The choice is ours. Our Lord invites us – He does not compel us. If we choose to ignore or even deny Him, He will do the same, eventually. Lord, teach us to pray.

Faith

Perhaps the saddest words spoken by Our Lord were concerning His return to earth: "But when the Son of Man comes, will he find faith on earth?" (Luke 18:8)

As Catholic people we learn that at the time of our baptism by water, we receive the gifts of faith, hope and charity. These are divine powers or virtues given freely to us to live our earthly lives in harmony with God. Literally, God raises us up to His supernatural level so that we are able to know, love and serve Him in this life. Yet these gifts need the daily nourishment of prayer to God. Otherwise, like any living creation without sunshine and water, they diminish and die. More than a few Catholics who stopped their regular prayer life have lost their faith and soon turned away from the Church and God.

I remember an elderly woman from France who left her prayer life and Catholic faith when she was nineteen years old. Mary traveled to America where she became the leader of Masonry in her neighborhood. A Catholic priest befriended her in her old age and invited her to return to her former practice of prayer. She returned, received the Sacrament of Confirmation and shortly afterwards suffered a stroke and died.

God our Merciful Father always invites us to be faithful – but some refuse His invitation. They are too caught up with the world around them. And then they die, leaving the world behind.

Over the past five hundred years, God has sent His Mother, Mary, to earth to invite all of us to return to Her Son, Jesus – beginning in Mexico with Our Lady of Guadalupe, to Lourdes, France and Fatima, Portugal, and on to Akita, Japan. Mary has come to remind us of God's Divine Love for everyone on earth and to invite us to return to God in prayer and penance. Mary promises that God will bring His peace to the world if enough of His children return in prayer to Him. It's a wonderful promise, but it depends on us.

You Are My Beloved

In most Catholic families, children learn their first prayer by signing their forehead, chest and shoulders with the fingers of their right hand with the words: "In the name of the Father and of the Son and of the Holy Spirit" – thus acknowledging the two greatest teachings of our Catholic faith – the Blessed Trinity and the Incarnation of Jesus. Whoever in the history of mankind could have imagined or conceived the notion and belief that Almighty God is three Divine Persons – Father, Son and Holy Spirit – and yet one God, possessing one divine nature? Yet at the baptism of Jesus, God revealed Himself as God the Father – "You are my beloved Son; with you I am well pleased." – and also as God the Holy Spirit – "[A]nd the holy Spirit descended upon him in bodily form like a dove." (Luke 3:22) All through the centuries since that time, the great theological minds such as St. Thomas Aquinas and his confreres have sought to comprehend and explain in words this great truth of God's inner divine life but eventually conclude: "It is a mystery."

Likewise, the great minds of the Catholic faith through the centuries have tried to fathom and explain the mystery of God as Son taking on the nature of man in the womb of His earthly mother, Mary. The Word became human and took up His dwelling among us. (John 1:14) Yet these two great mysteries of our faith, the Holy Trinity and the Incarnation, are expressed in faith by the smallest child with the sign of the cross.

The angels of heaven looking on from their place with God must be astonished at the simplicity which expresses mysteries of faith that even they do not comprehend.

How important to our spiritual growth and development and to that of our children that we approach this expression and sign of our faith with reverence and awe. We are marked with the sign of the cross by our priest, parents and godparents at our baptism, and we should be reminded that we are dedicated in a special way to the Father, Son and Holy Spirit.

The Deaf and the Mute

Jesus ministered daily to those who were brought to Him. On one occasion, the people brought to Jesus a deaf man who had a speech impediment. Jesus took him aside and put His fingers into the man's ears. He spat and touched the man's tongue and, looking up to heaven, said to him, "Be opened!" (Mark 7:34) Immediately the man's ears were opened, his speech impediment disappeared and he spoke clearly.

We as people are impressed with the physical miracles as were the people of Christ's time. The Lord, however, is more gratified with the spiritual miracles of our return to faith and belief. Many times during His public life, the scribes and Pharisees, the legal authorities, were blind and deaf to His merits and miracles. On one occasion Jesus chastised the scribes and Pharisees: "Woe to you, blind guides, who say, 'If one swears by the temple, it means nothing, but if one swears by the gold of the temple, one is obligated.' Blind fools…." (Matt. 23:16-17)

With our faith we see God; with our trust in Him we hear God and do His Divine Will. All God needs of us is our willing heart and our trusting will. "Here I am…send me!" (Is. 6:8) We need to respond.

Letter to God

Dear God,

I have a problem. Why are so many people afraid of you and why are they afraid to use your real name "God"? Many people, especially weathermen and women call you by the name "Mother Nature." Is this because they do not know or realize that you created and now control the movements of the earth and everything within it, especially the sunshine, rain and snow? "Mother Nature" gets all the credit for the nice days and blame for the bad days. Maybe, if they were to discover and pray to you, there would be more nice days than bad.

A lot of people who are referred to as "liberals" seem very afraid that you are being invited by some of our leaders into the secular and public schools. Maybe they think your presence will have a bad influence on the students who might even say a prayer or two somewhere in their secular schools. Maybe they think that people who do not believe you exist will somehow be offended. Maybe they think that these people might be influenced to pray also – and even with their children.

The liberal people seem to dislike those who are called conservative because conservatives seem to obey the Ten Commandments, which you gave to Moses a long time ago. Conservative people do not agree with the liberals that it is all right to kill the unborn child in a mother's womb, and also when the child is almost out of the mother's womb. The abortion doctor kills the almost-born child with his instruments. Liberals believe that all kinds of abortion are okay. Maybe they would realize how very offensive all abortions are to you and that everyone will have to answer to you someday soon.

God, you are so patient with all of us. It is a wonder that you remain so silent. Or maybe the earthquakes, tornadoes and forest fires are your way to wake up your people before it is too late to come back to you and begin living according to your commandments and laws. Please help us to become a good people again.

Signed,
Your many friends

Lip Service

In the Old Testament, the prophet Isaiah speaks of the downfall of the city of Jerusalem because the people draw near to God with words only, honoring Him with their lips alone, while their hearts are far from the Lord. (Is. 29:13)

In the gospel of St. Mark, Jesus reminds the Pharisees and scribes, the legal representatives of his day, that they are like the Jews of old who pay no attention to God's commandments but hold fast to human tradition. In effect, these people give lip service to God's laws while promoting the human traditions of washing hands before meals and the purification of dishes. (Mark 7:4) Jesus teaches them that nothing entering a person from outside can defile the person. (Mark 7:15) He says, "But what comes out of a person, that is what defiles. From within people, from their hearts, come evil thoughts, unchastity, theft, murder, adultery, greed, malice, deceit, licentiousness, envy, blasphemy, arrogance, folly." (Mark 7:20-22)

Today, our media – through television and computers, which are in almost every home in the country – promote and encourage a culture contrary to God's commandments and Christian virtue. Pornography and impurity are rampant in the computer world; abortion of the unborn infants is practiced and condoned through the millions of deaths of the innocents; the sacred and the holy are mocked in the modern movies and plays. Through all this sinfulness, God and His commandments are ridiculed in what passes as art form.

What can our Catholic faithful do in response to our worldwide crisis of faith in God? We can offer daily prayer, especially the prayers of the rosary – in honor of Jesus and Mary – to the Father in reparation for a sinful world and country. Like the city of Nineveh, which God was going to destroy for its great sinfulness, we can offer penance, even little penances of food and drink to God that He will spare our world and country from devastating punishment. We can offer daily and certainly weekly Mass to the Father that He will bless our world and country with peace. Our Father wants our clean hearts, not merely our lips, to praise and thank Him for His many gifts to us, especially His great gift of His son, Jesus, in the Eucharist. Otherwise, we can look forward only to severe divine punishment, maybe in our own lifetime. It is never too late to pray and do penance, but we should not delay too long!

Now I Can See

Some people will debate whether the condition of physical blindness is a more difficult handicap than total deafness, until they meet those who are both blind and deaf. For years, the Sisters of St. Joseph taught at St. Mary's School for the Deaf in Buffalo, New York. One young man was blind, deaf and physically impaired in body, but through the guidance and assistance of the school, was able to operate his own audio business.

Our Lord met a man blind from birth and told him to wash in the pool of Siloam. The man went and washed, and came back cured. (John 9:7) The man's blindness was physical, and hence was an easy miracle for Jesus to perform. But the Pharisees who questioned the man later about his cure possessed a different kind of blindness – a spiritual kind. Jesus said to the man who could not see, "I came into this world for judgment, so that those who do not see might see, and those who do see might become blind." (John 9:39) When the Pharisees challenged Jesus, He replied, "If you were blind, you would have no sin; but now you are saying, 'We see,' so your sin remains." (John 9:41)

Unfortunately, Jesus was unable to cure the spiritual blindness of the Pharisees, since they stubbornly clung to their prejudice and pride. They refused, like many in the world today, to open their hearts to the truths of Jesus Christ. So Jesus continues to stand at the door of their hearts and knock, waiting to be invited in. But their hearts remain closed in spiritual blindness to the truth.

Occasionally it happens that with God's grace some will open the door of their hearts to God and return to the light. If enough people will pray for those persons, they do return – thanks to God's grace. But some die in their pride and sinfulness.

Our world today yearns for peace, but most people do not look in the right direction. Instead of looking to God, they depend on their world of science and technology to bring peace. But it doesn't happen. Real peace of mind and body can be found only in God. Hopefully, people will discover that truth before it is too late. As St. Augustine, a convert to Christianity, once wrote, "Our heart is restless until it rests in you, O Lord." (Confess. Bk 1, 5)

Seeing Is Believing

Although Almighty God, Our Father, gifts each of His creatures with many gifts at birth – the least of which may be the ability to see the beautiful world we live in, the world of trees, flowers, lakes, sky, and people – we often take our gifts for granted and forget the God who gave us our bodily and spiritual gifts. Then we meet someone who was deprived at birth, like the man in the gospel who was born blind. (John 9) The Apostles immediately assume this condition of blindness is due to some sin in the family – even the man's own sin. But Jesus reminds them: "Neither he nor his parents sinned; it is so that the works of God might be made visible through him." (John 9:3)

Sometimes we only begin to appreciate this beautiful gift of physical sight when in our senior years of life we need glasses to see or when our eyes no longer can see to read or drive a car. Then we need to depend on others.

Faith is the spiritual gift of seeing with our soul the beautiful spiritual gifts of God which surround us, and living that gift of faith in daily prayer to God and in love for Him and for all He has created in His world. The Pharisees – the legal people of Christ's day – could see with their eyes, but they were blind to the works of Jesus. They had no faith in Him.

Today, physically well Catholics who say "We believe" but do not come regularly to Sunday Mass remain in their sins, like the Pharisees. Seeing is believing, and believing is living our Catholic faith.

Judas

It was at a dinner prepared for Jesus by Martha and Mary six days before Passover that Judas Iscariot showed his true appreciation – or lack of it – for his Master, Jesus. After Mary anointed the feet of Jesus with a liter of costly perfumed oil, Judas Iscariot questioned why the oil should not have been sold for 300 days' wages and given to the poor. He said this not out of concern for the poor but because he held the money bag and was a thief. Jesus said, "You always have the poor with you, but you do not always have me." (John 12:8) Judas departed and went to the chief priests to hand Jesus over to them. (Mark 14:10)

It is interesting to observe how history repeats itself in our modern society among some who echo Judas' thoughts and words. On more than a few occasions in building a church or chapel to honor God, the words are spoken, "Why not give the money to the poor rather than waste it on a church building or sacred vessel?" Probably the persons saying this are more concerned with their own pocketbook. Like Judas with his thirty pieces of silver, these righteous people will go to their eternity trying to hold on to their bags of money.

As we look back on the glories of the Church over the centuries, we find the magnificent cathedrals built on the faith of millions of ordinary Catholics, who wished to offer special praise and worship to God. It was God who merited the very best facilities of praise and worship – since everything we possess comes from Him and returns to Him eventually.

Judas lasted only a few years of life, and now is forgotten – except for his evil deeds of betrayal. We have only a few years to prove our generosity and love of God. Then we pass on into eternity to be remembered only for our few kindnesses and generosities. Hopefully, we will have a few.

An Invitation

One day the followers of Jesus complained to Him that there were some people not of their convictions who were casting out devils. Our Lord directed His followers to leave them alone. He said, "For whoever is not against us is for us." (Mark 9:40)

Today in the world there are many God-fearing people who live holy lives even though they do not follow the Catholic faith. Although they may not have the fullness of Christ's teaching, they love God and live according to their knowledge of Jesus. God not only appreciates the graces of their life but likewise blesses them for their faith and love.

It is important that pastors of souls reach out and invite those who come from a Protestant or Jewish lineage in the hope that a future interest in the Catholic faith be nurtured and encouraged. It is even more desirable that we encourage our priests to be open to all who inquire about our Catholic faith and never to refuse anyone who is open to ask. To the priests of the Old Testament, God warned the shepherds of Israel to strengthen the weak, heal the sick and bind up the injured. Otherwise, God said to the shepherds, "I myself will look after and tend my sheep." (Ezek. 34:11) The priests of Jesus Christ likewise are ordained to pasture Christ's sheep.

We can all help our pastors of souls by inviting the interested, the doubtful and the needy to come to know God's Word and His Divine Will as taught by our shepherds of souls, the Catholic priests.

More than one convert to the Catholic faith has confided that until now he or she had never been invited. You never know.

Conversion

When the zealous Jewish leaders stoned the new deacon, Stephen, for his faith in Jesus Christ, a young Jewish observer of the Mosaic Law named Saul was holding Stephen's garments and was assenting to the stoning death. Years later, the same Saul, a Jewish general with his army, on his way to imprison these new Christians, was blinded by a strange light and heard a voice speak to him. "Saul, Saul, why are you persecuting me?" (Acts 9:4) Saul said, "Who are you, sir?" (Acts 9:5) The reply came: "I am Jesus, whom you are persecuting." (Acts 9:5) Blind, Saul was taken to Damascus. Meanwhile, the Lord commanded a disciple, Ananias, to lay hands on Saul, who then recovered his sight and was baptized. Saul, now newly named Paul, became the great apostle to the Gentiles, the non-Jewish world.

Today, in our Catholic parishes, we welcome the "Sauls" in our world to see and embrace the light of Christ's faith and turn away from their former ways. This religious conversion takes place in a parish program called the "R.C.I.A." or the Rite of Christian Initiation for

Adults. The baptized and non-baptized who attend the instructions faithfully are welcome to become members of the parish at Easter time, if they wish and choose to do so.

St. Paul's conversion to the Catholic faith was perhaps more dramatic, given the circumstances of his time, but today's conversions are no less important. Our Lord shows no favorites. We need to understand that the same Lord who called Paul to the faith years ago continues to call many more people today to embrace His Catholic faith. Many need only an invitation from their Catholic neighbor – "Have you ever considered the Catholic faith?"

Does God Suffer?

Some parents in reflection on their children may say: "When they are young, they break our backs; and when they are older, they break our hearts." Certainly, this would not be true of all children, but it is a sad commentary even if it includes a small number.

In relation to God and His children, is it possible that as we grow older we are capable of breaking His Heart – the Sacred Heart of His Son and Immaculate Heart of His Mother? Is it possible that God, who rejoices in us when we are good and obedient to His commandments, likewise suffers in us when we are sinful and disobedient? Certainly God, who is Divine Spirit, is unable to suffer physically, but human parents suffer the pangs and anxieties of their children who reject them and choose a sinful lifestyle. Why cannot God, our eternal Father and Parent, suffer the pangs and anxieties of watching His children wander toward the fires of eternal hell through their sinful lifestyle? This remains a mystery of God. Abortion, pornography, greed, love of money, homosexual lifestyle, murder, stealing, etc. are all paths away from God and toward eternal damnation.

Since God has given us free will, He must respect our freedom to walk away from Him. In this refusal we disturb His eternal plan for us – as we disturb our human parents who love us. Only when we freely return to God in prayer, penance, sorrow and love do we bring Him joy and peace.

The Sacrament of Reconciliation provides us with the ability to return to God's love and is available to anybody that seeks it.

Strange Gods

When God dictated to Moses on Mount Sinai the first commandment – "I, the LORD, am your God…You shall not have other gods besides me." (Ex. 20:2-3) – Moses could not have foreseen the age of computer technology. False gods meant gold calves and numerous statuettes preserved in Jewish homes. But our false gods of money, worldly fame and material possessions that dominate our lives are now surpassed in every walk of life by our personal and business computers. While computers bring us convenience and efficiency in our schools and workplace, they also absorb our time and effort, leaving us with little time for our relations with our real God, our creator. Prayer and reverence to God are taking a back seat with many Christians and non-Christians today.

Sunday Mass and prayer services no longer occupy an important place in our busy lives. Yet many can find hours to spend on the Internet conversing with everyone all over the world. Is this today's "other gods" – in the mind of our Eternal God?

Recently the local TV newscast showed a man suffering from a disease who received into his arm a computer chip that would allow others to invade his body for medical reasons. The news commentator suggested this medical procedure may someday soon replace the use of credit cards – since the computer chip could not only be a medical tool but also a means for buying food and other necessities. Such an implanted computer chip could also be used by a government to control people in regard to their needs. We are already controlled in our Medicare and HMO prescriptions and medications at the pharmacies.

No one in his right mind should ever allow a computer chip to be implanted in his body, whether in the arms, hands or forehead – for whatever reason.

We may not always recognize the false gods of today, but they are there – daily in our lives, drawing our attention away from our One God by their constant presence and demand. Remember God's command from the beginning to have no other gods besides Him – strong words and wise advice.

Catholic Parents – Primary Educators

Since the development of Catholic schools in the U.S.A., Catholic parents have relied on them for the development of the Catholic faith in their children. Who is primarily responsible – the schools or the parents?

Catholic schools over the years, especially under the direction and teaching of the Religious Communities, have been very instrumental in the formation of the Catholic faith in their students. As a result, many Catholic parents have abdicated their primary duty to teach, by word and example, the Catholic religion to their children. Now that Catholic schools today are decreasing or are directed by the laity, parents necessarily are being made aware that, as parents, they must accept the primary care and responsibility for their children's faith and religious beliefs. No longer can Catholic parents shun their religious obligations to their families. Religious formation must begin in earliest years of childhood and continue throughout adolescence.

If Catholic parents do not provide the religious leadership for their children, Catholic schools cannot fill the void. They can assist, but Catholic parents must become the primary educators of their children.

Sign of Contradiction

Recently the Alabama Chief Justice was directed by a U.S. District Judge to remove a 5300 pound granite monument displaying the Ten Commandments from the State Building, since its presence violated the Constitution's ban on government promotion of religion. Can you imagine the uproar if the Justice had displayed a crucifix as well?

From His infancy to the day of His death on the cross, Jesus remained a sign of contradiction, as predicted by Simeon at the Temple:

"Behold, this child is destined for the fall and rise of many in Israel, and to be a sign that will be contradicted…." (Luke 2:34)

First, King Herod – fearing competition – tried to kill the newborn King of the Jews. Joseph and Mary were warned by an angel sent from God to flee with their infant son into Egypt. Later as an adult, Jesus was threatened with death by the scribes and Pharisees because He challenged their honesty and integrity. Finally, Herod's son teamed up with Pilate, the Roman governor, to successfully condemn Him to crucifixion because Jesus claimed to be God. Throughout His entire life, Jesus remained a sign of contradiction to the world – always in obedience to His Heavenly Father.

Our Catholic faith leads us along a similar path in life. From our infant baptism into the life of God, through our sacramental life – whether to marriage or priesthood – we are challenged by the Herods and Pilates of the world to follow their false teachings and practices of idolatry, artificial birth prevention, abortion, adultery, dishonesty, and impurities of every kind. The allurements of the earth are attractive but end up as a bag of wind. When we call upon the Lord in our need, He will always assist us. His presence in our life through prayer and the Eucharist will always make us stronger than our tempter. Jesus reminds us individually, "If you love me, you will keep my commandments." (John 14:15) He says, "This is how all will know that you are my disciples, if you have love for one another." (John 13:35)

It is one thing to say we love God and neighbor, and another thing to prove it by our actions. Actions always speak louder than words.

Evidence of a Catholic Home

When friends and others visit your home on occasion, is there any visible evidence that Catholic people live there? How about a large crucifix at the door or in the living room? Is the crucified Christ welcome in the home of a family he died for on the cross – opening for them for the first time since Adam the opportunity of a life in heaven forever? Maybe there is a picture of the Sacred Heart of Jesus or the Immaculate Heart of Mary or of the Holy Family of Nazareth somewhere on a wall.

Or are we ashamed or afraid to proclaim our friendship with them in that manner?

Our Lord reminds us very plainly: “Everyone who acknowledges me before others I will acknowledge before my heavenly Father.” (Matt. 10:32)

Our Catholic faith is a beautiful faith that deserves the attention of others who do not know or realize the treasure we Catholics possess. Our Lord desires that we proclaim our faith to everyone. Why not begin in our homes with the simple attraction of His crucifix or picture together with a blessed home? These externals of our Catholic faith will bring God’s blessing upon all who live in the home as well as all who visit there.

Let our home on earth reflect the heavenly home where all these externals of our Catholic faith will become a divine reality forever.

The Father Almighty

Feast of God the Father

During the last century, a petition was presented in Rome for the declaration of a special feast day for God the Father, but it was deemed inappropriate at the time. Now a new petition has been made in this century through the auspices of the Father of All Mankind Apostolate in Pittsburgh, Pennsylvania. Based on the dedication of the year 1999 to God the Father by Pope John Paul II and some private revelations from recent years, the Apostolate leadership has requested petitions from Catholic people and sent these petitions to Rome requesting the celebration of the first Sunday of August as a special feast of God the Father. What is amazing about this request is that it has to be made at all.

After years of Catholic worship, it would seem that the Church of the first few centuries should have declared a special annual day to honor God, Our Father and Creator. We seem to have a feast day for everyone else. St. Anthony, St. Jude and St. Francis have their special feast days together with novenas, holy hours and days of festivity. Where would we be without the feast of St. Patrick and St. Joseph, with the celebration of corn beef and cabbage and St. Joseph's table? Mary and her son, Jesus, are properly honored during the year. Pentecost Sunday belongs to God the Holy Spirit. But where is God the Father honored in a special way with days of prayer and a special feast day?

Is it too much to ask the Church – bishops, priests and religious men and women and all people of faith – to honor the Father of all Mankind in a special way? And while we honor the Father, how about doing His Will on earth? His Will is still waiting to be done and obeyed. God the Father is certainly very patient with us. Maybe some day He will be pleasantly surprised by His people.

God The Father Revealed

In 1932, as reported by Thomas Petrisko in his book *The Kingdom of Our Father*, an extraordinary but almost totally unknown event occurred in Italy that may some day be considered of unprecedented importance in the history of the Church and the world. A nun named Mother Elisabetta Eugenia Ravasio reported that the Eternal Father appeared to her in apparition on July 1, 1932 and again on August 12, 1932. Thirteen years later, the Church fully approved the visions as worthy of the faith.

On both occasions, God the Father revealed to Mother Ravasio His ardent desire to have a Feast of the Father of All Nations celebrated – together with a Mass and liturgical office on the first Sunday in August each year. Even though in 1935 a Church commission, after a lengthy survey, gave their approval, nothing was done to fulfill the Father's request. How poorly we treat our Eternal Father.

Perhaps it's a reflection of how we treat our earthly fathers. At one time, when television, computers and the Internet were still in the future, families had more time to enjoy each other around the dinner table and in the parlor, especially the presence of the father and mother. The father was the head of the house – to be respected and obeyed; the mother was the center of love – to be honored and loved. From such families came our present older priests and religious men and women. But our modern technology has drawn the family apart – leaving little time for the growth and enrichment of family life.

What may be said about our human family certainly reflects on our relationship with our Divine Family – Father, Son and Holy Spirit. It may well be that faithful Christian people over the centuries have turned to Jesus, Son of God, as well as the Holy Spirit. But God the Father continues to remain in the background of our spiritual life. Apart from the "Our Father" at Mass and in the rosary, we generally neglect our marvelous Father and Creator.

More recently in the mid-1990s, it has been reported that God the Father has maintained an ongoing relationship through locutions with a young Australian Catholic boy, Matthew Kelly, and an older grandmother in the U.S.A., Barbara Rose Centilli. In both cases, God the Father is reported as requesting a feast day of the "Father of All Nations" on the first Sunday in August, preceded by eight days (octave) of prayer. If this all proves to be accepted by the Church, is it not interesting that the Father is asking this favor in our time – a time that we as a nation and the world have turned our attention away from God towards the gods of technology and science? It will be interesting to see which side will win.

The Father's Will

Summer is a wonderful time for family celebration. The school year that begins again in September signals a return to study and work for young and old. So we need to appreciate the gift of family and friends during the summer months.

August is a special month which some Catholic people believe should be dedicated to honoring God our Father, since the month of June honors His Son and the Sacred Heart, and the months of May and October are directed toward the Immaculate Heart of Mary. Actually, the Church, since its beginning almost two thousand years ago, has yet to establish a special feast day or month in honor of God the Father. However, that should not dissuade individual Catholic members from offering their prayer of praise and appreciation for His daily grace and blessing upon all His children.

Like our human family, God the Father, Son and Holy Spirit is our eternal family – from the time of baptism onward. We need to acknowledge them as family. When we celebrate our life on earth, we need to realize that they celebrate with us – in fact, they are only "a heartbeat away."

Every day of His life, Jesus offered everything to His Father. From the temple in Jerusalem – "Did you not know that I must be in my Father's house?" (Luke 2:49) – to the cross – "Father, into your hands I commend my spirit" (Luke 23:46) – Jesus fulfilled His Father's Will. He did nothing apart from His Father. Jesus said to His disciples at the Last Supper, "[T]he world must know that I love the Father and that I do just as the Father has commanded me." (John 14:31)

We too are His sons and daughters, adopted at our baptism. How blessed our lives would become if like Jesus, His Divine Son, we would do the Father's Will on earth, as it will be done someday in heaven. Unfortunately, the Father's Will is yet to become the will of the many. Only a few fulfill His Will. Otherwise the world would change for the good. Abortion, pornography, adultery, murder and other acts of impurity would cease if the world fulfilled God the Father's Will. Maybe this will occur someday, but not without great punishment. Jesus reminds us: "How narrow the gate and constricted the road that leads to life. And those who find it are few." (Matt. 7:14) Do not delay any longer.

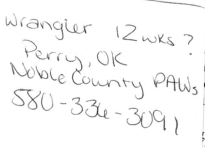

417-276-0280
Wagoner, OK

Wrangler 12 wks ?
Perry, OK
Noble County PAWS
580-336-3091

ou Pray, Say: "Father"

society which advocates same-sex marriages or ks with suspicion on permanent marriages that children, there is lost – at least for the moment of the faithful and loving Father of all, who is : think of our present pro-choice, pro-abortion noral responsibility or retribution?

ge that no longer respects and protects human forgiveness if we wish to avoid His strong arm . In Sodom and Gomorrah of Abraham's time, ded Abraham into Sodom, looking for only ten nsuccessful. So God destroyed the town and all 19:1-29)

gnore our Father in heaven, just as we are free to but there are always moral consequences from es. You may ask what are we to do to ward off begin by praying to Our Father daily, asking His merciful forgiveness for all who offend Him. We might invite our children to join us in prayer, since God is drawn to the innocence and goodness of children. On one occasion when His Apostles were trying to prevent some children from approaching, Jesus said: "Let the children come to me, and do not prevent them; for the kingdom of heaven belongs to such as these." (Matt. 19:14)

Also, we might write to our legislators, especially those who favor women's choice and abortion, to reconsider their legal but immoral position and become more open to life in all its stages from the womb to old age. Our Lady at Fatima in 1917 said to the three Portuguese children: "More souls go to hell for sins of the flesh than for any other reason." Killing the unborn in the womb of the mother certainly qualifies equally.

When Herod ordered the massacre of the infant boys in Bethlehem, he fulfilled the prophecy of Jeremiah concerning Rachel weeping for her children, since they were no more. (Matt. 2:18) It is sad that history repeats itself in our day. And we are all guilty. We are silent in the face of the ongoing and present massacre of our infants in the womb. It is a sad commentary on our culture and society. Pray constantly to our Father!

A Woman and a Well

Jesus Christ is our supreme teacher. By His example of friendship and love, Jesus encourages us to be open to others at all times. On one occasion, He meets a Samaritan woman drawing water at a well. He speaks to her, knowing fully that Jews did not speak to women, especially Samaritan women. Jesus invites her to do Him the favor of drawing water for Him. When she expresses surprise, Jesus invites her to ask Him for special water that will always quench her thirst – the water of eternal life. (John 4:10)

How many of our acts of kindness and love open the mind and heart of others to respond to our kindness? Sometimes a thoughtful telephone call to someone grieving or in need will open their hearts to respond in love. A visit to the sick or delivery of a hot dinner to a confined person sometimes triggers kindnesses within the family. I remember an elderly couple at a wedding celebration that had been away from church for nineteen years and returned upon receiving a blessed medal from a priest.

The woman at the well never thought that she would be the recipient of eternal life – simply by being open to a stranger who asked for a drink of water. But then Jesus reveals more to her. He reveals God, His Father, as worthy of adoration. "But the hour is coming, and is now here, when true worshipers will worship the Father in Spirit and truth; and indeed the Father seeks such people to worship him." (John 4:23) Pope John Paul II dedicated the year 1999 as "The Year of the Father." We are encouraged to love and honor the Father in a special way. For years we have worshipped His Son in the Eucharist and we have honored His Mother, Mary, in our prayer life. Now the Church invites us to pray the "Our Father," mindful that we promise to do His Will on earth as it is in heaven.

We do the Father's Will daily when we keep His commandments to adore Him and prefer Him to the strange gods of money, honors and worldly possessions. How many hours of attention do we give soap operas and sports on TV and then find an hour of prayer daily to the

Father too long? Let us find more time for God the Father in our daily life. He does not ask much of us – just the attention we should show to our loving Father. Then let us be mindful of the example of the Father's Son, Jesus, and extend to God's children the daily kindness of Christ.

The Holy Trinity

Many school teachers find their greatest enjoyment and challenge in the first grade or even in the kindergarten class. These young minds and hearts are always open to learn and eager to love. In Catholic school, the sign of the cross and the guardian angel prayer are memorized and said from the first days. When a priest, visiting first grade told them that if they never would commit a sin, they would go straight to heaven, one parent reported that her son came home to tell her that he intended never to commit any sin. Only time will tell. But the young are open to goodness – if parents will set the example.

The great mysteries and truths of our Catholic faith are readily accepted by our young children – even if they do not fully understand. Our greatest mystery, the Blessed Trinity – namely that God is one God but three Divine Persons: Father, Son and Holy Spirit – is learned and accepted by the young as they make the sign of the cross. Later in life, teachers and professors may put doubts in their head, but the truth is still there.

The scriptures speak often of God the Father – even from the early years of Jesus when His parents sought Him in the Temple, which He called His "Father's house." (Luke 2:49) Later, as an adult, Jesus said: "All things have been handed over to me by my Father." (Luke 10:22) God the Father is the object of everything that Jesus did on earth.

Likewise does the Father speak of Jesus as His Son. At the baptism of Jesus by John the Baptist, Jesus saw the Spirit of God descending upon Him like a dove, and He heard the voice of the Father proclaiming Him as His beloved Son. (Matt. 3:16-17)

Finally, after Jesus ascended into heaven, the Holy Spirit of the Father and the Son was sent upon the early Church on the day of Pentecost. (Acts 2:4)

We will meet the Father, Son and Holy Spirit in person as God someday. We need to take time each day now to become acquainted by reciting their blessing often – in the name of the Father, and of the Son, and of the Holy Spirit. Amen.

Show Us the Father

One day St. Philip the Apostle, whose feast day is May 3rd, challenged Jesus with the request to "show us the Father," to which Jesus responded: "Whoever has seen me has seen the Father." (John 14:9) Jesus continued, "Believe me that I am in the Father and the Father is in me…." (John 14:11) As Catholic people who profess faith in the Holy Trinity, sometimes we forget that God is Father, Son and Holy Spirit. Where One Divine Person is present, the other Two Divine Persons are also there. Consequently, when we visit Jesus in Perpetual Adoration of the Eucharist, we must realize that the Father and God the Holy Spirit are present with Jesus.

In the Old Testament before the birth of Jesus, God did not permit His chosen people, the Jews, to approach Him. Only Moses or the high priest was allowed. That is why it is remarkable and generous on God's part to allow His Catholic people, not only to approach Him in the sacrifice of Mass, but even to receive Him daily in Holy Communion.

It is difficult to appreciate and to understand why Catholic people refrain from coming to Mass often and receiving Him in the Sacrament of Holy Communion, unless they no longer believe. Then when they realize that God the Father and God the Holy Spirit are present with Him, it is an amazing event. It is only in heaven that we will understand this great mystery of the Eucharist to which we are invited daily. Meanwhile, despite our lack of faith and appreciation, God the Father continues to assist and support us daily. One day, however, in the near future, the world will acknowledge the Father and will do His Will on earth, as it is done in heaven. From the time of Jesus to the present day, the Father's Will has not been done on earth. When we all learn to do His Will, the world will receive a taste of "heaven on earth." We should look forward to that day.

The Father Waits for Us

When we as Catholics read the Bible regularly, even daily, we experience in our faith a growth much like a school child who begins in kindergarten and continues through high school and college and then graduates with a Ph.D. But unless we are faithful in study, we will remain in the area of third grade in our understanding of God and His relation to us. Many Catholics perhaps have never taken the time to open their minds and wills to God's Holy Word.

As Catholic people, we learn from the earliest years to practice our faith – from the Sign of the Cross to attendance at Mass, the sacraments and participation in religious studies in Catholic schools and religious education classes and events. Until we learn that God is Spirit who desires our love and devotion within our own spirit – our mind, will and memory – we remain always on the outward side of God's world, never allowing Him to visit us within. He remains for many Catholics an "Unknown Father" whom they have never met or have seldom spent any time with during this life on earth. As a result, this life remains a sad and joyless experience for some. Yet God our Father is waiting only for our invitation to Him to enter our hearts and be recognized.

God reveals Himself to us in the Bible from the first book of Genesis – through seventy-two writings – to the last book of Revelation, as a Father who loves each of us and desires that we return His love in prayer and service to Him. It does not seem to be a lot to ask of us.

God, Our True Father

There are some people in this world, young and old, who have never known the love of an earthly father – either because of death or abandonment. There are fathers who will never celebrate Father's Day because they have refused to accept and live the responsibility of fatherhood. This may also be true of some mothers who leave their children for others to support and raise. The worst scenario is when the father and mother permit the abortion or killing of their unborn son or daughter.

As a result of our U.S. culture of death, pleasure and freedom, many of our young people are left in a state of dejection, rejection and uncertainty. They lack the moral and spiritual roots of a loving family where they are truly loved. As a result, when they themselves accept the responsibility of life, they do not know where and when to start and are lost in their way to do what is right and moral in life.

But a true Father, God the Father, has always been with them – and us – from the beginning. From the time we left our Creator Father to the present moment, God our Father has been with all of us – protecting us from evil, encouraging us to do good, and repairing the damage of our sinfulness.

The major problem is not with Him but is with us. Like a parent that we take for granted, God our eternal parent and Father waits upon us to respond in love. We may say words in prayer, like "Our Father," but they remain only words – unless they come from our hearts. Too often we treat our Eternal Father as if He doesn't really exist or, at best, that He is someone who is too busy with His world and is not interested in what we have to say or do.

The truth is just the opposite. Not only is the Father interested, but like the Father of the Prodigal Son, Our Eternal Father will run to embrace us, if only we approach Him in sincere prayer. "While he was still a long way off, his father caught sight of him, and was filled with compassion. He ran to his son, embraced him and kissed him." (Luke 15:20) If an earthly father will respond in that fashion, how much more will our Heavenly Father respond to us. A pleasing response each day to our Eternal Father might be, "In praise and consecration, I love you Father, and I give myself to You." It will certainly get His attention.

The Father's Love

In recent years, parents who were frustrated in their efforts to train and educate their children in the ways of respect, obedience and cooperation within the family life, developed a program called "Tough Love." For years these parents had tried many things to contain and educate their children, but without success. So they banded together in this program that advocates severe measures to assist their children. This program might give the impression that the parents were acting without love, but it was the only way the children would respond. In some cases, parents would allow their children to be imprisoned for crimes committed so that the children would learn responsibility in jail.

Today in this world of sin and crime committed by His children, God may well have to adopt a program of "Tough Love" to gain a response from us of contrition from sin and conversion to His grace and life. For centuries, and especially in our twentieth century, He has sent His Son and His Mother to invite us to respond in prayer and conversion, from La Sallete, France in 1830, to Fatima in Portugal in 1917, and in hundreds of other places yet to be acknowledged. Despite His many invitations to prayer, goodness and holiness, His children continue to ignore His wishes with sins of murder, abortion, enslavement of youth, pornography, abuse of people's rights and many other sinful practices.

Is it not time for God our Father to begin to practice some form of "Tough Love," allowing His children to undergo punishment now – as He allowed His Divine Son, Jesus, to undergo the suffering of crucifixion for sin?

Maybe God needs to enter our conscience and show everyone our sinfulness so we will see ourselves spiritually as God sees us with all our faults, failings and sinfulness. Seeing the state of our soul and appreciating our final place in eternity, maybe God's children will respond. Maybe they will return to confession as in the past. Hopefully there will be enough priests available at that time. Better not to wait – but return now.

Obey the Father

Have you noticed in recent years in our media how little respect is given to our fathers in the family? Rodney Dangerfield is typical of the media in the TV world. We have allowed our TV and publications media to treat fathers with little concern and with minor importance. Perhaps the recent feminist movement, which emphasizes women's rights, has influenced our media, to the denigration of the father of the family. But we need to reemphasize the importance of fathers to our families and to society in general.

This same trend has been evidenced even in our Catholic faith. Perhaps, without intending to neglect God the Father, we have tended to concentrate our prayer life around Jesus, the Son of God. He assumed our human nature and lived among us for thirty-three years. His parents, Joseph and Mary, have been well known and loved by our Catholic people over the centuries. In recent years our devotional movements, like the Cursillo and Charismatic associations, have come to adopt the Holy Spirit as their source and center of prayer and worship.

Certainly no one should fault anyone or any devotional movement for their faithfulness to Jesus or to the Holy Spirit, for they are Divine Persons of God worthy of our adoration and prayer life. But when Jesus was on earth, He centered His prayer life and obedience around His Divine Father. He offered every prayer and deed to His Father.

If we are to follow Jesus, ought we not also obey the Father in heaven – a Father that we will live with for all eternity? What better way to prepare to meet Him someday in heaven than by consecrating ourselves to Him while we are on earth. We can begin by starting with our father on earth – in love, obedience and respect. If we learn to love our human father, it shouldn't be too hard to love and obey our Divine Father. Jesus sets the example for us. He was totally obedient to St. Joseph, His foster father on earth, and to his Father in heaven at the same time. "Follow me," Jesus invites us. He will help us.

Consecrate Yourself to the Father

Sometimes part of the reason that we do not know God, our loving Father, is due to our own poor relationship with our own earthly father. He may live in our homes but remains aloof or in the background of family life. How fortunate are those children whose father is daily present in their life. Unfortunately, daily demands that the world of business make on our father and mother draw them away from family life. It is no longer unusual in a family to have the father absent all week and the mother busy between her family and a full-time job. What child wants to go home to an empty house?

There was a time when mothers remained home with the children while the father worked during the day. Still there were evenings at mealtime and afterwards when the parents and children would enjoy their family life. Prayers at meals and at bedtime were a regular routine. Sometimes the family rosary was said immediately after supper. The father of the family was revered – though sometimes feared – if rowdiness took place too often. It was easier to relate to God as our father since we already experienced him in our own earthly father. If God is anything like our father, we learned to respect him. Never did we want to be called to task when we did wrong. So we tried not to do wrong. His commandments occupied a special place in our life. Our regular confession at church was a good reminder that we needed "to shape up or ship out." Most of us tried to "shape up" so as to please both of our fathers.

We ought to pray daily to God, our eternal Father: "For the greater glory of God and for the salvation of all, I consecrate myself to you, O Eternal Father, as one of your faithful. Behold, I come to do your Will."

Creator of Heaven and Earth

God Is Generous

If ever we were to doubt or deny the generosity of God, we need only look around at His creation. The abundance of flowers of every kind in every land, the oceans and lakes of fish and water, the multiple species of animals, vegetation and medicinal bushes and trees – all testify to the generosity of Almighty God. Who can doubt that we possess a generous God who provides abundantly for our material welfare? Then, when we become aware of the marvelous spiritual protection provided by God of millions of angel guardians, together with the daily food of His Eucharistic Body and Blood provided by His Son Jesus, and the prayer and intercession of Mary our Mother everyday, we must give thanks to God for this generous outpouring from heaven.

So how do we respond to all this generosity from God? If we are wise, we make this generous God the center of our lives, reflecting on Him daily and offering Him our prayers of praise, thanksgiving and contrition for sin.

How much does it take to recite the rosary as we drive along to work or the shopping center? Does an hour of adoration weekly in the chapel seem too difficult? When will we learn that a habit of unclean, vulgar or obscene language or behavior offends God very much? Even a person with a mouth of uncharitableness will live long in purgatory prior to entering heaven. Releasing our purse strings for those in need will please the heart of Jesus, just as He reached out to the poor in His day.

Seconds, minutes, hours and days pass very quickly. We should not lose a moment's opportunity to try to match God's generosity to us.

I Am

If you have read the Old Testament, you will recall that Moses spoke to God on the mountaintop and asked that God reveal His name so that Moses could tell the people. God said to Moses, "I am who am." Then He added, "This is what you shall tell the Israelites: I AM sent me to you." (Ex. 3:14) The Hebrew word for "I AM" is "Yahweh," but out of respect for the proper name of God "Adonai" – my Lord – is always substituted.

Recently at a televised AFC playoff game, there was a constant and continual commercial promoting a particular computer as "I Am." Individual people held up signs reading "I Am – super human," "I Am – intelligent," "I Am – all knowing." They were acknowledging a computer product. Whether consciously or not, the commercial was using the proper name of God to describe a computer. This, of course, is the sin of blasphemy – to substitute a false god in place of the only God, to attribute to a machine the power of Almighty God.

Yet upon further reflection, we have to be aware that our world has suddenly in the last twenty-five years turned almost 100% to computers in the business world, in our homes, and among our possessions. What food shopper can exit a supermarket without a computerized statement? How many students in school today require the use of a computer for their daily studies? How many laptop computers accompany the business world? We are people dependent on the almighty computer. The computer has taken over our daily lives and perhaps in some cases the place of Almighty God. As you watch the use of computers in the homes, do you wonder if regular prayer in the family has any chance? When we spend so many hours on computer games, does the family have equal time or any time for God? Very little activity of people today takes place without the almighty computers. The worldwide Internet is now available to our elderly and our very young. Even today our personal communication with each other is reduced to electronic mail. Our personal and private relationship with each other and even with God is exchanged for a creature-computer, something dependent on God's electrical power for its existence and operation. Yet the world has fallen in love with a computer and now allows the machine to dominate their life. When will we wake up to the reality of God and give Him equal time?

Let Us Sit with God

Let us imagine that we are sitting with God the Father watching over His world from the beginning.

First of all He had a bad beginning with His created angels – many of whom chose to follow Lucifer in his pride to hell forever. In His next try God did not fare any better with His creation of man – who, with all God's gifts, chose the way of disobedience and death. God in His mercy decided to give man a second chance. He chose the Jewish people to be His instrument of salvation under the leadership of Abraham, Isaac, Joseph and Moses. God made a covenant of faithfulness with the Jewish people, which they accepted. But in time they broke their covenant with God.

So God the Father turned toward His Son, as He promised when He spoke to the serpent in the garden of Eden, telling the serpent that He would put enmity between the serpent and the woman, and between their offspring. (Gen. 3:15) The woman's offspring is Jesus, the Son of the Father. God the Father made a new covenant in the bloody crucifixion of His Divine Son, Jesus, who offered Himself on the cross for the sins of all people.

God's people now are all who accept Him in the name of His Son and live their lives according to His Divine Will. Jesus teaches us to pray that God's Will be done on earth. So now we look down and observe with God's eyes the new people of God – everyone! Hence the word "Catholic," which means universal.

In the midst of great suffering at the beginning, St. Helena encouraged her emperor-son, Constantine, to accept Jesus and His teachings, and consequently the entire Roman world came to accept the Catholic faith.

Things continued pretty well until the 12th century when a Patriarch Bishop of the Eastern world disagreed with the Pope and, as a result, left the faith to begin the Orthodox Church. Most people of the East followed the direction of the Patriarch. To this day the Orthodox Church refuses to recognize the Pope as their spiritual leader.

Then in the 16th century a Catholic priest, Martin Luther, had disagreements with the Church and left it to found the Lutheran Church. Others followed Luther, including King Henry VIII, who started the English or Anglican Church.

As the Europeans followed Christopher Columbus to America, they brought their various Protesting Faiths with them. These eventually broke into many Protestant denominations that make up a great portion of religious belief in America.

Today God the Father looks down and sees His world split up into many faiths that disagree with the faith His Son, Jesus, communicated to the Apostles and disciples almost 2000 years ago. Certainly Lucifer was greatly responsible for the disarray of religious denominations, but man has to take some of the blame. We have not kept the covenant, made with God, through His Son, Jesus. We have shelved the Ten Commandments as outmoded and useless. We have brutally offended God in our total disregard today of His fifth commandment – "Thou shall not kill" – not only in wars but with our abortions, pornography and abuse of each other.

As we sit with God, we wonder when God the Father will justly say, "Enough," and take direct action to correct His world of broken promises.

The rebellious Jewish people, led by Moses, turned away from their Promised Land to spend 40 years of wandering. None of them, only their children and grandchildren, entered the Promised Land.

How many of God's people will enter the Promised Land of heaven? God is always ready to forgive, but how many will give up their sinfulness, pride, lust and greed? Time will tell. We should not wait too long. It must be interesting to see as God sees all things and people.

Do Not Be Afraid

Some people are afraid of the dark and seldom go outdoors after sunset. Those who do venture out after dark appreciate the roads and places that are well lit.

In the dark and windy sea, the boat of the Apostles was tossed about by the waves until Jesus came, walking on the sea, and entered their boat. Then the wind died down and Jesus said to them, "Take courage, it is I; do not be afraid." (Matt. 14:27) Who could be afraid anywhere, if we have the constant presence of the Son of God?

Unfortunately, many people in the world do not believe in God's Presence or that of His Son's Presence and miss out on such a privilege. Others who do believe are not too sure that God cares enough as to be constantly present to them in their daily life. Some others really do not trust God. They are like the young man who accidentally fell off a cliff but was saved by a large branch. As he clung to the branch, he called up to the top of the cliff ledge, "Is there anyone up there", to which a voice responded. When the voice identified himself as God, the youth cried out, "Lord, what shall I do?" When God responded, "Let go," the youth cried out again, "Is there anyone else up there?"

We are sometimes afraid to trust God and His Son, Jesus, with our lives. We need to change, placing ourselves in God's care and promising to do His Will in our daily life and tasks.

On September 11, 2001, suicide terrorists tried to instill fear and terror into our nation through their attacks on the New York Twin Towers and Washington Pentagon, but the resolve of the American spirit rose above their destructive actions and put down their leaders by force. As a result, America has become a stronger nation of people dedicated to peace and justice.

On the spiritual level, we have been engaged in a war with the devil and his evil spirits, who seek to terrorize us with their sinful tactics of impurities, murder, conflict and spiritual disorders. We need to call upon God and Mary in daily prayer, sacrifice and penance to put down these evil spirits and allow us to live in peace and harmony with God and our fellow men and women. Do not be afraid!

God Is Spirit

One of the most difficult things we deal with daily is the world around us. From the morning shower to the many tasks we face each day, our world takes up our time. Before we realize it, our daytime has evaporated and we face the night – and needed sleep. What to do about a God who is living the life of a Spirit?

Luckily, as Catholics and Christians, we have His Son, Jesus, who has become one of us in human flesh. But now for almost 2,000 years, He has returned to his Father. Nevertheless, we possess Him in His Eucharistic Presence under the form of bread, though many Catholics no longer believe in His Eucharistic Presence.

The rest of the world has little or no knowledge of Him. So many Catholics distract themselves from God by spending their free time watching TV, working the Internet, or visiting the bars. There is no time left for God. Besides, He is an invisible Spirit with whom we find it difficult to relate. Then the inevitable moment arrives. We die to this world and enter a totally spirit world. Now we are only spirits, having left our bodies behind to decay and decompose in the earth. Now everyone in our world is simply a spirit – from God, the Eternal Spirit, through all the angel spirits, to man who is also spirit. It is a totally different world from the one we left a few hours or weeks ago.

In the gospel of John, Jesus tells the Samaritan woman at the well of Jacob that true worshippers will worship the Father in Spirit and truth because God is Spirit. (John 4:23-24) Most of us have difficulty with this statement because we live in a "flesh and blood" community, with little or no relationship with our soul or spirit. If we cannot see, taste or feel something, we do not relate to it. So for us to live in the life of our spirit is difficult.

Yet the saints of the Church lived their entire life in the spirit. It does take a little practice, but prayer and adoration can be our daily food and habit. Like crawling, walking and running, we can become addicted to regular habits of prayer and union with the Spirit of the Father. We might learn to like it.

A Wake-Up Call

The great tragedy of September 11, 2001 was the loss of so many loved ones within minutes – as witnessed by millions of people watching on television. What disbelief and sorrow immediately entered the hearts and minds of their families and people everywhere. Where was our Loving God who would permit all this heartache? Our comfortable world was suddenly shattered and awoke to a new reality. Life suddenly appeared short and fragile. We had a need to return to a more important reality – our relation with God, our Creator, through a greater prayer life.

Some newspaper columnists and editorial writers referred to this day of September 11th as a wake-up call for America. Prior to that day, it seemed by our laws and actions in our communities, public schools, and town and city buildings, that God and His Ten Commandments were not welcome anymore in America, a country that had begun with Christian principles of life, liberty and the pursuit of happiness. From the founding of our country, "In God We Trust" has been written on our money. All of our schools were religious schools where prayer to God was a daily pattern. Then, in the 20th century, those religious values were uprooted and replaced with individual freedom and a false claim of separation of church and state. Freedom from a special state religion was translated to freedom from religion and God. A Supreme Court of nine voted 7 to 2 to allow the deliberate murder of the unborn child in the womb. Today, that has developed into the deliberate murder of the unborn child, outside the womb. And religious Americans say nothing or almost nothing about this horrible action. In addition, pornography on the Internet continues to flourish; vulgarity and violence are daily events on television; the sacred is mocked and belittled in public art and shows. And then we say in our public tragedy, "Where is God?"

As in the Old Testament, God was patient with the cities of Sodom and Gomorrah, and gave them time to repent and return to God. But when that did not happen, He sent fire upon the cities and destroyed them. They are now the site of the Dead Sea.

We need to pay more attention to our loving but just God. Hopefully we will learn.

A Masterpiece of God's Creation

Every morning when we look into our bathroom mirror with both eyes open, we behold a masterpiece of God's creation. It was on the sixth day of creation that God said, "Let us make man in our image, after our likeness." (Gen. 1:26-27) And so we behold in the mirror a person made to the image and likeness of the almighty and loving God. Externally when we examine this person, we find that he lives in a wondrous body that has a human brain to know and direct him, a muscular heart to energize his body with life-flowing blood, and hands and feet to assist and guide him.

Then we probe beneath the surface to discover his spiritual self, equipped with an intellect and mind to know and discover the universe around him, a memory that recalls his life and all its details, and finally a will that decides his everyday activity, whether good or bad. Then we marvel at the Divine Creator that created, structured and sustains such a masterpiece.

Then we discover another mystery. Each of God's human creatures – both male and female – has fingerprints, and no one has the same print. Each person is unique.

As we look beyond the human image of God to the actual Creator, we are not surprised to find a God who is Three Divine Persons: a Divine Father, a Divine Son and a Divine Holy Spirit. The same God who empowered our body and soul with three great powers of body and spirit is Himself existing as Three Divine Persons. When God the Father looks into His divine mirror, He sees His Son, and together they see and appreciate their Holy Spirit. Jesus said, "When the Advocate comes whom I will send you from the Father, the Spirit of truth that proceeds from the Father, he will testify to me." (John 15:26)

What a wondrous God we have. We certainly look like Him. Now we have to learn to act like Him. He will help us, if only we would ask Him.

Angels Are Our Best Friends in Life

It is interesting that only in recent years has the world discovered the existence of angels. Although God created the angel world long before He created this world, we have largely relegated the existence of angels to artwork and fantasy. Not too many people seriously thought of angels as real persons – living in our world, though invisible to our eyes. Now, suddenly, we have discovered their presence in our life. The commercial world provides all kinds of angel products – not only at Christmas but throughout the year. Our TV media features a very successful weekly series, "Touched by an Angel," with a happy male "angel of death" and several other angel messengers.

Most people with any religious appreciation believe that it is about time we opened our eyes to God's creations. The Holy Scriptures, from the beginning, describe angels as spirits created by God for His glory. Divided into nine Choirs – Cherubim and Seraphim, Thrones and Dominions, Virtues, Principalities and Powers, Archangels and Angels – God assigned each Choir to a particular task. Angels are assigned as messengers and guardians of man. Each person has an assigned guardian, protecting angel. When we are tempted to sin by a fallen angel/devil, we are assisted by our good angel. Each day we say: "Angel of

God, my guardian dear, to whom God's love commits me here. Ever this day be at my side, to light, to guard, to rule and guide."

On September 29th we honor the feast day of Michael, Gabriel and Raphael, archangels. When the angel Lucifer rejected God in the beginning, God called out to the angel world "Mica-el" which means "who is like to God." Hence Michael, the Archangel, came forth and with the power of God drove Lucifer and his fallen angels into hell.

This same Archangel, Michael, will confine Lucifer/Satan and his devils at the end of the world – never to be released. Men and women of our world who choose the devil and his values over God and the Ten Commandments will likewise be confined with the devils in hell. That is why it is very important to pray for people who live in mortal sin that they will come back to God before they die in their sins. Jesus is totally merciful to sinners who come back to Him. After death, it is too late!

The Angel Gabriel was sent on the great mission of announcing to the 14-year old Jewish virgin, Mary, that God had selected her as the mother of His Eternal Son. The angels of God waited to hear Mary's reply: "May it be done to me according to your word." (Luke 1:38) All heaven rejoiced! The worlds of heaven and earth have not been the same since that moment, when God became man and a new era of the world began – the Christian era.

The Angel Raphael, which means "medicine of God," was used to restore sight to Tobias in the Old Testament.

We celebrate October 2nd as the feast of the Guardian Angels who are our best friends in life and in death. They will escort us to God's throne as we leave this life.

Thank God for His angels. It will be our pleasure to live with them for all eternity. Perhaps one of the reasons the fallen angels resent us is that we are destined to occupy the places in heaven left vacant by their fall of disobedience. Too bad! But everyone is given free will to choose God or reject Him. We should choose wisely – with God's grace!

To Whom Shall We Go?

In our lifetime we are all faced with decisions. Usually, our parents make our decisions as we are growing up in our early years. But there comes a time when we have to decide things for ourselves. Very often at college age we are deciding where we can afford to go to school or perhaps a place of work. That decision will affect our future life or work style. A few may choose to begin religious studies or even begin to prepare for a life of marriage and family. Whatever we decide, we will be making life choices that will influence our entire life. We need to ask ourselves where God fits into our picture of life. If we do not include our God-Creator in our decisions, we will be like the person who began to build his house without the architect.

On one occasion when Jesus fed His people by multiplying five barley loaves of bread and two fish, the people returned the next day for more. When Jesus revealed to them the promise of eternal life if they would eat His flesh and drink His blood, they were greatly disturbed by His statements and questioned how He could give them His flesh to eat. As a result, many of the disciples stopped following Him. Although they had witnessed the miracle of the loaves and fishes, they refused to accept Jesus at His word. They made a life's decision and chose to walk away from Jesus.

We have Catholic young and old who make similar choices and decisions to walk away from Jesus and His Church because of disagreement on areas of birth prevention, abortion, remarriage in the lifetime of their spouse, and other aspects of the Church and God's moral law. Some never return. Jesus did not try to stop His people who walked away. Instead He turned to Peter, His future leader, and His Apostles and said, "Do you also want to leave?" (John 6:67) In matters of importance, Jesus demands our belief in His words and actions. Fortunately, Simon Peter answered Him, "Master, to whom shall we go? You have the words of eternal life. We have come to believe and are convinced that you are the Holy One of God." (John 6:68-69) Despite the unbelieving attitude and action of the crowd, Peter chose to believe in Jesus and chose to remain with Him.

So often some of our Catholic people are influenced by others to leave their Catholic faith, never to return. When one elderly man – a former Catholic who had chosen to leave his faith years prior because of marriage – was invited to return, he responded, "It's too late!" He died several days later. He chose to remain away.

Patient with God

A quality that is rare in the world among God's people is patience. Patient people are willing to wait in prayer and resignation for God in His mercy and justice to resolve situations and trials of disturbance in His own time, whether in the family, nation or world. When God does not seem to act to correct error and injustice right away, the patient person is willing to accept that decision of God, because God has lots of time. His time is not our time.

As people who want results immediately with the press of a computer button, we fail to realize that our Eternal God has been around from the beginning of time. As a matter of fact, He created time and years. And when He created us at one time, He created us perfectly in His own image and likeness. But He made us – unlike the animal world – free to choose His Divine Will or the will of the fallen angels – the devils; free to choose God or the devil; free to choose good or evil. Initially, our First Parents were happy to choose God and all His Divine gifts, but in time they turned from God and chose evil. As their children, we were born into that free decision.

It would be for a future "seed of the woman" to redeem us and offer each of us the freedom of choosing God's Will again. St. John, in vision, witnessed a great sign: a woman clothed with the sun, being with child. (Rev. 12:1-2) Some scholars believe this woman to represent the Church of Jesus Christ, but others see this woman as Mary, the mother of our Savior, Jesus Christ, who certainly lived her life in patient suffering – always accepting God's Will. Mary did not fully understand everything about God's invitation to be the mother of His Son, but she had faith in God and the patience to wait for God to unfold His Will for her. Meantime, "And Mary kept all these things, reflecting on them in her heart." (Luke 2:19)

As people of God, we too should be willing to wait for God to unfold His Will for us and be patient in prayer and expectation. "The kingdom of God is at hand." (Mark 1:15) Be patient.

Our Souls

When God created man in the beginning of time, He breathed into him an immortal spirit called his soul – the principle of life in the body. Thus, He destined us to live, body and soul, never to separate until one day we would be admitted to His presence in heaven. But Adam's sin of disobedience changed everything. Death, or separation of soul and body, was one of the consequences of sin. While other consequences of soul and body also occurred, the greatest punishment was the loss of heaven.

Now, with the passion and death of Jesus, God's Eternal Son, things have changed back. We have recaptured Heaven, our greatest gift. But the lesser punishment still remains – death – the separation of our soul from our body. However, even this will be remedied at the end of the world. We will be united – soul and body – never to separate again.

But in the meantime, after death, we live in our spirit or soul. We continue to love with our will, understand with our mind, and remember with our memory – all powers of our soul.

Let us be mindful, therefore, of the souls of our friends and family who have passed on into eternity and may be waiting to enter heaven. Our Masses to the Father, our prayers and good deeds offered for the Poor Souls, will help speed their way to Heaven. Meantime, our friends' and loved ones' souls in heaven continue to pray for us.

The Devil Is Strong

I believe that most people treat the devil and his evil cohorts as nonexistent or at most not very important to their world. And the devil likes that. He likes to remain unimportant and unknown. Yet from the time God created man and woman to occupy a place in heaven with Him, the fallen angels have tried in every evil way to draw man away from God and lead him to hell.

God said at the beginning of human creation to the serpent that He would put enmity between the serpent and the woman, and between their offspring. (Gen. 3:15) Consequently, Satan and the fallen angels have been the enemy of mankind from the very beginning.

In our daily life we seldom experience any sensible or visible evidence of the fallen angels. But as created spirits, they attack our souls, our mind, will and memory every day. We suffer impure thoughts, envious ideas and hateful moods toward our neighbor. As we consent, we fall into the trap of sin. Worry about our life, anxiety about our station in life, anger and impatience during the day, all are from the devil who tries to create an unhappy spirit within us. Those people who do not call to God in prayer every day will continue to fall ever deeper into despair and discouragement.

So our best cure is daily, constant communication with God, His Son, Jesus, Mary, and the saints – all of whom wait upon our free will for our prayer. God also appoints powerful angels to watch over, guard and guide us so that we will not fall into the traps set by Satan.

Certainly the devils do not appreciate or understand a happy face and disposition. Yet when we are doing God's Will daily and living out His commandments, we should have a happy appearance. We are on our way to heaven despite the best efforts of our spiritual adversary, the devil. The devil is strong, but God is stronger. We only need to call upon Him for help.

Mystery of the Trinity

How many times do we make the sign of the cross on our body without a thought to the Divine Persons – Father, Son and Holy Spirit – to whom we are speaking? It has become a careless habit that has little meaning for some Catholics as they begin prayer or enter church. One observer commented that it looked like some people were brushing away flies. This may seem like an exaggeration until you watch people entering church on Sunday. We need to remind ourselves once again that we are invoking Almighty God, who sent His Divine Son to release the graces of the Holy Spirit so that we would be invited to heaven forever.

The sign of the cross is our pledge to God the Father, Son and Holy Spirit that we are His adopted children and desire to live according to His commandments here on earth so that we may receive the inheritance promised by Him in heaven.

Father, our Creator;
Son Jesus, our Saviour;
Holy Spirit, our Sanctifier;
Help us to appreciate your
presence in our life on earth
so that we may enjoy your life
in Heaven forever. Amen.

The story is told of St. Thomas Aquinas, the great Doctor of the Church who wrote extensively on the Holy Trinity, walking the lake shoreline one day and meeting the Christ child who was making a hole in the sand and filling it with the water of the sea. When St. Thomas questioned the young boy, he said to Thomas, "I am putting the sea in this hole in the sand." When Thomas told him that this was an impossible task, the Christ child responded, "I will put this sea into this hole before your fathom and understand the mystery of the Blessed Trinity."

We will never truly understand, even in heaven, the mystery of the Holy Trinity, but we continue to honor, reverence and believe this great truth because Jesus revealed it to us. When we make the sign of the cross next time, let us appreciate to whom we are speaking – God the Father, Son and Holy Spirit.

And in Jesus Christ,
His only Son, our Lord

B.C. – Christian Time Begins – 1 A.D.

We live almost 2003 years after the birth of Jesus Christ. Over 1000 years prior to Christ, David – from whose lineage Joseph and Mary came – reigned as king over the City of Jerusalem – the City of Peace. Today, we acknowledge not the city of peace, but the Divine Peacemaker, Jesus Christ. After His bodily resurrection, Jesus said, "Peace be with you. As the Father has sent me, so I send you." (John 20:21) Three times He extended His peace upon His Apostles.

Today the entire world needs the peace of Christ. Our country is being threatened by terrorist attacks upon our people in a manner never before realized. Suicide-bent people, even within our midst, are planning to sabotage our normal workplaces, our centers of utilities, and even sensitive government buildings for the sake of creating fear and havoc among our people. Maybe it is time that we begin examining our collective consciences to discover how such an attitude of hate ever developed in our country. That some, in or out of our country, are willing to die as some did on September 11, 2001, to cause death and destruction, is reason to investigate and discover the reason for such hatred, and then to hopefully try to correct the cause. Otherwise, the cancer of hatred will continue for years.

In the year 1 A.D., our Savior, Jesus Christ was born into a society that, through the Roman emperor and empire, oppressed God's Jewish people. Jesus came to earth to bring God's peace to the world, but He was rejected even by His own people. Are we doing this same thing to God today? Is God welcome in our society, homes, public schools, market places, legislatures, Supreme Court – even in our own hearts? Can America – the home of life, liberty and the pursuit of happiness as well as the home of abortion of the unborn, pornography on the Internet and immorality of various kinds – show we are any different from the Roman Empire? There are some who would say we are the "Sodom and Gomorrah" of the present era. Yet, the all-merciful God invites us to change to our original state of goodness. It is never too late with God that we return as a people to Him. He alone will bring peace to our hearts and to the world. Peace be with you!

Behold, the Lamb of God

Practicing Catholics are familiar with the words of John the Baptist as he welcomed his Saviour at the Jordan River. "Behold, the Lamb of God," the priest at the altar proclaims at Holy Communion time, "This is the Lamb of God who takes away the sins of the world. Happy are those who are called to His supper." John recognized his cousin, Jesus, as the Saviour of the world. The priest and people at Mass recognize Jesus as the lamb-victim for our sins.

Each year at Passover time, the Jewish priest, together with all the Jewish families, would offer a lamb in sacrifice as a sin offering to God. It was called the Passover meal. After Jesus offered the Passover with His Apostles, He then took the bread and wine at the table and offered His first Mass. Then Jesus ordained His Apostles as priests to continue the offering of the Eucharist.

Jesus now has begun a new covenant with His people, a covenant that includes everyone in the world. We all are the new chosen people of God, as described and enacted in the Eucharistic sacrifice on the cross and in the Mass.

As the new chosen people of God, how do we respond to our leader, Jesus Christ? Like the chosen people of old, do we acclaim God with one voice and then turn away shortly in favor of our false gods?

Today we are blessed by God with the Real Presence, not only to offer Him back to God in the Mass, but also to receive Him under the form of bread and wine. We are also blessed with the sacraments of God whereby Jesus continues to wash us from sin, feed us with His Eucharist, and strengthen us with His sacramental anointing. Jesus invites couples in the enduring bond of marriage and confers His divine authority upon His new priests. We are a blessed people of God. Yet too many choose to ignore Jesus and turn away from the gospel teaching – preferring to seek their own gods of money, sexual pleasures and secular fame. Like the chosen people of old, many today have chosen to "do their own thing" – instead of God's Will. It is a poor choice.

Come and You Will See

Three times God called Samuel from his sleep in the temple, to which Samuel responded, "Speak, for your servant is listening." (I Sam. 3:10) What an obedient servant of God was Samuel. As a result, God made him a great prophet among his people.

What abundant blessings would be ours if, like Samuel, we would respond daily to God's inner call to us. When we rise in the morning, God speaks to our heart and mind to respond in morning prayer. Are we deaf to God's morning call? During the busy day, does our conscience respond to the right and wrong of the world about us? Do dishonest CEOs feel no obligation to their employees and clients – when they steal millions of dollars from their companies? Do employees who neglect to give an honest day's work for their pay feel no compunction? Do bishops, priests and religious reach out to the poor and neglected? Everyone is answerable to the Lord when He calls.

In the New Testament, Jesus Himself is our teacher. One day John the Baptist pointed out the Messiah as he approached along the Jordan River: "Behold, the Lamb of God." (John 1:36) As a result, Andrew and John followed our Lord. They asked Him where He was staying, to which Jesus replied, "Come, and you will see." (John 1:39) So the two stayed with Him that day.

How would you like to stay with Jesus at His home? It is possible today, for He lives in the Blessed Sacrament reserved or exposed in the tabernacle of your parish church. What an honor.

If like Samuel and the Apostles we would spend time with God as He reveals His daily Divine Will to us in prayer and work, how quickly we would learn to grow in wisdom, knowledge and grace. It may seem difficult to become a saint until we learn that saints are ordinary people who follow God's Will in their daily life. With God's grace we can all grow in sanctity. "Here I am Lord, I desire to do your Will", we say with Samuel. Our God will invite us to come and see where He stays. It's called heaven – forever.

The Breaking of the Bread

Our Catholic people are blessed with treasures, some hidden but real nonetheless. Because the world around us is so attractive and beautiful to our senses, many Catholics have failed to appreciate or even recognize the treasures in their midst.

The greatest treasure, of course, is the daily Eucharist that is present in every Catholic church in the world. Some countries that are pagan restrict and even punish Catholics from attending the Eucharist. But probably the main reason why our Catholic people ignore the Eucharist is their lack of faith. They no longer believe and accept the Catholic belief that Jesus Christ lives daily under the form of bread in the tabernacles of our churches. A great many no longer attend Mass on Sundays and Holy Days. It is the minority today who come to daily Mass. Even some Catholics who come every week to Mass seem to come out of obligation rather than love for Jesus. Yet the Mass – the unbloody offering of Jesus on the cross – remains the greatest treasure of the Catholic Church.

Next to the sacrifice of the Mass, probably our greatest treasure is Confession – the Sacrament of Reconciliation – whereby our contrite souls are forgiven and wiped clean of our sinfulness by God in the person of the priest. Catholic people burdened with personal sin are privileged to walk into a confessional and with proper contrition and resolution, walk out forgiven and cleansed. After His resurrection, Jesus appeared to His apostles and said, "Peace be with you. As the Father has sent me, so I send you." (John 20:21) He breathed on them and said: "Receive the holy Spirit. Whose sins you forgive are forgiven them, and whose sins you retain are retained." (John 20:22-23) We should be ashamed that we allow this great treasure of forgiveness to gather the dust of our neglect. How blessed is the person who confesses regularly in the Sacrament of Reconciliation. He will have fewer regrets and remorse as his soul approaches the judgment seat of Jesus.

One more treasure that we possess is our love for Mary, the Mother of God. Only Jesus, Her Son, and Joseph, Her husband, adequately honor her. But Mary still watches over and protects all her children as our spiritual mother. How lucky we are.

For Him or against Him

Forty days after His birth in Bethlehem, the infant Jesus was taken by His parents, Mary and Joseph, to Jerusalem to be consecrated to God. Waiting at the temple, the prophet Simeon blessed them and said to Mary: "Behold, this child is destined for the fall and rise of many in Israel, and to be a sign that will be contradicted...." (Luke 2:34) This prophecy followed Jesus all His life and beyond, even to this day.

With Jesus, there is no middle ground. You either love Him or you hate Him. You either follow Him in life or you go your own way. Either you are with Him or you are against Him.

How does our world today measure up to Jesus and His gospel? Our worldwide media, with its billions of dollars, is certainly on the other side – as it advances the cause of this materialistic and secular world. At home in the U.S.A., our government and court system that favors and promotes abortion, capital punishment, euthanasia and the activities of the gay community are also on the other side. What matters for each of us as individuals is our place with Jesus and His teachings. In every parish, priests experience a similar trend among their own parishioners. It is most noticeable with the attendance at Sunday Mass – which is a good barometer of our Catholic faith. Presently, only about half (50%) of parishioners attend Mass every week. Noticeably absent are our young adults, who may be moving from church to church. Failure in marriage, drug abuse, sexual friendships or simply loss of faith may be factors with their absence at Mass. Dissatisfaction with parish liturgies may also play a part. Whatever our reasons, "giving up" on our parish Eucharist certainly influences our relationship with Jesus Christ. Are we with Him – or against Him? You have freedom to choose.

A Prophet without Honor

Sometimes, nothing that we do is accepted and praised by families and friends. Yet people 500 miles away will publish and acclaim our expertise. Jesus had the same problem facing Him regularly. Jesus said to the crowds about John the Baptist: "For John came neither eating nor drinking, and they said, 'He is possessed by a demon.' The Son of Man came eating and drinking and they said, 'Look, he is a glutton and a drunkard....'" (Matt. 11:18-19) While people at a distance listened with respect and attention, His own townspeople found fault with Him. "Where did this man get all this?" (Matt. 13:56) The people were offended by Him. "But Jesus said to them, 'A prophet is not without honor except in his native place and in his own house.' And he did not work many mighty deeds there because of their lack of faith." (Matt. 13:57-58)

In our everyday Catholic life and work, we all encounter a similar response from family, friends and coworkers in the business world. Perhaps this apparent lack of appreciation from those most related to us might seem normal and natural because they see us every day and experience our daily humanness and faults. But, though Jesus was completely human, He had no faults or failings. As the Sunday Mass Preface (VII) reminds us: "You sent him as one like ourselves, though free from sin." For the Jews of His day to find fault with Him was based on fear, jealousy and ignorance on their part.

For our people to find fault with us may be God's way of chastising us for our own sinfulness. We need to accept it as a means of grace and blessing from God – instead of reacting negatively. We read in the life of David that a man named Shimei cursed David and threw stones at him, calling him a murderous and wicked man. When one of David's officers volunteered to cut off Shimei's head, David responded: "Suppose the LORD has told him to curse David...Let him alone and let him curse, for the LORD has told him to." (2 Sam. 16:10-11) David appreciated his own sinfulness and willingly accepted a rebuke and a reminder from God. Maybe we should do the same.

Daily Bread

Early each weekday morning, Catholic priests in every country of the world meet at the altar in their churches with a small number of men and women to offer the sacrifice of the Mass to God the Father. In the quiet silence of the morning this select group of Catholic people join with their priest, who represents Jesus Christ, to offer the Body, Blood, Soul and Divinity of their Saviour to the Father. It is the same sacrifice Jesus began at the Last Supper and then completed on the cross the next day.

It is difficult to understand why there is a relatively small number of Catholic people at daily Mass, given our Catholic teaching and belief that Jesus, the Son of God, is truly offered and received under the appearance of bread and wine daily. Why do not our Catholic people flock in great numbers to daily Mass? It is a mystery.

Then we recall how poorly God's people under Moses responded to God, though God fed them with the daily bread (manna) from heaven, and provided them with quail and water from the rock. Still they complained and murmured against God. If they had the graces and blessings afforded to our Catholic people today, perhaps they would have been more appreciative.

A wonderful blessing came to the Church under the decree of Pope Pius X in 1903. Up to that year our Catholic people made their First Holy Communion at the age of 12 or later, and then received Communion about once a year. Pope Pius X decreed that Catholics could make their first Holy Communion as early as they could distinguish the "Bread of Life" from ordinary bread. He also encouraged frequent Holy Communion, even daily.

We Catholics are so fortunate to have Jesus at Mass as our "daily bread" – a bread that becomes His body and blood. What a great gift – and it is freely given.

Kept at a Distance

I remember a young seminarian friend who was about to be ordained a priest and approached his professors for their blessing. The first priest refused to bless him and told him that he would disgrace his priesthood and the Church. Devastated by this refusal, the young man invited a blessing from another professor, who blessed him and predicted that he would do great things for God and the Church. And this prophecy came to pass – but not without many trials and tribulations.

When the Holy Family brought their 40-day old child, Jesus, to the Temple to be offered to God, Simeon predicted that He would be a sign that will be contradicted. (Luke 2:34) Ever since that day, the name of Jesus has evoked approval from many as well as disdain from others in the world. In our own secular America, the sight of the Christmas Crib near public parks or buildings causes a hypocritical outcry from the non-believer or even the politically-minded Christian. Some seem to want Jesus as a friend, as long as He keeps His distance and does not embarrass or require anything difficult. Otherwise, Jesus is not welcome. "Let Him stay at home where He belongs," say the public-minded.

However, when the earthquake or disaster occurs, then we welcome His help. In fact, we beseech His presence.

Jesus our Saviour never loses His love for us. He is always waiting for our response to His daily invitation to be His friend. Jesus is always the same, today, tomorrow and forever. His greatest joy is in our daily recognition of Him whether at home, in the public business world, in the parish church or in the confines of our soul. He is awaiting our greeting: "Jesus, Mary, Joseph – I give you my heart and my soul." He reminds us that if we acknowledge Him on earth, He will acknowledge us before God the Father in heaven. (Matt. 10:32) It is not difficult, and we will find it very rewarding.

Son of God

Some people by their own admission have difficulty discovering who they are on this earth. This attitude or puzzlement of mind very often occurs after some serious tragedy in their lives. Some begin to question their purpose and worth in life. Perhaps it is a form of grief upon the death of a loved one, but more often it is simply a result of living a long time without God in their lives.

Jesus Christ had no problem in this regard. He knew who He was and why He had come on this earth. He knew that He is the Divine Son of God, sent to earth by His Father to win back the entire human race by His death on the cross. But He still had to find believers among His people. And so He asked the simple question: "Who do people say that the Son of Man is?" (Matt. 16:13) After a varied response, Jesus asked

His Apostles the same question. Without hesitation, Simon the fisherman, brother of Andrew, said in reply: "You are the Messiah, the Son of the living God." (Matt. 16:16) In immediate response to Peter's profession of faith, Jesus changed Simon's name to Peter (the rock) and gave him His authority and keys to the kingdom of heaven.

Today in the turmoil of the modern world, Jesus asks each one of us the same question, "Who do you say that I am?" Do we come up with a varied response like the people of Jesus' time, or do we acknowledge Him as the Son of God? Maybe some people find God in the Internet technology of today, or in the feverish business of the money world or possibly in the media's fascination with sex, drugs and alcohol. While the Son of God remains quietly and serenely in the tabernacles of Catholic churches twenty-four hours each day, the people of world look everywhere else.

Let us acknowledge Jesus with our visits and our life while we have the opportunity.

Jesus, Our Divine Food

At the beginning of time, when God the Father with His Divine Son and the Holy Spirit worked out their plan of salvation for mankind, they had to decide on the most appealing way to attract men and women back to God after the fall of the First Parents. So they decided to offer us the one thing that everyone enjoys: "food." After a long period of waiting through Noah, Abraham, Isaac and Jacob, God blessed His people with daily bread from Heaven as Moses led them through the desert back to the Promised Land. "Then the LORD said to Moses, 'I will now rain down bread from heaven for you.'" (Ex. 16:4) Called "manna," this bread continued to feed God's people for over forty years until they crossed the Jordan River into the Promised Land. Then His people were fed in the "land of milk and honey" throughout the years of the Old Testament.

Fifteen hundred years later, when Jesus began His public ministry, He continued to feed the people. On one occasion, Jesus multiplied five barley loaves and two fish, feeding five thousand in number. Twelve wicker baskets of bread fragments were left over. (John 6:1-14) The next day, when the crowd of people found Jesus on the other side of the lake, they expected to be fed again. Jesus responded to them, "Do not work for food that perishes but for the food that endures for eternal life, which the Son of Man will give you." (John 6:27) The people retorted: "What can you do?" (John 6:30) They told Jesus that Moses gave them manna or bread from heaven to eat, but Jesus said to them: "Amen, amen, I say to you, it was not Moses who gave the bread from heaven; my Father gives you the true bread from heaven." (John 6:32)

When Jesus revealed that He was the bread that came down from Heaven, the Jews murmured against Him. Jesus explained that He was the living bread, that whoever eats of the living bread will live forever, and that the living bread is His flesh given for the world. This caused the Jews to quarrel and argue about how Jesus could give them His flesh to eat. As a result, many of His disciples walked away.

Today the Catholic world is experiencing a similar loss of faith in the Real Presence of Jesus in the Eucharist among some of its members. Although Jesus was very clear in His actions and words at the Last Supper – "[T]his is my body…this is my blood…." (Matt. 26: 26-28) – some Catholics today believe, like most Protestant denominations, that the Last Supper and hence the Eucharist was only a supper and not a true unbloody sacrifice – which culminated in the bloody sacrifice the next day (Good Friday) when Jesus died on the cross. These people, too, have walked away from their Catholic faith. How sad!

Hospitality

Usually we think of hospitality as entertainment with food and music. We all enjoy a good party with friends. Our Lord, in His human nature, enjoyed good friends. In the gospel of St. Luke, He finds this friendship in Martha and Mary, who lived near Jerusalem in Bethany. Mary brought joy to Our Lord by her loving presence, and Martha by her work in the kitchen. Both brought joy to Our Lord, but He preferred Mary's way. "Mary has chosen the better part and it will not be taken from her." (Luke 10:42) Our Lord enjoys the attention we give Him in our prayer life. He blesses us in our work, but prefers our prayerful attention.

In this sense, hospitality takes on a higher meaning – namely "Host," which implies a hidden victim. Jesus is the Eucharistic Host – hidden in the bread, who awaits our visit to the Church and who blesses us when we "choose the better part" like Mary. While Jesus understands our need to work, He simply prefers us as we visit Him in the Eucharistic Host.

This meaning of hospitality is missed by most people. In some ways we do this when we go to a party and hardly even greet the host or hostess as we make our way to the food. Jesus misses us as we daily pass the church and seldom stop to make a visit. Those who come daily enjoy the reward of Mary – who sat at His feet. They have chosen the better part, and it will not be taken away from them.

Listening to God

A recent article in the secular paper featured the active life of many younger parents today as they spend endless hours after school transporting their children to sports games, school events and various social commitments. Their daily lives involve one large car service for their children. Unless their children are raised and out of the house, many parents run the risk of becoming overly stressed and burned out – according to the newspaper article.

In the story of Martha and Mary as recorded by St. Luke, Jesus reveals His preference for prayer over the active life of all of us. Martha was preoccupied with preparing His dinner, while Mary sat at the Lord's feet, listening to Him speak. Our Lord was pleased with the work of Martha but preferred the listening prayer of Mary. (Luke 10:42)

Sometimes, as Catholic people, we fail to appreciate the value and effectiveness of prayer to God. Certainly, God does not need our prayers – since He is fully perfect and almighty. But God can use our prayers to help each one of us as well as others in need.

The perfect prayer is the daily Mass, where Jesus re-offers Himself under the form of bread and wine to His Father. In return, the Father grants us the great gift of His Son in Holy Communion. For those unable to pray the Mass, the Church encourages us to pray the daily rosary, offer various litanies of prayer, and speak to God in our own language. Like Jesus, the Catholic Church does not condemn our daily activism. Rather,

Jesus and His Church encourage each one of us to root ourselves in prayer and listening to God. Then our actions and our activities will take on new meaning and value. In European villages, the clock in the public square often says "Ora et Labora" – "pray and work." Notice which is first.

Lower Your Nets for a Catch

Some business people struggle all their lives with little or no success. The Apostles experienced that feeling on many days of fishing until they met Jesus – then their lives took on new meaning. Obedient to Him, the Apostles grew in their physical and spiritual successes. With Jesus in charge of their efforts, they were astonished at their catch of fish. (Luke 5:9)

If our business people were wise, they would put Jesus in charge of their day. Although Jesus never promised us heaven on earth, I am confident that if countries and nations consecrated and dedicated themselves to His Sacred Heart and the Immaculate Heart of His mother, they would prosper even in this world.

This would certainly work in marriage – where Jesus and Mary find a warm welcome in prayer and sacrifice. There would be fewer divorces and more attentive and faithful children. Instead of children at home who are glued to a television program or saturated with TV games or computer e-mail at night, a family rosary led by a father would bring Jesus and His mother into the home. Their presence would attract the angels and saints and even God the Father.

In the second chapter of John, the wedding feast at Cana was going smoothly until the hosts ran out of wine. The mother of Jesus said to Him: "They have no wine." (John 2:3) "Fill the jars with water," Jesus ordered. (John 2:7) It was the best wine at the feast. Jesus ordered it and it happened. It is a difficult – even impossible – task for us, but simple for the Son of God. Mary had only to ask and her Son responded.

We too have only to ask – "And I tell you, ask and you will receive; seek and you will find; knock and the door will be opened to you." (Luke 11:9) But unlike Mary, many have difficulty believing. Fortunately, there are homes and families that are faithful to God – and miracles occur.

When Peter lowered his net at the command of Jesus, he needed another boat to assist his great number of fish. Peter might not have received an A+ in arithmetic, but he knew his fish. Yet he left it all for Christ, and Jesus told him that from now on he would be catching men. (Luke 5:10) They are worth a lot more than fish.

Who was conceived by the Holy Spirit

God Became Man

"The sons of Noah who came out of the ark were Shem, Ham and Japheth…and from them the whole earth was peopled." (Gen. 9:18-19) Eventually it was the line of Shem that produced a man called Abram of the land of Ur. Historians trace this area to the present country of Iraq. God made a covenant with Abram and then changed his name to Abraham, "[Y]our name shall be Abraham, for I am making you the father of a host of nations." (Gen. 17:5)

Today the Jews, Arabs and Christians claim Abraham as their spiritual father. God tested Abraham, just as He tests each of us in our lifetime – by commanding or inviting us to do something difficult. Many of us shy away from the difficult task, but not Abraham. As ordered by God, Abraham took his only son, Isaac, into the mountain to sacrifice him to God. Even though an angel stopped Abraham's action, God was pleased with Abraham's obedience.

Our personal obedience involves a free act of our will. In effect, our obedient action tells God that we trust Him to do the best for ourselves.

God was most pleased with His Divine Son, Jesus, when obediently and freely He consented to become Man and eventually to offer Himself in sacrifice on a cross for the sins of mankind. He began His mission when a humble Jewish virgin in the town of Nazareth accepted His invitation to become His mother.

The world has not been the same since that moment when God became man in the person of Jesus, our Saviour. During the season of Advent – the approach to Christmas, Our Lord's birthday – let us be grateful for the great gift of Jesus in the world. Some day all the children of Abraham will recognize and accept Jesus as their God and Saviour. Let us pray for that intention.

A Special Lady

Mary, daughter of Anna and Joachim, lived her quiet life in Nazareth after her early education in the Temple school in Jerusalem. Although she was only fourteen years of age, she became betrothed in marriage to a carpenter in the village whose name was Joseph. She prayed daily that God would send a Messiah from Heaven to rescue her people from the bondage of the Roman law, and so it happened. God heard her prayers and those of her people and sent His Angel Gabriel to invite her to accept the responsibility of Divine Motherhood. Though Mary questioned how this could be, she immediately accepted the responsibility: "May it be done to me according to your word." (Luke 1:38) In that moment, the Son of God broke through the element of time to become present as God-Man in the womb of Mary, now His earthly mother. It was the beginning of our salvation from sin – a brand new era for mankind.

Each year on March 25th, we celebrate the feast of the Annunciation, nine months before Christmas, just as we prepare for Passion week – the days of our Lord's crucifixion, death and resurrection. Without Mary's "Yes" at the Annunciation, there would be no "Yes" of Jesus, her Son, at the crucifixion and no return from the dead on Easter Sunday. Without Mary's "Yes" to God, there would be no salvation for all of us and no invitation to eternal life in heaven. Without Mary, there would have been no Jesus in our world. Yet many Catholics show little or no appreciation for Mary, even to the point of ignoring her in their prayer life. Some Catholics even show disdain for her in word and action.

Mary is the mother of the Son of God and deserves our special honor and attention. If we are wise, we will pay attention to Mary. She will lead us to her Son, and He will lead us to His Father.

Mary, Conceived without Sin

She is known by the world of poetry as "our tainted nature's solitary boast," by St. Bernadette Soubirous of Lourdes, France as "The Immaculate Conception," by the angels of heaven as "their Queen," and by the Son of God as "My Mother."

Born of Anna and Joachim in Jerusalem, Mary entered this world – unknown to the world and known only by God – conceived without original sin – full of God's grace. She grew up in the Jerusalem Temple school from an early age. When she was ready for marriage, she lived in Nazareth. Joseph, a carpenter in Nazareth was selected to be her husband. Between the time that she married in the Jewish faith and the time after the dowry agreement, God sent His messenger, Gabriel, to invite her to be the mother of His Divine Son. Once she accepted, the Son of God took residence in her immaculate womb. It was only just and proper for the All Pure God to send His Son into a womb untainted by sin and full of His Divine Life.

From the moment of her consent as a young fourteen-year old Jewish girl, to the present moment, Mary has accepted and lived her vocation as Mother of God – though she probably did not understand her role for many years. From Bethlehem and King Herod to the Cross of Calvary and Pilate, Mary learned what was asked of her by God. Mary passed her test with flying colors.

At the proper time, as is the case with all of us, God called Mary to give an accounting of herself before the Throne of God. Again she passed with flying colors. She returned to her body and then body and soul she was assumed into heaven and crowned Queen of heaven and earth. At the side of her Son, Jesus, she reigns in heaven as our Spiritual Mother and Queen.

We need only ask her through her rosary or other prayer and she responds. Her Divine Son will refuse His mother nothing she requests.

On the contrary, Jesus grants her every wish. She is our great advocate before the Throne of God. She is the mediatrix of all grace. One person objected and said he prays directly to God, to which the priest responded, "Wonderful, but every gift to you from God returns through Mary." The Holy Spirit channels all graces to us through His spouse, Mary. Finally, as she stood beneath her Son on the cross, as He offered Himself as our Redeemer, Mary in her great pain and sorrow accepted her role as co-redemptrix. She cooperated with her Son as He reopened the gates of heaven once again for all mankind. Without Mary there would be no Christ. Without Mary there would be no redemption 2000 years ago. God would have had to go back to His drawing board had Mary said "No".

How many times do we send God back to His drawing board because of our many "No's" to Him? Every time we sin, we say "No" to God. Someday we will learn to say "Yes" every time He asks. Wouldn't it be pleasantly surprising to God if we would always change our words and actions with a positive answer?

Immaculate

The Latin language was the people's normal manner of conversation in the early centuries of Christianity. Although the seventy-two books of the Bible were written originally in the Greek and Syro-Chaldaic languages, St. Jerome in the fifth century translated the Word of God into the Latin language for the common people to read and understand. Eventually, the romantic languages of Spanish, Portuguese and Italian developed from Latin, and the Latin language still influences our language today.

The word "sincere" – a good example of the Latin influence – is derived from "sine cera" which translates "without wax." In the Middle Ages, in the repair of church bells, a bell worker might use wax instead of metal to repair a bell. But a bell with wax does not ring true. Only the bell without wax – hence only a sincere bell – would ring true. Likewise, a sincere person is one who rings true.

Another example might be the word "immaculate," which is translated "im-macula" – "without stain." Hence one who is immaculate is "without stain." The only human person that could qualify as being "without stain" is the Mother of Jesus. God prepared the bodily home for His Son in the immaculate womb of Mary, His mother. As a result of God's action, the Immaculate Heart of Mary and the Sacred Heart of Jesus beat as one. We say in prayer: "Sacred Heart of Jesus, be my love; Immaculate Heart of Mary, be my salvation."

The Catholic Church celebrates Mary's feast of the Immaculate Conception on December 8th each year with a special Mass of obligation for all Catholics. This feast day celebrates the Catholic dogma and truth that, by a special and singular gift from God, Mary was conceived in her mother's womb immaculate and free from original sin. At the time of the Angel Gabriel's visit to the young Mary, He revealed this truth. He said: "Hail, favored one! The Lord is with you." (Luke 1:28) In prayer, the Catholic Church says: "Hail, Mary, full of grace." The fullness of God's grace or life not only excludes all sin but reveals His divine presence in the soul. As Catholics we believe that God has been present fully to Mary from her conception. What a mother we have in Mary. Honor her in prayer.

Devotion to Mary

It may well be considered a compliment to the Mother of God that in the mundane world of football a final football pass of desperation at the end of a failing game is called a "Hail Mary," or it may well be another offense or slight to her marvelous personage. Certainly the term in football – "Immaculate Reception" – is offensive to the all-pure Mother of mankind. As these slights are permitted by the Catholic world, of which the world census records one billion, bigots and hateful people become more bold and present as art form our holy Virgin Mary covered with dung as if it were meaningful art.

The archenemy of Mary – the "woman clothed with the sun, with the moon under her feet, and on her head a crown of twelve stars" (Rev. 12:1) – is Lucifer, the archangel devil who will be trampled someday beneath her feet and cast forever into hell , as promised in the Scriptures. The devil presently incites mankind against Mary at his every opportunity and tries to draw us away from devotion to her. In this diabolical work, Lucifer is very successful. Even priests and religious men and women fall prey to these temptations. Very few religious communities in the U.S. today require their members to wear the rosary externally as a sign of their devotion to the Mother of God as they did from their foundation.

Even one Catholic college named after the rosary eliminated the name in favor of one of their predecessors. Little by little, the devil began winning the battle of discouraging Catholic devotion to the Immaculate Mother, Mary. In some ways, we became ashamed of her in our prayer life as if she no longer deserved to be next to her Divine Son. Jesus belonged in our religious life and devotion, but Mary had lost her place in our prayer life. We seemed, as so-called "Catholics," to allow her "out" for our May and October devotions since this time was considered "her time in our life," but she had to return to the "attics" of our prayer life during the rest of the year (Christmas being an exception).

Now we are invited to pray the rosary every day, all twenty decades – joyful, sorrowful, glorious and luminous, for peace, in our own hearts, in our families, and in the world. Mary never seems to give up. Despite all our disregard of her, like a caring mother, she continues to come back.

She does not seem to know when to take "No" for an answer. Thanks be to God!

In the Shadow of the Son

It may be that in some Catholic homes, and certainly in most non-Catholic homes, the name of Mary, the Mother of Jesus, has little or no importance. Nonetheless, in these same homes, the name of Jesus, her Son, merits a much higher applause. I am sure that Mary, from her place in heaven next to her divine Son, is not disturbed but rather is pleased that her Son, Jesus, is the center of attention.

In our life here, Mary always points us to her Son. From the moment that Mary accepted her role of Mother at the Annunciation and continuing to her own bodily assumption – twenty-five years after her Son's ascension into heaven – Mary has always remained in the shadow of her Son, keeping all things in her heart, never taking the limelight in place of her Son. "Do whatever he tells you," she said at the wedding feast of Cana. (John 2:5) Yet of all God's creation, Mary is the only creature of God that was conceived without sin and full of God's grace – in preparation for her destiny as Mother of God.

It is in Her Divine Motherhood that Mary of Nazareth excels all mothers. Jesus, Son of God and Son of Mary, is the difference. On August 15th, we celebrate the consequences of Mary's Immaculate Conception when her Son took her, after death, bodily into heaven. Together with her Son, who ascended bodily into heaven, Mary was taken up into heaven – and there shares the reward of her life of obedience on earth.

Mary, as Queen of Heaven and Earth, awaits our prayers so that she may pass them on to her Son, Jesus, for His response. "Holy Mary, Mother of God, pray for us now and at the hour of our death."

The Voice

The pilgrim visiting the holy land of Jesus may travel a short distance from Jerusalem to a small mountain village of Ein Karem – the home of John the Baptist. Presently, there exists in the village a church, dedicated to John, which was built over the site of the home of Elizabeth and Zechariah, his parents. Excavation has revealed a small home beneath the church. A short distance outside the village but within sight of the village church is a more modern church built in honor of the Annunciation of the Angel Gabriel to Mary.

It was to this village that Mary, bearing Jesus within, came and saluted Elizabeth, who was also with child. "When Elizabeth heard Mary's greeting, the infant leaped in her womb, and Elizabeth, filled with the holy Spirit, cried out in a loud voice and said, 'Most blessed are you among women, and blessed is the fruit of your womb.'" (Luke 1:41-42)

It was at this meeting of mothers that the infant John began his mission in life to announce and proclaim Jesus to the world. His leap in faith and grace was only the beginning of years of penitential preparation and vocal proclamation of the Messiah. John would tell the world that Jesus was the Lamb (John 1:29) and the Son of God. (John 1:34)

Is it not the mission of a follower of Christ to proclaim Him to the world as the Son of God? Why else would God the Father invite us into His family as adopted sons and daughters unless we acknowledge Jesus, His Divine Son, as our Messiah and Saviour?

Perhaps there are some Christians who are reluctant to acknowledge Jesus in their life, who are too busy to pray, to worship and proclaim their Lord. Too bad. Jesus will have no time for them in the next world. John the Baptist literally "lost his head" over Jesus. We too should be willing.

Rich Soil

When God the Father searched His world for a suitable home for His Eternal Son to begin His life as Man, He found one such young virgin in the town of Nazareth. Her name was Mary, daughter of Anna and Joachim. Already from her conception, God the Father had prepared the spiritual soil by filling her with the fullness of His grace and divine life. Mary was the rich soil that willingly received the Almighty Son of God into this world.

What an example we have in Mary as followers of Jesus Christ. From the time of her acceptance of God's will – welcoming His Son into the world – until her own death in the care of John the Apostle, Mary ranks number one as the perfect mother and Christian.

But then we examine Our Lord's words when Mary and other family members sought Jesus to save Him from apparent harm. He said, "Here are my mother and my brothers. (For) whoever does the will of God is my brother and sister and mother." (Mark 3:34-35) Christ does not discredit his physical relationship to Mary, but emphasizes the spiritual relationship as more important.

All loyal Christians and Catholics can join this sacred relationship if they wish. They need only start with their Catholic baptism and continue on, always open to God's Will.

To the degree that we allow God's Will to enter and affect our mind and will, we grow spiritually in the likeness of God Himself. Our Lord reminds us that the seed sown on rich soil is the one who hears the Word of God and understands it, bearing fruit many fold. (Matt. 13:23) These divine words of Jesus challenge all of us to strive always to do God's Will in our daily life on earth and also to try to attain a high place with the Lord. Jesus reminds us that there are many dwelling places in His Father's house. (John 14:2) Which place is yours?

Consecration to the Two Hearts

Today, in our modern medical practice, open heart surgery has become a very acceptable and successful event that occurs daily in our general hospitals. Patients with serious heart problems are dismissed for home within days of heart surgery. Yet, for the individual patient, this event is approached with a certain fear and trepidation – since the heart is the principal agent for sustaining life in the body. We may be able to live with the loss of other bodily limbs, but we die with the loss of our heart.

Apart from our own heart, there are two very important hearts that are vital to our spiritual well-being: the Sacred Heart of Jesus and the Immaculate Heart of Mary. The Sacred Heart of Jesus was formed in Jesus within the womb of Mary. As the child's heart was formed and began to beat, we can presume that His heart began to beat in harmony with His Mother's Immaculate Heart. We know from scripture that later, at age twelve, Jesus – found in the Temple by Mary and Joseph – "was obedient to them; and his mother kept all these things in her heart." (Luke 2:51)

When Jesus appeared in 1673 to Sister Margaret Mary Alacoque in her convent chapel in France, He revealed His Sacred Heart and asked that everyone show love and honor to Him by consecrating themselves to His Sacred Heart and by observing nine First Fridays in memory of His passion and death. Later, in 1917, Mary, His Mother, appeared to three young children at Fatima, Portugal, and requested that all persons consecrate themselves to Her Immaculate Heart and observe Five First Saturdays in her honor. She promised that God will bring peace to the world, if we fulfill her requests. To date, she is still waiting for the world to comply.

These two Sacred Hearts of Jesus and Mary hold the key to peace in the world – a peace that the world has never realized since before the disobedience of our First Parents in the Garden of Eden. Yet God – through Mary – will bring a great peace if we will consecrate ourselves to the Hearts of Jesus and Mary. Yet we are so occupied with our worldly activities that we do not find the time to do God's Will. It is a pity!

Our Hidden God

I was finishing my night prayer before the Eucharist in our adoration chapel late one evening when a father accompanied three of his nine children and a young friend for a weekly hour. I noticed that as his young daughter entered, she put on her head a simple but beautiful veil. I was impressed because her action reminded me of the reverence shown by women in church when I was younger. Every girl and woman wore a veil or hat in church in reverence to Jesus in the Blessed Sacrament. It was refreshing to see that this feminine custom has not totally disappeared. Who knows but someday the custom may return?

It is interesting to note that from the time of Adam and Eve, Almighty God has veiled Himself from our visual sight and only shows

Himself in heaven. In the time of Abraham and the prophets, God remained veiled in cloud and fire. He led the Jewish people under Moses out of Egypt with a cloud by day and a fire by night. Although God allowed Moses to approach Him in a special way, He still remained veiled.

Then God sent His Divine Son to earth, revealing and unveiling Himself to the world through the Son. Jesus is the perfect image of God his Father. "Whoever has seen me has seen the Father." (John 14: 9)

But it still remains for God the Father to reveal and unveil Himself. He is a pure uncreated spirit who has never assumed a human form, so we must recognize and see Him with the eyes of our spirit/soul. We need to see Him with our spiritual mind. This may only be when we enter heaven in our spirits/souls. Then in spirit we will see God as He is. At the end of the world when our bodies are reformed by God's power and joined to our souls once again, then we will see and experience God with all of our bodily senses as well. Meantime God remains veiled in His Divine Nature. He continues to reveal Himself through His Son, Jesus. Today Jesus remains veiled under bread in the Eucharist. The veil continues to be a sign of the sacred on earth. He promises to reveal Himself to us someday.

Thy Will Be Done on Earth

From the time of the fallen angels who refused to do God's Will – "I will not serve," responded Lucifer, the archangel – through the creation of Adam and Eve, who refused to do God's Will and ate of the tree of the knowledge of good and evil, men and women have consistently refused to do God's Will, with one exception. Only Mary, the teenage village girl from Nazareth, accepted God's Will and persevered throughout her life in maintaining God's Will.

So it is ironic that we Catholic/Christian people pray that God's Will be done. Perhaps we might be made more aware of the importance of doing God's Will if we continued the complete sentence of Jesus' prayer. "Thy will be done *on earth*" might be more understandable and enlightening, since His Will is *never* disobeyed in heaven. Can anyone imagine the saints and angels in heaven saying "No" to God and refusing to do

His Will? But on earth the Will of God – with a few exceptions of Mary and some saints – has never been accomplished.

Our Blessed Mother in 1917 promised to Lucy, Francesco and Jacinta at Fatima that finally after great turmoil and chastisement God would grant a period of peace to the whole existing world. It would be a peace that would resemble the world before Adam and Eve sinned. Finally, the people of the world would do God's Will for the first time and enjoy a world of love of God and love of neighbor.

Real peace has taken a long time to come but, with God's power and Mary's intercession, it will finally come. What a blessing we await.

Mary, Co-Redemptrix

Some years ago the business world encouraged people to collect green coupons to be used to obtain various merchandise in their businesses. It was a business way of inviting potential customers to become involved in their products. In effect, customers used the coupons to redeem merchandise.

God the Father's divine product is eternal life in heaven. When Adam and Eve rejected this wonderful prize and gift, the Son of God volunteered to join the human race in order to redeem and win back eternal life.

Through an angel he invited Mary, a humble maiden, to be his mother and his channel into this world. Mary in her humility accepted the invitation and God's process of redemption of the human race began immediately and continued for thirty-four years, to the moment of crucifixion. The cross is the sign of our redemption, opening again to mankind the prize and gift of eternal life in heaven.

From the moment Mary accepted her role as mother, she continued throughout her Son's life to assist and nurture Him even to her sorrowful presence under the cross. She perfectly cooperated with and obeyed all of God's wishes and designs for His Son, Jesus.

Because she perfectly assisted in the work of Jesus' redemptive acts, she stands now with Him as co-redemptrix. In a much lesser way we too are invited by Jesus to assist in our own redemption. Jesus invites each of us to follow Him to our own cross in this world that we may enjoy the reward of heaven some day. As the poet says, "No cross, no crown." Our daily prayer and works can be the green coupons of eternity – assisting us in our own redemption.

Advent – A Time of Preparation

The world is "all dressed up" but does not know where to go. And yet the place is right before our eyes – the eternal home of God our Father. For centuries God has been preparing for our visit. Everything is ready: the choirs of angels have been practicing for years; the banquet has been "in the making" by God; His mother, Mary, and foster father, Joseph, are in their places; our families have gone on ahead and already are celebrating – all that is needed are the guests. What is holding us back? One person quipped, "We are all dying to get there, but nobody wants to go."

Our Blessed Mother is said to have informed Estela Ruiz of South Phoenix, Arizona since 1988 that, "The world is in the need of the goodness and love of God. As Mother of God, Jesus, our Saviour, I come to touch men's hearts so that out of those who hear me and answer, God can raise up great saints, men and women of great faith, strong in their love of God, trusting God implicitly, men and women obedient to God's commandments. These holy people will become the light of God, bringing peace and joy to all, in God's name." (March 20, 1993) Nine months later, Mary spelled it out even more clearly, "I, as your Heavenly Mother, come to invite you, to encourage you to open your hearts to God's spirit that He may change you from weak humans to great soldiers of His work. If you say 'Yes' to Him, He will fill you with His spirit and will do great things through you."

During the Advent season, as we prepare for the coming of Jesus in our hearts, Mary offers each of us a wonderful opportunity for holiness and spiritual greatness. It only takes a joyous and ready "Yes" to God and we will be on our way. Why wait around doing nothing, when we could be busy with God?

Abortion

In a recent ABC program on abortion entitled "A Civil War," with Peter Jennings and a panel of experts, one of the panelists pointed out that in most cases of abortion the woman involved is presented with no choice in the abortion clinics. What is the Catholic Church's teaching about choosing to abort a child in pregnancy?

The Catholic Church continues to teach that abortion, for whatever reason, is killing an unborn child. The Church believes that we are a created person of God from conception and, even though we have not been born, we are truly God's child and have every right to be born. No one, including our mother, ever has the right to choose to put us to death by whatever means. On the contrary, mothers and fathers must do all in their power to preserve and maintain the life of their child in the womb and continue their care and vigilance after our birth.

We honor our Blessed Mother from the moment of her conception and celebrate her feast of the Immaculate Conception. Likewise we honor her son, Jesus, from the first moment that the Angel Gabriel announced His conception in Mary's womb by celebrating the feast of the Annunciation.

Our world, especially the United States, has done a serious disservice to God's creation by legalizing the abortion of children in the womb. All who believe in everyone's right to life from the womb to old age need to pray diligently that our country "wakes up" and begins to respect the life of all its citizens, both born and unborn.

Born of the Virgin Mary

Who Was Born on Christmas Day?

It is the day after Thanksgiving and suddenly it is Christmas, at least in the media and business world. Who are they celebrating? Red Nosed Reindeers and Santa Claus; Snowbirds and Christmas sox; new toys and Christmas trees – but where is the Divine Infant, Jesus, and His new parents, Mary and Joseph?

The local town hall does not want them, the school board voted them down, the government does not know what to do with them, and they remain an embarrassment for most people. But how can anyone celebrate Christmas without Christ? It is not easy to do, but our world does its best to ignore Him and His parents. The members of the Holy Family were outcasts from the very beginning with Herod, the local king, and remain so with the Herods of today.

Is there any decent believer willing to stand up and applaud in the public area the beauty and mystery of the Holy Family? Perhaps that can be our birthday gift to the Lord.

Christ's Birth – A Divine Event

Every year on December 25th, the Christian world is privileged to celebrate the birthday of the God-Man, Jesus Christ. At the same time, the business world celebrates its financial profits generated by this divine birthday. The non-Christian world usually shows disinterest in the event. As Catholic people, we believe that something wonderful has occurred – God has sent His Divine Son into the world through a Jewish virgin-mother so that He would redeem mankind through His Son's painful death on the cross. The death of Jesus would be the price to pay Almighty God for the many sins of mankind from Adam to the end of the world. Each of us is included in this payment and necessarily must participate by our daily response to God.

Unfortunately, our Catholic people in large numbers look to the celebration of Christmas as a time to offer gifts to one another instead of offering gifts to the Christ-child. While some Catholics will prepare themselves through the Sacrament of Confession and daily Mass, many limit their response to God on His Son's birthday in the world by a few gifts to family and perhaps with a family dinner. Generosity to the parish does increase at Christmas time. Instead of a weekly contribution of $10 or $15, many Catholics will double their gift on Christmas Day, but their average weekly contributions return to the weekly norm after the holiday. Every parish has at least one or two parishioners at Christmas time who give a very generous gift of money and food to be distributed to poor and needy families. But by and large our Catholic parishioners are very minimal in their weekly gift to Christ's Church. An exception to the rule is a parish of 2,500 families in Kansas City, Kansas which averages weekly support of $75,000, most of which pays for a health clinic and all parochial and high school tuitions of parish students.

Certainly, every birthday is a cause for celebration, because everyone created by God affects the development and growth of the world around us. We celebrate the birthdays of the pope, great presidents like Washington and Lincoln, our parents who brought us to life and other important people. But who can compare with the importance of the God-Man, Jesus Christ? And who can compare with the virgin-girl, Mary of Nazareth, who fully cooperated with God's plan for our redemption by permitting the Son to be conceived within her? The first Christmas arrived nine months later, and the entire world changed for the better from that day. Hopefully, with Christ, we will continue to change for the better.

Mary, Our Spiritual Mother

I know that I should be more understanding of people outside the Catholic faith who have a problem accepting the mother of Jesus as their spiritual mother, but it is difficult. We read in John 19:26-27: "When Jesus saw his mother and the disciple there whom he loved, he said to his mother, 'Woman, behold, your son.' Then he said to the disciple, 'Behold, your mother.' And from that hour the disciple took her into his home." In that moment of agony, the suffering Son, Jesus, committed the care of His mother to John, the Apostle and to us, his spiritual brothers and sisters. Mary became our spiritual mother from that moment. Just as she accepted her Son at the moment of her Annunciation, so she accepted all of us as her adopted sons and daughters – at the invitation of her Divine Son on the cross.

I am aware that some non-Christians such as the followers of Mohammed have a great respect and love for Mary. Nonetheless, other non-Catholics shy away from loving her. It will be interesting when these people meet Mary someday in heaven. How surprised they will be at her motherly love for them.

Prior to their reception into the Catholic faith, Scott Hahn and his wife, Kimberly, both Presbyterians and ministers as well, admit that they were both anti-Catholic and very anti-Mary. But as they studied the scriptures and the early Fathers of the Church, their early bias disappeared and was replaced with love and admiration. In their story of conversion, *Rome Sweet Home* (Ignatius Press), they quote Archbishop Fulton Sheen in their preface: "There are not over a hundred people in the United States who hate the Roman Catholic Church; there are millions, however, who hate what they wrongly believe to be the Catholic Church."

Once people discover the real Catholic Church, they also come to love and accept Mary as their spiritual mother. Even so, like a true mother, Mary loves all her children – no matter their lack of response. She is like our own natural mother who loves us no matter what. Before a special mother died, she sent a card to her son that read, "I like you just because you're you; But what the heck, I'd like you even if you were somebody else...Love, Mother." Mary would say the same.

Apparitions of Our Lady

Increasingly, over the past century, Mary, the mother of Jesus, has appeared in frequent apparitions to young people in France, Portugal, Ireland and other countries. What is the significance and message of her appearances?

Our Christian faith finds its very beginnings in the apparitions of the Angel Gabriel to Mary of Nazareth, the young girl engaged at the time to

Joseph, the carpenter. With Mary's consent, God sent His Divine Son into the world, which had great need for a Saviour and Redeemer.

Today, our present world, immersed in the selfishness and sinfulness of abortion, euthanasia, drugs, pornography and illicit sex, truly needs Jesus as Saviour and Redeemer. It would seem that Mary's frequent apparitions in this century are God's approach to draw the world back to His Son, Jesus. Mary's message includes: return to daily prayer, conversion of our hearts, repentance for sins, fasting and peace of soul.

Mary's role today seems to be one of a Messenger of Peace and Reconciliation. She calls herself "Our Lady of Peace" and promises peace to the world that responds to her requests.

Secret to Peace

We all love to know a secret about others but are offended if our personal secrets are revealed. Our Eternal Father has had secrets from all eternity which He has finally revealed to a world that will listen and believe. From the moment that the peace of the Garden of Eden was disturbed and broken by the disobedience of our First Parents, God began to reveal the solution to recovering that heavenly peace.

In our time, in 1917, three young shepherds in Fatima, Portugal, met in apparition and vision a beautiful Lady in the fields who revealed that "she came from Heaven" and promised a wonderful peace to the world if the people of the world would consecrate themselves to her Immaculate Heart and return in prayer and penance to her Son, Jesus.

In more recent times, since 1981, six young people in Medjugorje, Bosnia, claim that Mary, the Mother of God, appears daily as Our Lady of Peace. She asks that we return to the weekly Eucharist, monthly Confession, fasting on bread and water (Wednesday and Friday), and praying the full rosary daily for peace in our hearts and in our world.

If we believe all the many claimed apparitions of Mary in the last 150 years from Lourdes, France to the present moment, we have to believe that God's secret from eternity for restoring the shattered peace of the Garden of Eden to civilization today is in the hands of Mary, Queen of Peace. Through our love and devotion to Mary, we will come to Her Son – who is Peace Himself – a peace attained by His Blood shed on the cross. Jesus will then present us to His Father, and Our Father will then dispense His heavenly peace once again to the world. It seems like a simple solution, and it is. It is a great secret – now revealed in our time.

Mary, Our Advocate

How many times in our life have we invited the Mother of God to intercede for us with her Son, Jesus? As children, we repeated her beautiful prayer: "Hail, Holy Queen, Mother of Mercy, our life, our sweetness and our hope…Turn, then, most gracious advocate your eyes of mercy toward us." Mary is and has been our advocate before God in all our endeavors. When Archbishop Fulton Sheen spoke of his moment after death when he would appear before Jesus, he said that he hoped that Jesus would say to him: "My Mother has often spoken about you." How consoling to have the Mother of God as your friend and advocate before God.

It all began with Mary's acceptance of God's invitation to become the mother of His Son. From that moment and throughout her life on earth, Mary continued to respond affirmatively to God's Will. Finally, from His cross, Jesus, Her Son, entrusted His mother to the care of St. John, the Apostle. Consequently, from that moment, Mary accepted her task as spiritual Mother of us all. After the Ascension of Jesus, Peter and the other ten Apostles met in the upper room in Jerusalem: "All these devoted themselves with one accord to prayer, together with some women, and Mary the mother of Jesus, and his brothers." (Acts 1:14)

To this day – from the early days of the church – Mary, our Spiritual Mother, has taken an active role in the Church and specifically in the lives of all its members – interceding for us with Her Son.

While Mary continues to do her part, sometimes we fail to respond to her. Many Catholic people fail to appreciate her presence in their daily lives – even to the point of ignoring her presence, or even disbelieving in her place with God. Unfortunately, the modern world has little time for the Mother of God and, at times, even mocks her God-given attributes of perpetual virginity and Immaculate Conception.

Consequently, Mary depends on the minority of her children to offer praise, devotion and obedience to her. Like our mothers of today – whose children when young "break their backs" and when older "break their hearts" – Mary, the spiritual mother of all, suffers similarly. Perhaps only in Heaven will we appreciate the daily attention and devotion that Mary provides for all of us. She is our daily Advocate before God. Let us acknowledge her now while we have time. It is not too late.

A Great Mother

In the Holy Family of Jesus, Mary and Joseph, there were many moments of happiness and joy. Although the prophecy of Simeon hung over their heads from the Lord's presentation in the Temple eight days after His birth – "Behold, this child is destined for the fall and rise of many in Israel, and to be a sign that will be contradicted (and you yourself a sword will pierce)...." (Luke 2: 34-35) – yet the Holy Family remained in peace and obedience to God's Will.

Later at age twelve, the young Jesus began to manifest His mission in life. Staying behind in Jerusalem three days, He countered His mother's worry – "Son, why have you done this to us?" (Luke 2:48) – with the response "Did you not know that I must be in my Father's house?" (Luke 2:49) As a matter of fact, Mary and Joseph did not know or understand.

Some teenagers presume that parents understand their mysterious and unpredictable actions. They come home late at night without any explanation of where they have been and why they are late. Meantime, parents are worried and upset, thinking that their children have been in an accident and are hurt. The very least that young people owe their parents is a phone call that all is well.

We wonder why Jesus put His parents through this three-day trial. Maybe He was preparing them for the day of His great trial – as Mary would be called to watch Him die on His cross. At the crucifixion, Mary might ask Him again why He had done this to us, and Jesus might respond: "Did you not know that I came to save the world from sin?"

As baptized people, we are privileged to have this strong suffering woman as our spiritual Mother. No wonder God has made her our advocate and mediatrix of all His graces. A great mother is Mary.

Holy Family – Jesus, Mary and Joseph

It is good to honor God the Father of all mankind. He is our Divine Father who creates, protects and nourishes everyone on earth with His marvelous grace and love. In return, He asks only that we acknowledge Him in prayer and obey Him in love. He provides much and asks very little of each of us. Yet we are very stingy in our response to Him. Still He waits in eternal patience for our daily response to His invitation of love.

Meantime He sends us His greatest gift in the person of His Son, Jesus. He began on the first Christmas by entrusting Jesus to Joseph of Nazareth, a new father through adoption, and to Mary, a young virgin of Nazareth, now married to Joseph. These two people accepted their role as parents of the Father's Only Son, Jesus. In obedience to God the Father they loved and raised their Son with the greatest care and protection. As parents they showed Him by their example of marital love and affection how parents should live in harmony with God and their neighbors. They instructed their son in the daily tasks and duties of everyday by both word and example. Mary's chores in the home and Joseph's tasks in the carpentry shop helped Jesus to form the illustrations of many of His instructions in later life.

While Joseph and Mary provided their son with much human instruction, their greatest contribution to Him was their love and obedience to His Heavenly Father. Would that parents today, and everyone, would look to God the Father in the same way. He is only a prayer away.

St. Bernadette and "The Lady"

Bernadette Soubirous was a twelve-year old French peasant girl in Lourdes in 1858 when she met a beautiful Lady outside her village. The Lady instructed her to have the priest build a church in her honor. Obediently, Bernadette instructed the priest, who was not impressed with the demand but told the little girl to ask "The Lady" for some sign of her identity. In return, "The Lady" said, "Tell the priest I am the Immaculate

Conception." Upon hearing the response, the parish priest knew immediately "The Lady" was Mary, the Mother of God. It was only four years previously in 1854 that the Holy Father with the bishops of the Church had declared the dogma of the Immaculate Conception of Mary. Now Mary had come to confirm the Church's teaching.

The result of that meeting with Bernadette is the beautiful Basilica of the Immaculate Conception at Lourdes, France. In the past 140 years, millions of people have visited Lourdes to be bathed in its miraculous waters and honor the Mother of God and her Son. Evidenced in the corridors of the huge basilica are rows of crutches and various bodily helps left by people who walked away without them. In honor of His Immaculate Mother, Jesus has restored thousands of people to bodily and spiritual health as He did years ago on the shores of the Sea of Galilee.

Just as Almighty God prepared the future mother of His Son, Jesus, by filling her soul from the beginning with His divine life, so too God invites everyone created by Him to share in His divine life through baptism and the sacraments of the Church. "The image and likeness of God" lost through the sin of Adam and Eve are returned to each of us at the moment of baptism. And for those people who do not recognize the presence of Jesus, God still graces them when they freely return their love and honor to Him and live in love with their neighbor. The merciful God never excludes anyone from His friendship on earth and in heaven. Some people, however, may choose to exclude themselves through their sinfulness. Despite the Mercy of God, some may choose freely to go to eternal hell. Our Immaculate Lady asks everyone to pray for great sinners that they will be sorry and return to God. Prayer works!

May Crowning

A most beautiful and impressive moment each May is the crowning of the statue of Mary, the Mother of God, in the parish church. In the presence of the First Communicants, parents and parishioners, children honor their heavenly Mother with a crown of flowers, and all present consecrate themselves in prayer to Mary. Almighty God – Father, Son and Holy Spirit – must be very pleased when we honor Mary. For Mary of Nazareth was selected from all ages to become the daughter of the

Father, the mother of the Son and the spouse of the Holy Spirit. Then, from the cross, Jesus gave Mary to all of us as our spiritual mother.

It is the hope of many in the Church that soon our Holy Father, Pope John Paul II, will affirm the role that Mary accepted from God and has fulfilled throughout the years of the Church, that of being the Co-Redemptrix, Mediatrix and Advocate for God's people. She accepted and cooperated with the mission of her Son to offer Himself in sacrifice on the cross. It was Mary and John beneath the cross who suffered with Him and who accepted His dead body for burial. It was Mary who spoke out in intercession to her Son for the bridal couple, "They have no wine." (John 2:3) And so now it continues in heaven when Mary, our Mother, is the channel of God's grace and blessing to us – and has been from the beginning of the Church. She is the Mediatrix of all grace to us from God.

God has chosen to answer all prayer and favors through His mother. We cannot tell God how He should answer our prayer. He has His own way, and Mary is involved. From the moment she said her "Yes" to God, she became involved. It is much like the "Yes" of the saints such as St. Theresa and St. Bernadette, who committed themselves to God in their lifetime. Now God allows them to bring His graces and favors to us when we pray. It is claimed that St. Theresa sends a rose in evidence of her assistance.

It is never too late for anyone of us to say "Yes" to God in our lifetime and eventually join Mary and all the saints someday. God invites everyone!

The Mothers of the First Priests

As the month of June completes its celebrations in honor of the two Sacred Hearts of Jesus and His mother, Mary, we come to the first leaders of the Apostles, Simon Peter and Saul/Paul – both of whom gave testimony to their love and loyalty to Jesus and His newly-founded church. As our first leaders – Peter to the Jewish people and Paul to the Gentile people – we admire them and try to emulate them in their courage.

But then as we look deeper, we wonder what their mothers were like. What kind of example of love and prayer did these men receive in their early youth? Although their mothers are not mentioned in scripture, Peter's mother–in-law is listed in Matthew as being sick with a fever when Jesus visited their home in Capernaum by the sea. (Matt. 8: 14-15)

Although we cannot compare their mothers to the mother of Jesus, still they must have instilled the seeds of great virtue in their sons for them to grow in the marvelous spiritual strength they manifested.

Would that mothers today and all parents would emulate the mothers and parents of these first Apostles and disciples of the Church. Would that today parents would pray for the gift of a priest-son or religious-daughter. Our seminaries and convents are almost empty of new candidates for the priesthood and religious life. Where are the future "Simon/Peters" and "Saul/Pauls" to lead our Catholic Church and people? Have our Catholic mothers and fathers stopped praying for a priest-son or religious-daughter? Have they ever begun to pray for and encourage their family?

There is an old poem entitled "His Mother's Monument" which tells the story of a priest who made his way one evening to the graveyard where his mother's body lay in a tomb. The priest made excuses and apologies to his mother for the fact that no monument had yet been erected in her honor. Then her voice came sweetly from the tomb saying: "My monument was built in my womb, my greatest praise was won, the hour that you became my priestly son. For all the souls in heaven whom you have sent, forever proclaim you as my monument." Amen.

Mary's Garment

Recently during the Sabres division playoff, almost every teenager was wearing a Sabres sweater or jacket. It is the same thing with Buffalo Bills shirts and caps during football season. We call it Sabres/Bills fever. All the sports fans want to acknowledge their favorite sports heroes.

About 700 years ago, in a mountain monastery of Carmelite priests and brothers, Mary the Mother of God presented to Fr. Simon Stock her own special cloth garment for us to wear. It is called a scapular because it is worn around our neck, near our scapular bone. Just as the Sabres/Bills clothing demonstrates loyalty, Mary's scapular around our neck testifies to our love and loyalty to her. And Mary can win more battles for us than the Sabres and Bills put together!

Mary promises that those who wear her scapular faithfully will never go to hell, but at the hour of death, she will personally protect them and even escort them to heaven. In effect, if we root for Mary in life and wear her brown garment, she will watch over us in a special way. Neither the Sabres nor the Bills can make such a promise to any of their fans.

It is usual for children making their First Holy Communion to be enrolled by a priest in the brown scapular of Our Lady of Mt. Carmel. Where this does not happen, Catholics of any age can request their parish priest to perform this enrollment at any time. The original scapular is cloth and is preferred by the Church. However, the Scapular Medal may be worn instead. The promises of Mary remain the same. Catholic sports fans are proud of their special heroes in the sports world; they should give at least equal time to their spiritual mother by wearing her garment – the brown scapular.

Even the honored sports world acknowledges her special abilities once in a while when, with all the odds against them on the very last play of the game, someone throws a "Hail Mary pass." Why wait for the end? Let us honor Mary now and every day. Wear her scapular now!

The Promise of Peace

In 1917 and again in 1929, the Blessed Mother appearing at Fatima, Portugal promised the entire world a great gift from God – the gift of peace on earth. Such a gift would literally do away with sin, since the devil would be banished for a period of time. Wars, hatred among people, and crimes against life would be non-existent during this period of peace. Some knowledgeable readers of Mary's promise foresee a return to the original happiness and joy of our First Parents – though like them, people would retain their "free will."

Mary's promise of peace, however, was preceded by a prediction of war and persecution that would take place first, unless the world changed its way of sin and returned to prayer and consecration to her Immaculate

Heart. "I ask that the Holy Father in union with the bishops of the church consecrate Russia to my Immaculate Heart, and that people come to Mass and confession on five first Saturdays for peace." She told the three children that World War I would cease soon but a more terrible war would begin in the time of Pope Pius XI unless people responded with prayer and the rosary. Then she revealed a message, prior to her promise of peace. That part of her message, known to the Pope, was not revealed until June 2000, when Pope John Paul II made it known. It contained two visions: the first of an angel with a flaming sword which was extinguished in contact with our Lady; the second of a bishop in white who was killed at the foot of a cross. "The Holy Father will have much to suffer," Mary said at Fatima. But Mary also promised peace: "In the end there will be peace," she said.

Over the past thirty years there has been a large falling away of Catholic people, especially younger people. Many priests and religious women have left their vocations for marriage and for other pursuits. Mary has apparently continued her apparitions in many other areas of the world, apart from Fatima, and continues to ask for a return to her Divine Son. But her words fall on deaf ears. People are reluctant to hear and respond. In most cases of apparent Marian apparitions, the local bishops are quiet or slow to approve. Consequently, Mary's message remains unheard and unknown. It is the gospel message of repentance of sin and return of the prodigal son to his father in prayer and forgiveness. Some Marian apparitions do have church approval – Knock in Ireland, Lourdes in France, Fatima in Portugal, Akita in Japan, Betania in Venezuela and some others. Yet people in great numbers remain away, and true peace has yet to arrive in the world. Perhaps peace will come finally after 2000 years. Let us pray and respond to Mary, Our Mother.

Mother's Day – Beginning with Mary, The Mother of God

Mothers are special people to their children. Our father is very important to us, but our mother is special and unique. We might forgive someone who is nasty toward our father, but we will not tolerate anyone who offends our mother. We will protect our mother at all costs.

If this is true with human beings, it is more true with God. Almighty God loves and protects His Mother. When she was in danger of being stoned by her own villagers, God sent the Angel Gabriel to Joseph: "Joseph, son of David, do not be afraid to take Mary your wife into your home." (Matt. 1:20) When Joseph arose from sleep, he wedded Mary and protected her from being stoned to death. In heaven today, Mary, our spiritual Mother, occupies a place next to her divine Son.

While we have the opportunity in life to show special honor to our earthly mother, we should take every advantage. We should help her at home and ease her burden of work. As we grow older, we should find the time to honor her with our presence and love. When she is unable to be independent, we should attend to her needs.

Likewise, those who are wise will learn to relate to our wonderful spiritual Mother, Mary, in prayer and deed. Mary is our Lady of Grace and Holiness during our life, our motherly companion leading us to Her Son, Jesus, and our advocate at the Throne of God.

It is unfortunate that many in life do not know or appreciate Mary. One such person approaching a priest said that he did not see any difference between Mary and his own mother, to which the priest replied, "You may not see any difference between the mothers, but there is a great difference between the sons."

We need to pray for others that they may appreciate their spiritual Mother.

Faithful Disciple

It was on the feast of All Saints, November 1, 1950, that Pope Pius XII proclaimed to the world that Mary, the mother of Jesus, having completed her earthly life, was taken up into heaven, body and soul. Christians have believed in Mary's bodily assumption from the earliest times of the Church. We find it in the writings of the early Church Fathers. We even find this truth depicted by a ninth century artist in the basilica of St. Clement's in Rome.

As Catholic people, we accept this proclamation of the bodily assumption of Mary after death as an infallible teaching of the Church. While we may not totally understand this great gift of God to Mary, we believe that it happened shortly after her death. We believe that Jesus ascended into heaven by His own power as God, and we likewise believe that Mary in her resurrected body was taken up to heaven by God's power.

Just as Mary was at her Divine Son's side in this world, so shall she be at His side in the next world. From her Immaculate Conception in the womb of her mother, Anna, to her own death in the care of St. John, Mary remained a faithful servant to her son, Jesus, and to His Church.

One day while Jesus was speaking to a crowd, a woman called out: "Blessed is the womb that carried you…." (Luke 11:27) Jesus responded, "Rather, blessed are those who hear the word of God and observe it." (Luke 11:28) While Jesus appreciated His physical relationship to Mary, His mother, He praised her spiritual gift of faithfulness and obedience to His father's Will. It is the same with all of God's children. While He loves all of His children, He relates most to those who are obedient to His Will. "Whoever has my commandments and observes them is the one who loves me." (John 14:21) Who more than Mary, His mother, observed and kept His commandments? We need to imitate Mary.

Mary's Dormition

The sacred writings of the New Testament contain references to Mary as a young Jewish virgin girl who accepted the awesome task of becoming the mother of God. Mary appears again several more times in scripture: presenting her infant son in the Temple, finding her lost 12-year old Son in the temple, reminding her 30-year old Son of the lack of wine at a Cana wedding, seeking to protect her 31-year old Son from the crowds, standing at the foot of the cross of her 33-year old crucified Son, and finally joining with the Apostles in the newly energized Church on Pentecost Sunday, when the Holy Spirit in tongues of fire came down upon the believers.

After that first Pentecost Sunday, there are no more references to Mary in the sacred scripture. Oral and written tradition in the early writings of the early Fathers of the Church have Mary living out her remaining 25 years of life with St. John the Apostle, to whose care she was entrusted by her Son on the cross.

The city of Ephesus in modern Turkey claims the home where Mary and John lived after the death of Jesus. Eventually, Mary died a natural death. But again, the scriptures are silent. We need to rely on the writings of the early Fathers of the Church, who referred to Mary's death as a "falling asleep" or dormition. Tradition has a number of the Apostles present at her death. But Mary had no burial. Shortly after her death, according to oral and written tradition, her body was taken up with her soul into heaven by God. Hence the Church celebrates the feast of the Assumption of Mary into heaven every August 15th as a holy day of obligation.

As Catholics, we believe that at the end of the world God will call all of us to the final judgment, body and soul – either to heaven or to hell. Concerning Mary, God did not wait for the end of the world to bring her body and soul to heaven. Mary received a special privilege in the beginning of her life – her Immaculate Conception – and then again at the end of her life – her Bodily Assumption. She deserved both honors.

Little Christmas

Long before the Church adopted December 25th as our annual celebration of the Birthday of Jesus, the feast of Epiphany was the official celebration of Christmas. On this day, people of the Catholic world exchanged gifts in honor of the Christ child, in imitation of the Magi, or kings from the east. The Magi brought to their newborn infant king gifts of gold, frankincense and myrrh as a testimony to the Divine King, born of woman, who would someday die for the sins of the whole world.

When we come together on the feast of Epiphany, Jesus looks for our gifts to Him – not gold, frankincense and myrrh, but our hearts filled with charity, prayer and penance. Our Lord has no need from us of gifts of material things since He owns the world, but He greatly desires our love and devotion. The rich are poor indeed if they think our Lord is attracted by their material wealth, and the poor are rich indeed if they can only offer Jesus their gifts of love, reverence and obedience to His Will.

When the crippled man at The Gate Beautiful in Jerusalem asked St. Peter for alms, St. Peter responded: "I have neither silver nor gold, but what I do have I give you: in the name of Jesus Christ the Nazorean, [rise and] walk." (Acts 3:6) St. Peter possessed the wealth of Jesus Christ, the power of the Holy Name of Jesus, through whom all peoples have received their eternal salvation. What a treasure to possess reverence for the name of Jesus in a world that uses the Holy Name as a vulgar expression in everyday life.

Today, more than at any other time in history, Jesus invites all of God's creatures to return to Him and to His Father in prayer, sacrifice and obedience to His Will. These are gifts that all of us are capable of giving to our Creator – no matter our state in life – whether we are rich or poor.

We need not wait for an Epiphany feast to respond to God. Today, even, would be a suitable time. Why not begin now?

Visitors to the Home

The custom of marking the front door at Christmas time comes from an eastern world tradition that popularizes the three Magi, or kings from the east – Caspar, Melchior and Balthasar. Eastern Christians and now a number of Western Catholic people mark in white chalk the initials of these three with a cross in the middle and the current year in order to welcome the Magi, together with Christmas and New Year visitors, to the home. During the year some Catholic people proudly welcome Jesus with a crucifix displayed in the living area. Others at Christmas time place a crib with the infant Jesus and parents, Joseph and Mary, beneath the Christmas tree. One Vietnamese family in Florida displayed a large statue of St. Martin, their patron, and Our Lady, completely lit, outside their home. Some Catholics are not ashamed or afraid to manifest their Catholic faith to others. Unfortunately, many Catholics seem to hide their faith with bare walls or walls laden with worldly art.

The Magi of old were not afraid or ashamed to show their faith in the Infant Jesus. In fact, they brought gifts of gold, worthy of a king; precious frankincense, whose fragrance ascended to the heavens; and myrrh, a symbol of death. Despite their fear of King Herod, who sought the death of the infant king, the Magi completed their homage and returned home by a different route.

We live in days of fear and terror due to the Herods of today. Yet we need not live our lives in fear and trembling, since we possess the Prince of Peace and the King of Kings, Jesus Christ. Jesus is our divine leader and the head of the Church, of which the Pope is His Vicar. We need only turn our minds and hearts toward Jesus and invite Him into our daily life. "Come to me, all you who labor and are burdened, and I will give you rest." (Matt. 11:28) He will come if you will invite Him. And He will bring with Him God His Father, His Holy Spirit, together with Mary and Joseph. It doesn't get any better than that. Try it. You will like it.

Suffered under Pontius Pilate, was crucified, died and was buried

And Jesus Wept

The death of a loved one – a father, mother, brother or sister – is a traumatic moment for anyone. It is a time of pain and sorrow as we experience the loss of someone we love.

It was equally a difficult moment for Jesus as He met His close friends, Martha and Mary, as they came in sorrow after the death of their brother, Lazarus. Saint John tells us, "And Jesus wept." (John 11:35) Jesus remembered the enjoyable hospitality of Martha, Mary and Lazarus at their home in Bethany. They were his good and loyal friends. Now Lazarus had died without the consolation of his good friend, Jesus, at his bedside. It would seem that when He was needed most, Jesus deliberately remained away. While His Apostles must have wondered, Jesus had a purpose. He intended to reveal His divine power as God's Son. Saint John tells us that after He called upon His Father, Jesus cried out in a loud voice, "Lazarus, come out!" The dead man came out, tied hand and foot, with his face wrapped in a cloth. Jesus said to them "Untie him and let him go." (John 11:43-44) Little did anyone suspect by His miraculous action that Jesus was preparing for His own death and then His bodily resurrection from the dead on Easter Sunday.

It was shortly after this that Jesus was invited again to Lazarus' home for a special dinner. The Passover celebration was within a few days. Mary took costly perfumed oil and anointed the feet of Jesus – in preparation for His death. (John 12:3)

Today our priests anoint with a special olive oil on the foreheads and hands of our people who are in any danger of death from old age, infirmity or accidents. This Sacrament of the Anointing of the Sick is meant to bring God's spiritual forgiveness and grace as well as any physical assistance that God permits and provides. Wise is the Catholic person who requests this grace-filled sacrament during his lifetime. Unfortunately, out of fear or misunderstanding, some Catholic people delay or put off this special gift from God. It comes too late after death.

Jesus was grateful to Mary for her service of anointing: "Let her keep this for the day of my burial." (John 12:7) We should express our gratitude to our priests and to God. It is a great gift.

Get Behind Me, Satan

The mystery of the Incarnation of Jesus, taking on human nature and living as God-man, is inexplicable and difficult for us to understand and explain. We believe in it but cannot fathom or explain it.

Years ago a cartoonist developed a very popular character called Superman, who could leap over tall buildings, fly like a jet plane and yet, during the day, would work as a reporter for a daily newspaper. Young people were fascinated by this superhero who would rescue people in distress and subdue the thieves and bad guys with his super powers.

In one sense, Our Lord is like a divine superman. Though He is God, yet He lives in human "flesh and blood," and eventually He dies very horribly on a cross, is buried, rises from the dead, and returns to His Father. The difference, however, between Jesus and other ordinary men is that, by His Divine Power, He can and did return from the dead.

To prepare His Apostles for His death, Jesus reveals to them the manner and circumstances involved with His death and resurrection. "From that time on, Jesus began to show his disciples that he must go to Jerusalem and suffer greatly from the elders, the chief priests, and the scribes, and be killed and on the third day be raised." (Matt. 16:21) This revelation was too much for Peter who exclaimed, "God forbid, Lord! No such thing shall ever happen to you." (Matt. 16:22) Jesus retorted to Peter: "Get behind me, Satan! You are an obstacle to me." (Matt. 16:23)

The same Satan had come to Jesus as He was preparing in the desert for His public ministry. Three times Satan tempted Jesus until Jesus finally dismissed him, commanding Satan to get away. (Matt. 4:10) Now the devil comes again in the person of Peter and tempts Him to give up His mission of dying for us. The same devil tries to tempt and dissuade us in our Christian mission of living and dying in Christ. He tries to lure mankind toward hell by promising the easy life of comfort and sin. But Jesus asks us what profit there would be for one to gain the whole world and lose his soul. (Matt. 16:26)

We need to always choose Jesus over Satan – light over darkness.

The Crucifix

Since the time of Abraham when God commanded him to sacrifice his beloved son, Isaac, on the pyre of wood in obedience to Him, there has been the cross in our life. In the desert, in the time of Moses, God healed His people who looked upon the bronze serpent mounted on a pole. (Num. 21) Jesus refers to this moment when He told Nicodemus that just as Moses lifted up the serpent, so must God's Son be lifted up. (John 3:14)

In the time of Jesus, Mary and Joseph, the cross of the Romans was reserved for criminals of the state. Although Jesus did nothing to merit the title of a common criminal, the people of the legal system hated Him and taught others to do the same. They did this because He claimed to be God. When Jesus stood before the Jewish high court, Caiaphas, the high priest said to him, "I order you to tell us under oath before the living God whether you are the Messiah, the Son of God." Jesus said to him in reply, "You have said so." (Matt. 26:63-64) They said in reply, "He deserves to die!" (Matt. 26:66) The next morning Jesus was taken outside the city and was crucified. Since that day the cross became a symbol of victory – victory over sin and death.

From early Christian years the sign of the cross became the introduction to all Christian prayer and also to all the sacraments of the Church. Christians began and ended their Christian life with the sign of the cross. What had been a sign of fear and hatred in Roman times became, because of Christ's death on the cross, a sign of hope and love. Today, Christ continues to invite us to take up our cross daily and follow Him.

In many Catholic homes a crucifix is prominently displayed in the family room as a reminder of our obligation as Catholics to follow Him during our lifetime. Archbishop Fulton Sheen said on one occasion that the communist governments impose the cross on their people, but without Christ. They have great hardships but do not acknowledge Jesus Christ. America, however, honors Jesus but without the cross. America has the benefits of Jesus in the Mass and sacraments without accepting the pain and hardship of the cross. True Christians accept Jesus with and on the cross.

Our Cross

One day the mother of the Apostles James and John approached Jesus and requested that her sons sit at His right and left in His kingdom. Jesus then asked the two sons, "Can you drink the cup that I am going to drink?" to which they replied, "We can." (Matt. 20:22) Little did they understand and realize that Jesus was referring to His "cup of suffering and crucifixion" within a few weeks.

In time, all of the Apostles drank that same "cup of suffering" for their Catholic faith, and all but John, who cared for Mary, suffered a cruel death by crucifixion or the sword.

In Luke's gospel, Jesus speaks of this "cup of suffering" as a baptism that will cleanse the earth. "I have come to set the earth on fire...." (Luke 12:49) He then invites all of His followers to join Him in His mission to cleanse the earth of its sinfulness, pride and impurity. If we are truly His Apostles and disciples here in this world, we will join Him now.

When St. Francis of Assisi in Italy told his parents of his intention to follow Christ in a manner of poverty, chastity and obedience, they locked him up in a room until he would come to his senses. Today we thank St. Francis for his persistence in establishing the Franciscan Order of priests, sisters and brothers all over the world.

Catholic people are naive and misinformed who accept a Christian life without the trial, tribulations and sufferings that their leader, Jesus, endured as a price for our sins. If we are to follow Jesus properly, we are to follow Him to the cross. Any other way – a way of pleasure and ease – is not Christian. Although God permitted His Son to enjoy the fruits and joys of the earth, as He does His human creation, these things are only consolations that eventually lead to the cross. We all need to suffer and die in union with Jesus on His cross. We may try to run from our cross in life, but it will eventually catch us. "Without the cross, there is no crown." We need to offer up our daily crosses to God so that He will accept them in union with His Son's cross for the sins of the world.

Daily Cross

Perhaps the most difficult part of our Catholic faith to accept is the cross of Jesus Christ in our daily life. The joy and celebration of our Baptism, Eucharist and Confirmation stand in contrast to our acceptance of death, burial and resurrection in the life of our family and friends. Just the word "cancer" causes ripples of fear and unrest in our hearts. The thought of pain over a period of years is not something that most Catholics can embrace without fear and worry.

Yet the cross was the ultimate goal of our Saviour, Jesus Christ. When He invited us to follow Him, He held up His cross as a goal in life. He reminded us, "Whoever loves his life loses it, and whoever hates his life in this world will preserve it for eternal life." (John 12:25)

The Lenten season that occurs during springtime gives us an opportunity to live our particular cross of life in preparation for the Good Friday death and the Easter resurrection to eternal life with God. We need only invite the Presence of God into our daily life beginning with our morning prayer and continuing with every action during the day. As we live our daily union with God, we pledge to Him our love and devotion. Then every thought, word and action becomes our daily penance.

Someone remarked one day that it is not easy to live the Catholic faith, to which we reply "but it is wonderful to die in the Catholic faith."

Our Lord does not invite us to a world of joy and happiness now. Jesus promises that at the end of the age "the righteous will shine like the sun in the kingdom of their Father." (Matt. 13:43) It seems worth waiting for.

The Lamb

In countries where shepherds watch over their flocks of sheep, the lamb is a favorite among the flock, not only because it is somewhat defenseless but also because it is a victim for sacrifice. In the time of God's deliverance of the Israelites from Egyptian slavery, God ordered

Moses and his people to sacrifice a lamb as a victim for sin and celebrate a Seder supper every year in thanksgiving to God for their deliverance from slavery in Egypt.

In compliance with the Law of Moses, Jesus and His Apostles celebrated the Seder with an unblemished lamb at the Last Supper. Then He offered Himself as the True Lamb of God in sacrifice for the sins of the whole world when He took the bread and wine and instituted the Eucharist. (Matt. 26:26-28) Today, Christ's eternal priesthood continues daily to offer Jesus, the lamb, in the sacrifice of the Mass. "This is Jesus Christ, the Lamb of God, who takes away the sins of the world," the priest celebrant says at the time of Holy Communion. "Happy are those who are called to His supper."

As Catholic people, we believe that Jesus Christ is present at every Mass both as priest and as victim. He offers Himself as priest and is offered as victim to His Father. He is both the Good Shepherd who tends His flock and, likewise, the lamb-victim offered for the sins of the world. He voluntarily ascended His cross on Good Friday and was offered as a bloody sacrifice.

When Jesus invited His Apostles to follow Him, He had His cross in mind. We too are invited to share His cup of suffering on earth that we might enjoy His risen life in heaven. There is no suffering in heaven. Thanks be to God!

The Hospitality of Christ

During the months of May and June, there seems to be an endless run of parties and celebrations, from First Communions, to graduations, to birthdays and wedding anniversaries. And they are all important and pressing, especially for family members and close friends. Priests and religious are usually included. Then come the more leisurely months of July and August, with continual relaxing backyard barbecues and picnics.

For a parent to play host at these enjoyable and hospitable events requires work and sacrifice. In addition to purchasing and preparing the food, there is also the additional task of cleaning the house and yard in order that family and guests will be properly honored with clean facilities.

When Our Blessed Lord invites us daily to His sacred sacrifice and meal, there is likewise a great deal of work and sacrifice in preparation. In the early years, He showed us how very much He loved us by laying down His life on the cross and then daily repeated His sacrificial offering through the ministry of His priesthood. Today He chooses to feed us with His very Body and Blood, Soul and Divinity, under the external form of ordinary unleavened bread and wine. And like a host at a celebration here on earth, the Son of God, with the assistance of God the Father and God the Holy Spirit, presides over the Eucharistic celebration. Unlike a host at a party serving ordinary food, Jesus serves Himself as our Divine Sacrifice and heavenly food.

The twenty-foot crucifix that occupies the sanctuary wall at St. Bernadette's Church in Orchard Park shows a large white host surrounding the figure on the cross. Its presence testifies to the reality that Jesus crucified continues to live in the Sacred Host of the Mass and Holy Communion. Our Divine Host, presiding over our lives, continues to offer Himself daily in the Eucharist as our sacrifice and as our food. What a celebration our Divine Host, Jesus, invites each of us to – daily and forever. Can anyone top this invitation? Why do we not respond daily?

Communion in the Hand

Today many Catholics receive Jesus Christ in the Eucharist in their hands. Is it not more proper to receive Holy Communion on our tongue?

It is true that our parents and grandparents received Holy Communion on their tongue and that they knelt at the time of Communion. It is also true that, at the beginning of our century, Catholics received only once a year and made First Holy Communion at a later age. Our Lord has given Himself as our food for now and all eternity, and whether we kneel or stand, whether we receive Him as our food on our lips or in our hands, means little to Him. What matters is that we receive Him in respect and love and that we live our lives in harmony with His commandments of love of God and neighbor. Our Lord looks beyond our hands and lips and into our hearts.

Ridicule – A National Disease

The American Heritage Dictionary describes the word "ridicule" as words or actions to evoke contemptuous laughter at the expense of another person. Other words of mocking, taunting and deriding another person complete the meaning of the action of ridicule, a human disease invading our modern society.

Results of ridicule are seen in the recent and not-so-recent shootings of students in our schools. Students who have been the objects of ridicule and verbal abuse have ventilated their feelings by shooting their fellow students and teachers.

Authority figures have called in psychiatrists and psychologists to examine this phenomenon among our students. But I do not think we need to look too far for the source. Apart from parents at home, who spend their conversations in the presence of their children demeaning and criticizing their neighbors and their associates at work, there is another large and more vocal group whose profession seems to be constant ridicule of others.

Beginning with the media evening talk shows whose time on the air is spent in constant ridicule of our government leadership and anyone else with whom these so-called comedians disagree, to the very liberal editorial writers in our nation's newspapers, there is a constant flow of this national disease of verbal abuse. Our people who open a newspaper or turn on a television are fed a diet of ridicule aimed at those with whom the writers and reporters disagree. And there is no defense for the person involved.

Recently, it was reported that a local Catholic college sponsored at some expense a speech by a very liberal woman editorial writer who spent her time ridiculing and vilifying the new President and his wife – to the laughter of those present. This is a sad commentary on our Catholic higher education system. And then we fail to understand where our students are learning this vile practice of conduct.

Our Lord Himself suffered from the effects of this practice of ridicule from the Pharisees and Sadducees, legal representatives of the law in His day. He said to His Apostles, “Behold, we are going up to Jerusalem, and the Son of Man will be handed over to the chief priests and the scribes, and they will condemn him to death and hand him over to the Gentiles who will mock him, spit upon him, scourge him, and put him to death….” (Mark 10:33-34)

Jesus used strong words in describing the scribes and Pharisees, who appeared righteous on the outside but were filled with hypocrisy and evildoing on the inside. (Matt. 23:27) These strong words from the Son of God show how Our Lord feels about the practice of ridicule and verbal abuse. Our society, especially the media, needs to listen better to the Lord.

The Crucified King

When the remaining kings and queens of this world are presented to their subjects – as with the Queen of England – great pomp and ceremony accompany them. The finest wines and dinnerware are prepared at the table. The guests wear their finest clothing out of respect for their queen or king. But the Lord of heaven and earth, Christ the King, merits only a crown of thorns and a cross of cruelty. “Are you the king of the Jews?” Pilate asked Jesus, to which Jesus responded, “You say so.” (Matt. 27:11) Then the soldiers, kneeling before him, mocked him saying, “Hail, King of the Jews!” (Matt. 27:29)

Our eternal King deserves better treatment than we have given Him. As our King who freely accepted mockery and abuse for our salvation and freedom from sin, Jesus ought to be the center of our praise and thanksgiving every day. No other king or ruler has ever endured such pain and suffering for His people as did Christ our King.

Yet many people – including Catholics – show in their daily life little respect and regard for their eternal King by ignoring the Eucharist and daily prayer, by their disobedience to the commandments and their uncharitableness and injustice toward their fellow workers and neighbors.

St. Dominic Savio, who died as a young boy, lived his short life in Italy. On one occasion a priest, carrying the Eucharist to the sick, approached, so Dominic immediately knelt down while a soldier nearby remained standing. Dominic said to the soldier, "Kneel down, He is more than a general."

In Jesus we possess the King of Kings, the ruler and judge of the entire world. We need to acknowledge Him with our prayers and our actions.

Christ the King

In our democratic society today, we no longer have kings and queens, together with a royal family, although this was not true centuries ago. In England, there remains a remnant of royalty in the persons of Queen Elizabeth and her family – but they do not exercise any real authority as did the kings and queens in the past. In years gone by, the king had supreme authority over his subjects; his word was the law of the land. He could order life or death for his people.

When St. Patrick entered Ireland as bishop, he encountered the King, who through St. Patrick's word and example, became a convert to the Catholic faith and ordered all of his people to become Catholic. That is one reason why so many Irish people became Catholic at once. They followed the example of the King.

When standing trial before Pilate, Jesus was asked if He was the king of the Jews. Jesus replied: "My kingdom does not belong to this world." (John 18:36) Although God places each of us in this world, He intends that we spend only a short time and eventually return to His heavenly kingdom where His Divine Son, Jesus, has complete authority as King and Ruler. The difference between kings on earth and Christ the King is eternal love, joy and happiness. Jesus, our Heavenly King, will rule through love. His great sign on earth is His passion and death on the cross – the crucifix. Everywhere there is a crucifix, there is evidence of the King's love for us. His crown is made of thorns, His body is impaled with nails, His side is open from the soldier's lance – all these in recompense for our sins. "No one has greater love than this, to lay down one's life for one's friends." (John 15:13) Jesus, our King and Saviour, shows

His great love for us by laying down His life on the cross. For all eternity in heaven, we will be reminded of this great gift of our King. We shall be eternally grateful to Him.

I Was in Prison and You Visited Me

It is interesting that four of St. Paul's letters in the New Testament were written from a prison. They are called "captivity letters." He was a captive because of his testimony for Jesus Christ. In the final outcome, St. Paul was beheaded for his Catholic faith. Jesus, too, spent His last night on earth in a dungeon/prison – awaiting His fate of crucifixion the next day.

So Jesus, who can identify with those confined today in our prisons, reminds all Christians that whatever we do for the least brothers and sisters, we do for Him. (Matt. 25:40) A simple visit to someone confined in prison helps not only the prisoner but also the visiting friend or relative. The friend brings a sense of affection and love to someone who has lost a sense of worth and esteem. Prisons – with their impersonal identification numbers – reduce a personality to a number and a cell. Consequently, prisoners can quickly lose respect for themselves as well as for others. Certainly, our Lord does not restrict our deeds only to prisons, since we meet people daily in all avenues of life, but the loneliness and restricted life of a prison is a good place to begin.

We might identify with the dying prayer of St. Dismas, the good thief. When the other crucified thief taunted Jesus on the cross to save himself, St. Dismas responded, "Jesus, remember me when you come into your kingdom." (Luke 23:42) Jesus replied, "Amen, I say to you, today you will be with me in Paradise." (Luke 23:43) With a simple gesture of comfort and faith in Jesus, the good thief literally stole heaven. If we accept our Lord's invitation to welcome Jesus in others in need, we shall – like the good thief – do the same.

Feast of the Cross

In the early days of Christianity, St. Helena, the mother of the Emperor Constantine, organized a crusade to Jerusalem to find the true cross upon which Christ was crucified. The followers of Christ had buried it in the earth to protect its destruction by the Roman soldiers and the Jewish leadership. According to the tradition of the time, St. Helena unearthed a cross which manifested at touch many cures and miracles.

Today there are many Catholic churches which display a relic of this true cross encased in a beautiful reliquary. The cross was, in our Lord's day, a sign of suffering, punishment and disgrace until the Son of God ascended His cross as a means of suffering and expiating the sins of the world. Then the cross became a sign of victory over sin and His trophy of victory over the devil and his agents of evil. His painful death on the cross opened for all of us the gates of heaven which had been closed with our First Parents' sin of disobedience in the garden.

When you enter a Catholic church today, Jesus on His cross should be the center of your focus at the altar of sacrifice. On the cross, Jesus shed His blood for us. On the altar at Mass, Jesus continues to offer Himself under bread and wine – but in an unbloody manner. Jesus began His sacrifice on Holy Thursday at the Last Supper and continued His sacrifice for us on the cross on Good Friday. Jesus offered only one sacrifice, and He offered it forever.

It is interesting that today the Risen Christ occupies our attention in many Catholic churches, especially the newly built ones. Our liturgists and artists seem to have forgotten that before Jesus could rise on Easter Sunday, He necessarily needed to die on the cross on Good Friday. The crucifix reminds all of us that before we attain the glory of our resurrection into heaven, we need to follow Christ to our own cross in life and die to ours sins of selfishness, greed, uncharitableness and disobedience. Without living our cross today, we will not share His glory tomorrow. When Jesus invites us to follow Him, He takes us first to His cross and then to His joy – and His joy is forever.

Stations of the Cross

A popular devotion in the early Church was to visit the places of Our Lord's crucifixion and death on the cross in Jerusalem. Since the death and resurrection of Jesus represent His central contribution to our salvation, the Church has always blessed the devotion to the Stations of the Cross.

After the fourteen stations were erected in parish churches by the Franciscan priests, the Church granted a plenary indulgence (a full pardon of punishment due to sin) to everyone whenever they walk the fourteen Stations of the Cross, meditating on the events that occurred and praying for the intentions of our Holy Father, the Pope. The Church also asked that the people go to Confession and Holy Communion at that time.

Catholics who are devoted to the Stations of the Cross receive a very special appreciation of the great love of Jesus, who died for us. All that is required is a brief meditation at each station on the passion and death of Jesus and prayers of the Holy Father. All spiritual benefits are given to the Holy Souls in purgatory.

Sacred Heart of Jesus – First Friday Devotion

In the apparitions of Jesus to St. Margaret Mary Alacoque (1647-1690) at the Visitation Convent of Paray-le-Monial, France, beginning in 1673, twelve promises were given to increase devotion to the Sacred Heart of Jesus. They are:

1. I will give them all the graces necessary for their state in life.
2. I will establish peace in their families.
3. I will bless every home in which an image of My Heart is exposed and honored.
4. I will console them in all their difficulties.

5. I will be their refuge during life and especially at the hour of death.
6. I will shed abundant blessings upon all their undertakings.
7. Sinners shall find in My Heart a fountain and boundless ocean of mercy.
8. Tepid souls shall become fervent.
9. Fervent souls shall rise to great perfection.
10. I will give to priests the power of touching the hardest hearts.
11. Those who propagate this devotion shall have their names written on My Heart never to be erased.
12. I promise you, in the excessive mercy of My Heart, that My all powerful love will grant to all who communicate on the first Friday of the month for nine consecutive months, the grace of final penitence; they shall not die in My displeasure nor without their sacraments; My Divine Heart shall be their refuge in this last moment.

As a result, today – after more than three hundred years – people display prominently in their homes a picture of the Sacred Heart of Jesus and attend Mass and receive Holy Communion on nine consecutive First Fridays in their parish church. It is a practice worth following.

He descended into Hell

You Are My Beloved Son

Although God the Father was very evident in the Old Testament with Abraham, Isaac, Jacob, Moses and David, He remained aloof when His beloved Son took center stage in the New Testament. Only occasionally did the Father appear for a moment and then withdrew to allow us to absorb His Son, Jesus. One of those moments was as Jesus rose from the waters of baptism, when the Spirit descended upon Him, and the voice of the Father was heard proclaiming Jesus as His beloved Son. (Mark 1:10-11) Father, Son and Holy Spirit all together as one God – all in agreement for us. Later, when Nicodemus questioned Jesus about eternal life, Jesus told him that a person must be born again of water and the Spirit to gain everlasting life. (John 3:5) Through baptism we too become the beloved sons or daughters of the Father.

It is amazing that after centuries of rejection and broken covenants by His people in the Old Testament, God would – with His Son's entrance into this world as God-man, born of Mary – adopt each one of us at baptism as His son or daughter. It is equally amazing that He would invite us then to live forever with Him in heaven. Certainly we are not an improvement over His people of the old law. But the difference is Jesus, His eternal Son, who willingly offered Himself as our sacrifice to God the Father for our sinfulness. Without Christ's sacrifice on the cross, we would continue to wait with the people of the Old Testament in a place of darkness.

Our Catholic Creed tells us that after His death on the cross, Jesus descended into hell – a place of waiting, not the hell of the damned. "He descended into hell." (Cath. Cat.) He announced to all the just of the Old Testament that "He had arisen" and would come soon to lead them into heaven. From the first Adam to John the Baptist, all the just rejoiced at His appearance.

How blessed we are to be God's new people. We best not take God for granted and treat Him like the first people of God did. Nothing is sure. We need to be faithful and obedient.

A Great Chasm

When Almighty God created the beautiful earth with its rich resources of food and medicine for His beloved creatures, He did it for our pleasure and enjoyment. God said: "See, I give you every seed-bearing plant all over the earth and every tree that has seed-bearing fruit on it to be your food...God looked at everything he had made, and he found it very good." (Gen. 1:29-31) When He created man, man chose to disobey Him; so God banished him from the Garden of Eden to till the ground from which man had come. (Gen. 3:23) Yet God, a forgiving and merciful Lord, gave Adam a second chance.

When we read the story of the creation of the angels, we find no forgiveness for them. When Lucifer rose up in disobedience against God and said "I will not serve," God created hell and banished Lucifer and all his cohorts into hell forever – never to return to heaven. God created "a great chasm" between heaven and hell, which will always exist. It is not our place to question the All-knowing God for this apparent discrepancy. He forgave man but not the fallen angels. One possible reason might be found in the greater intelligence of angels over man. They are far superior to man.

In any case, there exists an eternal place of hell for the fallen angels and for those human beings who reject God by word and deed. In the parable of the rich man and Lazarus, Jesus tells us there is a great chasm established. (Luke 16:26) I cannot imagine anyone who would desire to go there. Yet some people live a daily life of sinful practice without a thought of punishment in hell. Won't they be surprised when they find themselves suddenly thrust into eternity to be judged by Jesus? As Catholics we need to pray daily for people who have committed themselves to the dangers of hellfire forever.

Peace Be with You

In a world that has not enjoyed a real peace of mind and soul for more than 100 years – suffering through world wars, country conflicts and hatreds in all parts of the world – Our Lord's words of peace bring a hope of true peace. But the world needs to accept this God-man of peace.

Thomas, the Apostle, said to the other disciples: "Unless I see the mark of the nails in his hands…I will not believe." (John 20:25) Thomas represents the unbelieving world, which needs a sign. When Jesus is asked one time to produce a sign that He is authentic, Jesus responds, "An evil and unfaithful generation seeks a sign, but no sign will be given it except the sign of Jonah the prophet." (Matt. 12:39) Then Jesus reveals His resurrection from the dead as His sign to them. "Just as Jonah was in the belly of the whale three days and three nights, so will the Son of Man be in the heart of the earth three days and three nights." (Matt. 12:40) Still the scribes and Pharisees refuse to believe in Him.

It is unfortunate that the greater portion of the world refuses to acknowledge God's Son, Jesus. Instead, they are caught up with the gods of this world – money, honors, sports, sinful pleasures and practices, TV and the Internet. These occupy most of their time. At the same time, those who acknowledge Jesus as Lord have so little time for Him. As a result, God allows the devils of hell to roam freely in this materialistic world – drawing many away from Him.

We need to come back to God through daily prayer, penance and almsgiving – beseeching God to welcome us home to Him. We need to show Him that we truly are His family and desire to live with Him forever.

A popular prayer for peace is the rosary – now twenty decades of prayer and praise, thanksgiving and petition. A priest who worked tirelessly to support the family rosary, Fr. Patrick Peyton, used to proclaim, "The family that prays together, stays together." I believe that is true today.

Reverence in Church

Some friends returned recently from their experience of meeting Pope John Paul II in his chapel in the Basilica of St. Peter's Cathedral in Rome. They were excited and enthused as they recalled every detail of the event. However, they had not been prepared well for the meeting;

the women did not have the proper dress and had to call a shop in Rome; the men also had to shop a little; otherwise they would not have been allowed to attend. This is a change for many of our Catholic people who are invited daily to meet, not the Vicar of Christ, but Christ Himself at the parish Eucharist. It would seem that rules of deportment and dress no longer seem to apply as we meet the Son of God under the appearance of bread and wine. Some young and old, men and women, boys and girls are dressed for the beach or an athletic event with little regard or respect for their Divine Creator. In a meeting with the Pope, President or some special dignitary, these people would not be welcomed or admitted. God's presence, however, does not seem to merit proper attire in the minds of some. It is true that Jesus is more interested in the internal clothing of God's life of grace than the bodily external dress, but there is importance to both.

At the parable of the wedding feast, the King met a guest without a wedding garment and ordered him to be cast out: "Bind his hands and feet, and cast him into the darkness outside...." (Matt. 22:13) The wedding garment of heaven is the sanctifying grace of God's life – the image and likeness of God. Without the presence of God's image and likeness in our soul, we cannot enter God's home, heaven.

Catholics who live in mortal sin are without the wedding garment. Unless prior to death these Catholics repent of their serious sins and confess them with true sorrow in the Sacrament of Confession, they will not enter heaven upon death. If they are living in an occasion of serious sin, such as remarriage during the life of their spouse, a habit of impurity such as pornography, or assisting in the practice of abortion of infants and the like, they will be barred from heaven unless they express true sorrow and leave their occasion of sin. An eternity in hell is certainly not a good choice.

The third day
He rose again from the dead

Risen from the Dead

In their lifetime, the twelve Apostles did not understand or accept Jesus' plan to suffer, die and rise from the dead. After Peter had made his profession of faith in Jesus – "You are the Messiah, the Son of the living God." (Matt. 16:16) – Jesus revealed to him that He must go to Jerusalem, suffer greatly, be killed, and on the third day be raised. Peter began to argue with Him, and Jesus rebuked him, saying: "Get behind me, Satan!" (Matt. 16:23)

For ordinary fishermen and a tax collector to appreciate the true mission of God's Son was beyond their understanding and belief. It was only after they physically touched His wounds and then ate with Him in the upper room after His death on the cross that they began to accept Him and believe in His resurrection from the dead.

Equally astounding to the Apostles and those who were fed bread and fish on the mountainside about one year prior to His passion, death and resurrection, was His challenge to them, "Whoever eats my flesh and drinks my blood has eternal life, and I will raise him on the last day." (John 6:54) This is the promise Jesus makes to each of us who receives the body and blood of the Son of God in the Eucharist.

Knowing this promise, it is hard to understand the indifference and lack of faith of some of our Catholic people who fail to attend Sunday Mass. It is not an understatement to say that only 50-60% of Catholics attend the Eucharist regularly every week in the United States. A visiting European Cardinal of the Church recently revealed that only about 4% of his people attend Mass weekly. What a shame that so many knowledgeable Catholic people fail to appreciate their great gift of faith. The Judgment Day should be very interesting.

They Recognized Him

As the years pass, we lose track of the companions of our youth. Then what a joy it is to meet them again after years apart. I remember one boy with whom I played sports daily and then he disappeared from my life, until a day thirty-three years later when we met unexpectedly on the street. He recognized me and called me by name, and I did the same. We walked together for several blocks exchanging memories of the past. Then he crossed the street and disappeared again. But at least we enjoyed a few minutes with each other again.

Something like that happened to two of our Lord's disciples. As they were walking out of the city of Jerusalem on the day of the Resurrection, they were joined by Jesus but were prevented from recognizing Him. As they walked with Him, He spoke of the prophecies of the Old Law that described Him as the Messiah. Then when they invited Him to stay for dinner, Jesus took bread, blessed and broke it, and gave it to them. With that, their eyes were opened and they recognized Him in the breaking of the bread, but He vanished from their sight. They said to each other, "Were not our hearts burning [within us] while he spoke to us on the way and opened the scriptures to us?" (Luke 24:32)

Today, in every Catholic church in the world, we have the joy of recognizing Jesus, our divine friend and Saviour in the Eucharistic "breaking of the bread." At every celebration of Mass daily, we are privileged to listen to His words and receive His body and blood in the intimacy of our body and soul. More than being in His presence, as His disciples experienced, today we are privileged to have His divine presence within us – raising us to the level of the divine life of God. In the Eucharist we enter the life of heaven for a moment while still remaining here on earth.

Our Catholic people are so privileged to have the sacrifice of the Mass daily. We should pray for our priests and for young men to enter the priesthood. Without the priesthood, there would be no Mass. Without the Mass, the Catholic faith would lose its heart. St. John Marie Vianney, patron of parish priests, said one day, "Were I to meet an angel and a priest, I would bow first to the priest." Jesus never ordained an angel to represent Him at Mass, only His human priests – from the Last Supper to the present day. While the priest remains human, Jesus graces him with divine power to act in His name. Only in heaven will we begin to appreciate the greatness of the Eucharist and the priesthood.

Passover and Easter

It is interesting that in the year 1999, Jews and Christians celebrated Passover and Easter on the same day. Jewish people commemorated the Passover of God's angels over the Egyptians, which forced Pharaoh to release the Jewish people from their slavery and allow Moses to lead them to the land promised by God. Christian people commemorated Jesus Christ, the new Moses, who by His death on the cross paid for our sins which had enslaved us and won for us the right to the Promised Land of heaven. Both events were historic and eventful for the world, so it is significant that they both come together on the same day at the end of the century.

Forty years ago at the first Mass of a newly-ordained priest whose father was Jewish, I was invited to give the homily. The first two rows of the parish church were occupied by the priest's Jewish relatives. When I pointed out that before Jesus at the Last Supper offered the First Mass, He celebrated the Passover meal with His Apostles according to the Law of Moses, the Jewish relatives were surprised and remarked at how close we were in our celebrations.

Jesus was always a faithful Jew and followed the Law of Moses – as did the Jewish people of His day. But Jesus took us a step higher and invited us to a new Promised Land – a place with God in heaven. By His death and resurrection, Jesus shows everyone – not only the Jewish people – the way from this life of pain and suffering to His life of joy and eternal happiness. At the time, apart from a few Apostles and disciples, His Jewish people refused to follow Him. As a consequence – with St. Paul leading the way on earth – the rest of the world was invited to follow Him.

Now, almost 2000 years later, it is sad to note that the non-Jewish people of the world have decided not to follow Jesus anymore. They have decided to follow their own world of technology and science instead of Jesus Christ. Maybe it is time for God to invite His original chosen Jewish people to return and occupy the places in God's kingdom abandoned now by His former Christian people. Something like that happened when the fallen angels followed Lucifer and left their places in heaven to mankind. Something like that happens even in the Catholic faith. It seems that when a Catholic leaves the Church by the back door; there is always somebody knocking on the front door to his place.

He Is Risen

Although the inspired scriptures do not mention the event, it was a tradition in the early Church that the first person the Risen Jesus visited upon His Bodily Resurrection on Easter morning was His mother, Mary. Who was more involved and concerned in His life and cruel death than Mary, His mother? From birth to death, Mary was there – in His joys and in His sufferings. Who cared the most but His mother? So it would seem fitting that she would be the first to see Him in His glory.

Many people call themselves Catholics but they have long since given up on their faith in Jesus and His Church. If the truth were really known, other things (little gods) like TV, sports, money, fashion and self-indulgence, occupy their leisure time. Daily prayer to God, Sunday Mass, and Lenten observances are not important to them. God, our loving Father, remains in the background for many Catholics, but nonetheless He is always there waiting for some sign of love – eager to welcome back to His love those Catholics who have wandered away from Him and His Church.

Faithful Catholics who live daily to please God and do His Will everyday need to pray for those living apart from God, that they may return.

Mary is the perfect follower of God who will always lead us to her Divine Son, Jesus. Pray to Mary that she will lead everyone back to her Son.

The First Day of the Week

The Lord said to Moses, "For six days you may work, but on the seventh day you shall rest; on that day you must rest even during the seasons of plowing and harvesting." (Ex. 34:21) From the time of

Moses to the present, the Jewish people have observed the Sabbath, the last day of the week, as their day of rest and their day to honor God.

When Jesus was born of a Jewish mother, He too observed the Sabbath – as did His Apostles. But then when Jesus approached His death on the cross, He gave His followers a new law to observe. At His Last Supper with them, He took a cup and said, "This cup is the new covenant in my blood, which will be shed for you." (Luke 22:20) The old covenant with Moses and his people had been completed. The new covenant with His Apostles and everyone united with them began. When Jesus rose from the dead on Sunday morning, His followers began to observe Sunday, the first day of the week, as their new day of rest and prayer.

From the earliest Christian years, Catholics attended Mass on Sunday and observed their day of rest from active manual labor. The Church considers it a serious obligation to observe Sunday with the sacrifice of the Mass and abstinence from hard labor.

In our modern times, Catholics in many countries, including the United States, have become lax in their weekly attendance. They seem to have lost their sense of reverence and obligation. Other worldly occupations have distracted mankind everywhere away from God.

In Old Testament times, God allowed His people to suffer for their sinfulness. In one instance He sent serpents to bite His people until they called out to Him for mercy. (Num. 21:6) Quickly His people returned to God.

Today our Catholic people need an awakening to a new and better appreciation of our obligations to God and His Divine Son. It is unfortunate that we wait for God to act until we respond.

Easter Sunday

A group of businessmen were discussing the technique of starting a successful business when one of them, a Catholic, offered a suggestion. He said that a successful leader should surround himself with twelve associates and, after a period of instruction, allow himself to be put to death and then raise himself from the dead. He said Jesus Christ did this and now enjoys a worldwide organization of 900 million people.

Naturally, no one but God could accomplish such a feat. But with His Father's authority and power, the Son did just that through the presence of the Holy Spirit. Having risen from the dead on Easter Sunday, Jesus commissioned His Apostles to go out in the whole world and bring His gospel message to everyone, baptizing them in the name of the Father, Son and Holy Spirit.

Today, through the Apostles' efforts, the Catholic Church is in every country and nation in the world. If Jesus had remained in His tomb after His death on the cross, the Apostles would have gone back to their homes and families. But He rose as He promised.

Today Catholics and all Christian people celebrate Holy Week and Easter Sunday as the highlight of the life of Jesus, without which there would not have been a Christianity in the world. The world, like the Jewish people, would still be looking and waiting for a Saviour and Messiah.

In heaven, the Risen Christ awaits His people. In a time chosen by God, He will return in glory to earth and, after a general judgment, will lead His people to an eternity of happiness and joy in heaven. It is a place worth waiting for.

He ascended into heaven,
and sits at the right hand of God,
the Father Almighty

Return to the Father

Thanksgiving Day and similar special days like Christmas and Easter are generally family days, when people enjoy returning for a feast to their parents' and grandparents' homes. Generally, they and their children are welcomed with open arms. Usually, the best chinaware and wines are brought to the table. It is a celebration of homecoming.

Can you imagine the homecoming welcome the Son of God received when He returned to His home after 33 years? Not only were God the Father and God the Holy Spirit on the front porch of heaven, waiting to welcome Him home, but nine choirs of angels were bursting the heavens with song. In addition, coming with Him were all the saints of the Old Testament, beginning with Adam and Eve. It must have been quite a show of love.

Something like Christ's homecoming will happen to each of us who live on earth in accord with the Will of the Father. Having been purified through suffering either here on earth or after death in the suffering in purgatory, our soul will be escorted by our guardian angel and Mary, our Queen, to the immaculate presence of God's heaven.

On one occasion, Jesus said: "If anyone wishes to come after me, he must deny himself and take up his cross daily and follow me." (Luke 9:23) Our Lord does not reveal to us what our particular cross in life will be. But as we continue our life on earth, our cross will be presented to us, whether physical, mental, psychological or moral pain. How we embrace our cross in life in obedience to God will determine our reward place in heaven.

Immediate entrance into heaven is possible for everyone who will live a life in accord with the eternal Will of God. We make the decision while we are living on earth. If we refuse God's wishes now, He will respond accordingly after we leave this world in death. He reminds us: "Whoever is ashamed of me and of my words, the Son of Man will be ashamed of when he comes in his glory and in the glory of the Father and of the holy angels." (Luke 9:26) Jesus will remember His friends.

Ascension

It has been said of people who love God and are looking forward to heaven that "everyone is dying to get there but nobody wants to go." As Catholics, we learn from our earliest years that "God made me to know Him, to love Him and to serve Him in this world and then to be happy with Him forever in heaven." So it should come as no surprise that eventually God will call us to judgment and to heaven. The only problem we have is that, to reach our eternal goal, we have to die and leave our well-cared-for body behind on earth.

Death is not attractive to most of us. Yet it is a necessity – as it was even for Jesus, the God-man.

Yet Jesus did not leave His body behind for very long. As He predicted to the Pharisees who challenged Him in the Temple area: "Destroy this temple and in three days I will raise it up." (John 2:19) The Jews responded that the Temple had been under construction for 46 years and how could He raise it up in three days. But Jesus was speaking about the temple of His body. When Jesus was raised from the dead, His disciples remembered what He had said and came to believe the words Jesus had spoken. (John 2:20-22)

Having risen bodily on Easter Sunday, Jesus continued to be present with His Apostles and Mary for forty days – after which He ascended bodily in their astonished midst back to His Father in heaven. "So then the Lord Jesus, after he spoke to them, was taken up into heaven and took his seat at the right hand of God." (Mark 16:19)

As Catholic people, we believe that after our individual death, we will have a similar spiritual experience. Leaving our body behind until the final judgment at the end of the world, we will ascend in our souls before the particular judgment before Jesus, the Son of God, who will reveal to us the state or condition of our souls. If we are without sin and have made up for our sinfulness with lives of prayer, charity and good deeds, we will be welcomed immediately into the eternal joy of heaven, where we will meet God the Father – face to face. If we have minor sins and faults on our soul and have not yet made up for the sins of our life, we will necessarily need to be purified in the place of purgatory – prior to entering heaven. If our souls are in the state of serious sin without repentance, we will be immediately consigned to hell for all eternity. It is a horrible thought, yet it is our choice in life and in death. Later, our bodies will join our souls whether in heaven or in hell. We need to pray daily for a happy death.

Ascension of Jesus

It was a very difficult Thursday as the Apostles watched their Master and Teacher, Jesus, ascend on a cloud before their very eyes into the heavens. He had come into the world quietly through His birth to the Virgin Mary, His mother. He had obeyed His Heavenly Father by establishing His Church on Peter and the Apostles. Now He was leaving them to carry out His work that He completed by His death on the cross and His Resurrection from the dead.

Now it is up to us as His followers to assist Jesus in His task of leading all people to Him and His Church. Eventually, we will follow Him in His death and resurrection.

The task is really overwhelming and beyond our own powers to accomplish. We need the assistance of God the Holy Spirit, just as the Apostles and early church depended upon the coming of the Holy Spirit on that first Pentecost Sunday. Our prayer today should be, "Come Holy Spirit, fill the hearts of your faithful people, enkindle in us the fire of your divine love. Send forth your Spirit and we shall renew the face of the earth."

With the presence of God, the Holy Spirit, we can do mighty things for the Lord and His Church. Then, when our task is completed, we will close our eyes in death and ascend to our friend and Saviour, Jesus, in Heaven.

He invited all of us to follow Him in life and in death to unending life in heaven. Let us be faithful in this journey.

Prepare the Way of the Lord

When the President of the United States announces his intention to visit a city or a country, intensive preparations by the Secret Service are made weeks and even months in advance for purposes of security. Buildings and homes on the President's motorcar schedule are visited and checked, lest there be a potential danger to the President. Bodyguards surround the leader at all times during public appearances. In addition to security measures, other preparations for food and shelter surround a President's travel. Similar preparations are made in other countries of the world for their kings and rulers.

If these preparations are necessary for earthly leaders, what preparation must be done for the King of Heaven and Earth, Jesus Christ? John the Baptist prepared the way before Jesus, making ready the coming of the Son of God in this world. (Luke 3:4-5) John's preparation begins in our hearts as we open them to allow our Saviour to enter – hearts that are swept clean in anticipation of the visit of our King.

As Catholic people, we need to renew our reverence for our Eucharistic Lord. Apart from preparing our physical appearance to greet Him on Sundays, we need to prepare our hearts and minds through prayer and frequent confession. We need to rid ourselves of the daily anger, jealousies and uncharitableness that harass us in our everyday lives. Prepare the way of the Lord with a clean heart and a generous manner. Then God will come to us and live in us. "Whoever loves me will keep my word, and my Father will love him, and we will come to him and make our dwelling with him." (John 14:23) Presidents and worldly leaders rule for a brief time, but Our King, Jesus Christ, rules forever. He merits our preparation now.

The King of Kings

Apart from the Queen of England and a few princes and princesses of Europe, our generation has grown up without any perceptible knowledge of the royalty of the past. Our democratic governments elected by the people extend only a courteous and respectful nod to the royalty still alive in European and Asiatic nations. They no longer govern their nations as did their kings and queens of the past. Today, royalty seems to be a symbol of past glory.

But there is still one person who remains a powerful king: Jesus Christ, the eternal King of heaven and earth. Pilate addressed Him boldly before sentencing Him to death on the cross, asking Him if He was the king of the Jews. Jesus responded that His kingdom is not of this world. (John 18:33-36)

There is a pronounced difference between the past kings of this world and our eternal King, Jesus Christ – and the difference is Divine love. While many of them were kings who were benevolent rulers, many were not. Rather, some exercised worldly power over their subjects. King Henry VIII left his Catholic faith for a woman and established the Church of England. He then imprisoned and executed the bishops and priests who disagreed with his decision. Most of England lost the Catholic faith. In contrast is our Eternal King, who invites us to His kingdom of justice and peace in heaven. Our Eternal King exercises His authority from the pain of the cross and invites us to follow Him in this world to joy and happiness in His eternal kingdom in heaven. His crown is a crown of thorns that leads to a crown of blessedness. He rules with a scepter of love for the poor and the sick and invites us to care for them now and share His authority forever. He rules with an eternal love that He shares with us. Not too bad a gift – forever.

Christ the King

When Jesus revealed His Sacred Heart, crowned with thorns, to Sr. Margaret Mary Alacoque over 300 years ago, He mourned the world's indifference, coldness and thanklessness and asked Sr. Margaret Mary for a communion of reparation on nine First Fridays. He said, "Behold this heart which has loved everyone so much that it has spared nothing in order to testify its love." The Sacred Heart of Jesus deserves to reign as King over the hearts of His people. As our Divine King, Jesus has no desire to rule over any material possession we have – but only over our hearts. He desires only our love.

In addition to the First Friday Sacred Heart devotion, the Church promotes a Sunday each year at the end of October to remind people of the Kingship of Jesus Christ. As King, Jesus wishes to reign over His people with His Divine love. Yet most people do not pay any attention to Him.

There will come a time when our indifference to Christ our King will result in our choosing someone or something else as our King – the devil, worldly possessions or fame. It will be a sad day for any individual to choose passing value over the eternal God. The wise Christian will hand over and consecrate his heart to the Divine Heart of Jesus – depending always and only on Him. The average life of man according to Scripture is 70 or 80 years, if we are strong. (Ps. 90:10) Imagine someone trading an eternity of joy for a short lifetime of passing value.

Blessed Are the Peacemakers

Since the act of terrorism against the nations of the world and specifically against America on September 11, 2001, the people of America have become much more patriotic and prayerful. Approximately 3000 persons in the World Trade Center, representing many of the countries of the world, lost their lives as two large passenger planes deliberately dove into the twin towers in a suicidal action. America has never in its history been attacked on its soil before with such a violent and destructive act. Not only was precious human life taken, but the country's economy was severely affected. While the President and Congress have been responding to this deliberate action, the leader of the terrorist attack continues to threaten even more dire actions against America.

Many nations of the world have expressed sympathy and support for combating terrorism in the world, yet such a task to eradicate this disease of the mind and will of some people of the world seems too big for a single nation. Since this disease of terrorism has spread throughout many nations of the world, including within the United States, any lasting cure must come from every peaceful person in every land.

Ultimately, the only successful peacemaker is Jesus Christ, the Prince of Peace. When He was born in Bethlehem, the angels sang about peace on earth. (Luke 2:14) God, our Father, through His Divine Son, will bring peace if we all ask Him in prayer.

We are all His children – even the terrorists – but God desires that we all return to Him in prayer and action. In the story of the prodigal son, the father was filled with compassion and ran to meet his son, embracing him and kissing him. (Luke 15:20) Our Heavenly Father will treat all of us in the same way, if only we return to Him with sorrow for our sinfulness. If we place ourselves prayerfully within our Father's Divine Will, He will work miracles in the world and bring true and lasting peace to all. Everyone on earth is invited to assist in bringing peace to the world.

I Am with You Always

Our belief in God's created world of angels is a truth of our Catholic faith. Another truth of our faith is the protection and daily presence of the angels, as guardian spirits for every human. Our Lord Himself reveals this message of the presence of angels appointed to watch over us: "See that you do not despise one of these little ones, for I say to you that their angels in heaven always look upon the face of my heavenly Father." (Matt. 18:10) It is also believed that our guardian angels will accompany us upon our death to meet with Jesus, our eternal judge.

As comforting as is our Catholic belief in angel protectors, Our Lord's assurance of His own presence with us until the end of the age is an even greater blessing. After Jesus rose from the dead, He commissioned His Apostles to make and baptize disciples of all nations, and then He promised to remain with us until He comes again in glory at the end of the world: "And behold, I am with you always, until the end of the age." (Matt. 28:20)

This Divine promise is fulfilled in His Eucharistic Presence under the appearance of consecrated bread. In every Catholic church throughout the countries of the world, Jesus is present to us, inviting everyone to visit with Him and offer Him in a daily or weekly Mass. In some parish churches there is the practice of Perpetual Eucharistic Adoration of Jesus, whereby the Eucharistic Bread is exposed in a golden monstrance twenty-four hours daily throughout the year. People sign up to spend one hour a week in His Presence.

This daily Divine Presence of Jesus was made possible when Jesus celebrated His Last Supper with His apostles and instituted the Eucharist by consecrating the bread and wine. He shared His body and blood and then ordered His Apostles to do this in memory of Him. (Luke 22:19) From that moment on, His Apostles and the bishops and priests who followed have offered His Eucharistic Presence under bread and wine so that He could remain with us until His return in glory. As Catholic people, we are truly blessed.

From thence He shall come to judge the living and the dead

Our Particular Judgment

On August 15 we celebrate the bodily Assumption of Our Lord's Mother – the day that God called Mary in her body and soul to heaven, after her death here on earth. The early Fathers of the Church referred to her death as a "falling asleep" or "Dormition" out of respect for her relationship as Mother of God. We will differ with her at death in that we will go before Jesus only in our soul – the body being left behind in the ground.

Later, at the end of the world, God will join our reformed and resurrected bodies to our souls – to live forever, whether in heaven or, by our choice, in hell. Purgatory will release all its suffering souls to heaven by God's command and they too will be joined in body and soul again.

In St. Luke's gospel, Jesus reminds everyone to stay ready and be prepared for that great day when He will return to earth and invite us all to follow Him to heaven. "Blessed are those servants whom the master finds vigilant on his arrival." (Luke 12:37)

Realistically, however, our own personal death will precede that great day. It is our day of death that we need to prepare for. Just as the day of the Lord's return is unknown to us, so too is the day of our death. Perhaps people with a terminal illness have a fair idea of the time of their death. But most of us do not. A sudden, unforeseen accident or heart attack can happen to anyone – especially older people. Will we be prepared – living God's grace and life – through our faithful observance of the Sacraments of Confession and Holy Communion? Only we can answer that question.

A timeless and true method of preparation for the Lord to call us is a daily prayer life: morning, afternoon and evening prayer to God. Such a divine communication will plug us into the eternal life and grace of God. Like a cell phone that remains charged, we connect to God through our prayerful conversation. Death then provides simply a continual connection with God and His eternal home. Our immediate appearance before God in our particular judgment will continue our relationship and will influence the Lord to welcome us into heaven.

The Narrow Gate

If you have had the good fortune of visiting Bethlehem, the village of Christ's birth, you know that the front entrance of the church built over the cave of His birth is a small narrow opening which forces everyone to bow down to enter. It is similar to the size of the backyard entrances of Jewish homes referred to as the "eye of a needle," a small open area which prevented the hump of the camel from entering.

In the gospel of Luke, Jesus refers to the narrow gate of heaven: "Strive to enter through the narrow gate, for many, I tell you, will attempt to enter but will not be strong enough." (Luke 13:24) Unless we are willing to follow the path that Jesus walks and accompany Him on His journey to suffering and death, we may be shut out of His kingdom.

Jesus reminds His Jewish listeners that the chosen people of old do not have any exclusive claim to His kingdom. People of every nation will be able to enter if they devote themselves to Jesus' message. "And there will be wailing and grinding of teeth when you see Abraham, Isaac, and Jacob and all the prophets in the kingdom of God and you yourselves cast out. And people will come from the east and the west and from the north and the south and will recline at table in the kingdom of God." (Luke 13:28-29)

Like the chosen race – which failed to recognize and accept Jesus, the Son of God, as their Messiah – there are some Catholic people who have been blessed at birth with the faith and teachings of Jesus Christ but who treat Jesus and His Church with indifference. Some Catholics by their lack of daily prayer, their disregard for Sunday Mass, their attitude toward the Holy Father and the Church especially in relation to artificial birth prevention, abortion, women priests and other similar teachings, put themselves in jeopardy spiritually. As Catholics we must maintain our loyalty and consecration to Jesus and His teachings if we wish to merit His friendship and His kingdom. The gospel of Luke does not mince words in demanding our wholehearted devotion to Jesus. As Jesus tells His chosen people in response: "Depart from me, all you evildoers!" (Luke 13:27) What will He say to the new chosen people today, who fail to acknowledge Him in life? Perhaps the same words!

Who Is My Neighbor?

Most of us consider a neighbor as the person next door or down the street. Many people do not know their neighbors nor have they made any attempt to show them any kindness or hospitality. The neighbor in this case is some nameless person who lives nearby.

When the lawyer in St. Luke's gospel asks Jesus who is his neighbor, Jesus tells him the story of the Good Samaritan who stopped to assist a man, beaten by robbers. A priest and Levite passed the man by, but the Samaritan treated him with mercy. The Samaritan was a true neighbor because he cared for another in need and showed him kindness and mercy. Jesus said to the lawyer, "Go and do likewise." (Luke 10:37)

Jesus does not limit the obligation of becoming a good neighbor to any single place or to any particular people. As the world becomes smaller and smaller through the medium of the airplane, car or train, we can meet people in need anywhere in the country or even the world. The computer age with access to the Internet allows us to know and meet people from all over the world almost daily. Human needs are plentiful everywhere. Every day people in some countries are dispossessed of their homes and possessions and need assistance.

How good a neighbor are we to the rest of the world, not only down the street but across the oceans? We may plead that we are in need ourselves, but we can always pray for others, and most of us can divest ourselves of some of our many possessions for another's need. Or like the priest and Levite we can simply ignore the needs of others who are hurting.

Just prior to His death on the cross, Jesus spoke of the Last Judgment. At the Last Judgment, He will identify with the neighbor in need, saying: "For I was hungry and you gave me food, I was thirsty and you gave me drink, a stranger and you welcomed me, naked and you clothed me, ill and you cared for me, in prison and you visited me." (Matt. 25:35-36) Jesus our King will remind everyone that whatever we did for one of the least brothers of His, we did for Him. Some people in need may not look or act like Jesus, yet Jesus identifies with everyone.

Saints and Sinners

So very often when we think about saints or sinners, we look to the past years of the Church to those great saints like St. John of the Cross, St. Theresa, and St. Anthony or the great sinners like St. Augustine, Judas and the Roman emperors who persecuted the early Christians. But, in truth, the saints and sinners live today, though we fail to acknowledge them.

We need only to look to Rome, Italy where one of our greatest saints lives today. Pope John Paul II is not only acclaimed by heads of state but by millions of young people who flock wherever the Holy Father visits in the world. "John Paul II, we love you" the youth chant. What a great testimony to a great man and priest of God. Then we look to other leaders of their countries, who in their pride of power and greed cause the death of thousands of people they wish to cleanse. It is proof that the devil continues to provoke these government leaders to destroy and subjugate their people. The Lord will judge these leaders – much like He judged the leaders of His day. And Jesus said to the Pharisees: "You justify yourselves in the sight of others, but God knows your hearts; for what is of human esteem is an abomination in the sight of God." (Luke 16:15)

Then we look to our homes and parishes where we will be surprised to find honest-to-goodness saintly people who live their faith and charity daily: mothers with their many children who attend daily Mass; men and women, young and old, who spend hours in adoration before the Blessed Sacrament; married people who live their sacred vows for 50 years; numerous individuals who minister to the sick, the hungry, the impoverished, the lonely, the imprisoned – all in the name of Jesus. In every country we will find these saintly people.

Unfortunately, in every country, state, city and town we will find the drug dealers, the abortionists, the murderers, the thieves and just plain great sinners. What was Our Lord's solution? He said: "Let them grow together until harvest; then at harvest time I will say to the harvesters, 'First collect the weeds and tie them in bundles for burning; but gather the wheat into my barn.'" (Matt. 13:30) It is really our own decision as to where we will eventually end up – heaven or hell.

Sacrament of Marriage

In the time of our grandparents, the Sacrament of Marriage was a sacred vow and promise that lasted until death. Even when circumstances dictated that a husband and wife had to live apart, they continued to respect and keep their solemn marriage vows.

Then came the "throwaway" era of discarding everything we use – including marriage vows. Now if spouses, with or without children, disagree or tire of each other, they often seek a divorce. Many feel justified in remarrying again during the lifetime of their spouse. Jesus faced this question with the Pharisees: "I say to you, whoever divorces his wife…and marries another commits adultery." (Matt. 19:9) God made it clear in the Old Testament that such actions are wrongful when He commanded us not to commit adultery. (Ex. 20:14)

Not only does this sin of adultery offend God in a serious way, but it attacks the sacredness of marriage and, where children are involved, divorce and remarriage cause a great psychological harm to the family.

Children in a divorce situation sometimes are forced by the circumstances to take sides with their parents. Generally, children love both parents and do not want to be compelled to choose one over the other.

Another development of recent times is the growing practice of living together prior to marriage. This habit of living together is known as the sin of fornication, which offends God as much as divorce and remarriage. In the Old Testament God destroyed the cities of Sodom and Gomorrah for their sinful immorality. The Lord rained down sulphurous fire upon these cities, overthrowing Sodom and Gomorrah and the whole plain, together with their inhabitants. (Gen. 19:24-25)

Since He is the same God, how will He treat countries and nations today that are no better than Sodom and Gomorrah – the present site of the Dead Sea? Are not parents and priests and ministers of the Gospel who do not speak out against this immorality guilty of sinful silence and acceptance? It is better we refuse these couples the Sacrament of Marriage than offend God by our silence.

Lord, Lord, Open the Door

Priests who live their priesthood in the daily life of a parish are blessed with abundant opportunities to gain experience and wisdom. Their greatest lesson in their priestly life is to learn to live their priesthood, based on the life and death of Jesus, the Eternal Priest, and to assist their parishioners, young and old, to do the same. If the priests, deacons, religious women and their parishioners are daily in tune with Jesus, their Priest, the parish will be on the right track to heaven and will be blessed by our Heavenly Father.

Unfortunately, every parish consists of some who live without God in their homes and in their working places. Their children – some not baptized – grow up without the blessings of the sacraments, daily prayer, and Sunday Mass. These parents are very busy in their worldly pursuits of work, sports and pleasure. They have little time for God during their time on earth. They are like the foolish virgins in the gospel story who, when taking their lamps, brought no oil with them. They will at the end of their lives cry out to God: "'Lord, Lord, open the door for us!" (Matt. 25:11) Our Lord will reply, "Amen, I say to you, I do not know you." (Matt. 25:12)

Very often the relatives will reach out to the church in petition for help for the deceased, but it is too late. Their loved ones have already passed on to eternity. Only our prayers will assist them at this time. Our Lord concludes His parable on the wise and foolish virgins by urging us to stay awake, for we know neither the day nor the hour. (Matt. 25:13)

Apart from negligent parishioners who hardly relate to their Catholic obligations and duties, the greater consolation, joy and experience of the parish priest are the majority of families who live their daily lives in tune with God's Will and inspire their parish and neighborhood with saintly children and parents. They will be like the wise virgins who, when the bridegroom came, were ready and went into the wedding feast with Him. (Matt. 25:10) We are all free to choose wisely.

The Righteous and the Accursed

Years ago when young boys prepared to play a neighborhood baseball game, they chose sides until there were two equal teams. In our lifetime, we are also invited to choose the side that suits our spiritual life. On the one side is Jesus, the Son of God, whose team is led by the great Archangel Michael; on the opposite side is another team led by the archangel, Lucifer, who has chosen to oppose God. We are always free during our lifetime to switch teams and join the other side. But when death arrives, we remain confirmed on the team we have chosen, and either enter heaven with Jesus or enter hell with Lucifer – forever. The choice is always ours, but death confirms our choice.

According to St. Matthew's description of the general judgment, Jesus who is our King in this world and in heaven, will say to the accursed who chose Lucifer, "Depart from me, you accursed, into the eternal fire prepared for the devil and his angels." (Matt. 25:41) But to the righteous He will say, "Come, you who are blessed by my Father. Inherit the kingdom prepared for you…." (Matt. 25:34) So it is vitally important that we learn to choose the right team in our lifetime.

Our Lord teaches all of us how to do this – to be on the right team. He tells us to find and assist Him in the hungry, the thirsty, the stranger, the naked, the sick and ill, and the prisoner. Whatever we do for the least brothers, we do for Him.

This admonition from the Son of God seems at first to be a relatively reasonable and normal request until we are faced on a daily basis with our neighbor who is in need. We balk at doing even a small request sometimes because of our prejudice and temperament. As a result, we fail to please God and miss out on fulfilling God's Will. Our pride and our judgmental manner draw us away from pleasing God. The archangel, Lucifer, wins again.

God and Neighbor

In the very beginning of our life, every created person, male or female, comes from our Almighty Father and is placed in the protective womb of our earthly mother. When each of us leaves this world at the end of our earthly life, we immediately return to the presence of God's Son, our appointed judge. He will repay each of us according to our deeds. (Rev. 22:12)

Although our First Parents lost God's image and likeness through their refusal to do God's Will, we are privileged by the death of Jesus on the cross to regain through the Sacrament of Baptism this beautiful image and likeness of God within our souls. While our Eternal Father never leaves us during the allotted time between birth and death, He allows us to freely live out our time on earth and holds us accountable for our actions, good and bad.

We are free to continue to grow in God's image and likeness through our daily prayerful communication with our Eternal Father. "Our Father who art in heaven, hallowed be thy name. Thy kingdom come. Thy will be done on earth, as it is in heaven." If we live as a saintly person on earth, we are certain to continue our holiness into eternity. We need only the approval of Jesus at the entrance into heaven.

What better way to live our time on earth than to follow Our Lord's commandment to love the Lord our God with all our heart, soul and mind. (Matt. 22:37) How sad life can be for those who live their time on earth without God. What do those people say to Jesus at the end of their earthly lives?

But love of God is only the first commandment. Jesus continues His response to the Pharisees by commanding us to love our neighbor as ourselves. (Matt. 22:39) Suddenly, the rest of the world becomes important to our life of sanctity. Since we do not always like our neighbors, this commandment to love our neighbors requires a lot of prayer and effort. Is heaven worth it? Each person has to answer for himself.

Caesar vs. God

No one enjoys being taxed. The Jews under Caesar's rule truly resented the government taxes, which were excessive. Likewise, in paying taxes to Caesar, the Jews were acknowledging a sovereign other than God ruling over them. Yet taxes were a way of life for the Jews, as they are today.

A bone of contention for Catholic parents who choose to send their children to religious rather than secular schools is the school tax. By law, these parents are taxed to pay for secular schools without much benefit and likewise pay for the religious schools that are their choice. It would be more equitable if these Catholic school parents could direct their school taxes to their school of choice. There are some signs of change for the better, however. In June 2002 the U.S. Supreme Court upheld the constitutionality of a school voucher program in Ohio.

When the Pharisees tried to entrap Jesus in speech, Jesus used the Roman coin to confound them, saying "[R]epay to Caesar what belongs to Caesar and to God what belongs to God." (Matt. 22:21) Jesus reminds everyone that we are obliged to observe the laws of this world as well as observe the laws of God. Our Catholic faith instructs us that where a conflict exists between our world and God, our God must be preferred. We need always to obey God and His law.

One such conflict would be the legal sanction of abortion of the unborn in the womb of the mother, which is totally contrary to God's fifth commandment "Thou shall not kill." If we foster, assist or allow abortion, we are guilty of serious sin. People who live in a country like China – which punishes citizens for having more than one child – face a difficult decision. Birth prevention and abortion are a way of life in those countries. The same can be said of America and Europe.

Our Lord will have His "hands full" on the Day of Judgment, when the people of these countries come before Him for the final judgment. It will not be a pleasant task.

Our Choice in Life

In the Old Testament time, approximately 175 years before the birth of Jesus, there lived an evil Syrian King, Antiochus IV, who bitterly persecuted the Jews. "It also happened that seven brothers with their mother were arrested and tortured with whips and scourges by the king, to force them to eat pork in violation of God's law. One of the brothers, speaking for the others, said: 'What do you expect to achieve by questioning us? We are ready to die rather than transgress the laws of our ancestors.'" (2nd Macc.7:1-2) All of the sons with their mother were put to death in a most painful and horrible manner. It was not long after this that the king himself died a very painful death.

Today Jesus reminds His followers not to be afraid of those who kill the body but cannot kill the soul. Rather, we should fear the one who can destroy both soul and body in hell. (Matt. 10:28) Our only fear is falling in the grasp of the devil and his evil ways. But if we acknowledge Him before others, He promises that He will acknowledge us before His Heavenly Father. (Matt. 10:32)

Every day of our lives we are faced with challenges to our Catholic faith. Our morning and evening prayers offered regularly are a challenge. It becomes easy to neglect them, unless our faith in prayer to God is important to us. Even prayer in a public place – before lunch or dinner – is an acknowledgement of the Father.

Our daily response to our family and employees at work allows Christ to become visible in us. Our care and concern for the poor and the sick people we meet daily are of greatest importance to Jesus.

Holiness of mind and body is not a difficult task. We need only reach out daily to God through prayer and good deeds. Holiness is noticeable when we do these things.

Living In

The devil in hell has done a neat trick on many of our Catholic young people who are preparing for marriage by inviting them to live together physically and by convincing them that the money saved and convenience obtained justify such very offensive and dangerous conduct. It is offensive to God as well as to our world; such sinful conduct seriously violates the sixth commandment of God and provides the world of young people with a scandalous example. Living together is also dangerous spiritually because, through this practice of seriously sinful living, it places our souls in danger of eternal separation from God. Catholic couples living in mortal sin together miss out on all the lost graces and blessings from God during their engagement period. Unless they, with sincere sorrow and repentance, make a good confession sometime before their Catholic marriage, they continue to live in the darkness of serious sin after they marry. The devil has really sold them a bill of evil goods and, in a real sense, owns them for himself.

Another group of Catholics that has been tricked by the devil are those Catholic spouses who have separated or divorced from their partners and remarry another during the lifetime of their spouses. Jesus counsels us that the man who marries a divorced woman commits adultery. (Matt. 5:32) Years of living together in adultery will gradually dull any sense of guilt for some and even convince them that God approves. Yet Our Lord reminds us that anyone who looks with lust at a woman has already committed adultery with her in his thoughts. (Matt. 5:28) Our Lord continues: "[B]etter for you to lose one of your members than to have your whole body thrown into Gehenna." (Matt. 5:29)

The devil's best trick is saved for last, when he convinces these Catholics in sinful relationships to go without shame and without fear to receive Holy Communion – the sacred body and blood of Christ – while continuing their sinful relationship. The Jewish people of the Old Testament did not dare enter the temple without washing, yet some Catholics dare to approach their God while in serious sin. The devil has really won – at least for now.

The Value of the Poor and Lowly

One day the Apostles were discussing among themselves as to who was the greatest among them. Jesus took a child and placed it in their midst, saying: "Whoever receives one child such as this in my name, receives me; and whoever receives me, receives not me but the One who sent me." (Mark 9:37) In effect, Jesus used the symbol of a child to represent the poor and the lowly in the Christian community and to identify Himself and His Eternal Father with the poor and the lowly of the world.

How freely and quickly in our daily lives do many Catholics ignore and shun the poor and lowly in their midst as if they are not their Catholic responsibility. In our travel through the city, some of us avoid the poorest neighborhoods lest their presence might remind us of our obligation to assist them. Even the people of the night who walk the streets during the day in our downtown areas are looked upon with suspicion as alcoholics and drug users who are looking for a monetary handout.

If we wish to identify with the Father, Son and Holy Spirit during our lives here on earth, Jesus reminds us that we will discover them in the poor and lowly of the world. Our greatness in God's eyes at the general judgment and for all eternity will be determined by how we treated, respected and assisted the poor and lowly.

St. Louis de Montfort – who traveled through France in 1700 as a poorly-clad priest, preaching true devotion to Mary, the Mother of God – returned home on one occasion to visit his priest-brother living in a monastery. When his priest-brother opened the monastery door, Fr. Louis addressed him as "brother." Since he was also a priest, he resented being called "brother" because the religious brothers occupied a very lowly place in the community. Every day for a week, Fr. Louis addressed him as "brother" and as a result received very little attention. When the priest-brother finally learned that this poor priest visitor was actually his real brother, Fr. Louis suddenly received the special treatment a brother deserves.

Is Jesus truly our real brother? Perhaps – with some.

Until Death Do Us Part

Recently, a Catholic married couple approached to express their gratitude for 48 years of marriage. They were not only happy for their family but especially happy that they were still in love with each other. They certainly meant their vows "until death do us part." On the other hand, there was the couple that married Catholic, expressed their vows "until death do us part," and parted after the wedding reception. Now they are dating again – but with someone else. Where was their permanent commitment? Apparently, it was never present – nor will it exist perhaps in the future with someone else.

Today, in our "throw-away" society that recognizes very little permanence in many lives, we are evidencing a daily attitude toward "dispose all" – life, marriage and commitment. "Until death do us part" is accepted as long as we do not disagree. Otherwise, we say "goodbye" and look for the "next one" in our life. To the question "Are you married?" some will reply "No" until they are asked "Have you ever married?" Apparently these people once or twice married – even in the Catholic Church – are convinced in their mind that a civil divorce invalidates their marriage vows and allows them to remarry someone else validly. Will they not be surprised before God's judgment?

When Jesus told the Samaritan woman at Jacob's well to call her husband, the woman answered Him that she did not have a husband. Jesus said to her: "You are right in saying, 'I do not have a husband.' For you have had five husbands, and the one you have now is not your husband." (John 4:17-18)

These people of the time of Jesus lived without the benefit of the Catholic Sacrament of Marriage and perhaps will be judged accordingly. But we Catholic people have enjoyed the blessings of the Catholic faith and certainly should know better. Catholics who live together prior to marriage, as well as Catholics who divorce and remarry outside their Catholic faith, are responsible before God for their actions. While they are welcomed and encouraged to attend Mass, they are not privileged to receive Holy Communion until they remedy their lives and behavior. Otherwise they compound their sinful lives with a sacrilege. Why would Catholic people disdain and insult God so? Some day they must answer to Him. They need our prayers.

My Words Will Not Pass Away

At every funeral Mass, the priest celebrant blesses the deceased person at the end of the Mass with the words: "Eternal life grant unto them,

O Lord. May perpetual light shine upon them." Yet as Catholic people we have great difficulty in understanding "eternal life." Our lives are made up of 24 hours of eating, working and sleeping – which comes to an end in death. As our body returns to the earth, our spirit disappears from this world of hours and minutes. For a short time we are living in this world and then suddenly we seem to vanish. No wonder people without a belief in God and His eternal life in heaven or hell despair and live in a state of ignorance.

Yet we believe that God is an infinite, uncreated Spirit whose words in the scripture will live forever – "Heaven and earth will pass away but My words will not pass away." (Mark 13:31)

When we accept this great truth of eternity, we realize that our short time on earth of 25, 50 or 75 years is brief in relation to "forever." Should we not then live these years preparing for our life forever – uniting our mind, will and heart to God, our creator and to Jesus, our judge? Should we not acknowledge our Spiritual Mother, Mary, in our prayer life, especially through the daily rosary? Instead of hours in front of the TV or Internet, learning all about this secular – and at times immoral – world, would it not be better to learn about God and His eternity of joy in prayer, daily Mass or Perpetual Adoration? We really begin to choose heaven or hell while we are living in this world.

It is a sad commentary on our Catholic upbringing and education that some choose hell by their sinfulness. Couples who live together prior to marriage, couples who live in a second marriage without the benefit of the Sacrament of Marriage, offend God even more by receiving Holy Communion; individuals who promote or assist in the abortion of the unborn infant; those who deal in pornographic material – these are some of the Catholics who are already choosing hell in this world. Yet, like many in our Lord's day, they walk away from the truth. It is sad.

These Least Brothers of Mine

Jesus reminds us that we are to recognize Him in others in need. "[W]hatever you did for one of these least brothers of mine, you did for me." (Matt. 25:40) Christ identifies Himself with our neighbor in need.

Yet most of us have difficulty with recognizing Jesus in our neighbor, principally because our neighbor does not speak, act or resemble Jesus. In one rectory when the cook told the priest at dinner time, "There is a bum at the door," she was reminded by the priest, "He might be St. Joseph." The cook returned to the back door, then closed the door and told the priest, "He doesn't look like St. Joseph."

Outward appearances very often are our measure of determining need. Consequently, many people do not qualify. Also our own suspicious nature helps to determine our acceptance or rejection of another possible "St. Joseph." We tend to believe that our generosity toward others will end up in the cash register of a bar or the pockets of the drug dealer.

In Our Lord's words, He never mentions the bar or the drug dealer. He merely identifies with anyone who is in need.

"Need" does not have to be purely financial. I remember a grandfather who requested as his Christmas present one hour of his grandchildren's time. To visit Christ in your grandparents or relatives is fulfilling a very important need. Likewise, to visit Christ in the Eucharist as in Perpetual Adoration is to fulfill a supernatural need. Unfortunately, many of us are too concerned for our own interests and pleasures that we do not look or recognize "need" beyond our own nose. We are basically too selfish to recognize and fulfill our neighbor's needs. We should consider how we treat Him in others.

The Vast Crowd

The story is told of two young people walking along the sea amidst thousands of fish washed ashore. The one remarked that there was nothing he could do to make a difference for the dying fish, to which the other, picking up one of the fish, threw it back into the sea and remarked, "I made a difference for him."

Often times in our life we have to face serious challenges both physical and spiritual which might tend to overwhelm us and even cause us great stress of body and soul. When Jesus saw "the vast crowd" of people approaching Him, He could have panicked and got back into His boat, but instead He began to teach them. (Mark 6:34) He then proceeded to feed them with five loaves of bread and two fishes.

Our Holy Father, Pope John Paul II is a splendid example and inspiration for the world in this regard. Facing the great physical ailments of older age, partial facial paralysis, and other infirmities, together with the challenge of facing a sinful world, our Holy Father travels the globe to bring the Word of God to others. Nothing stops the efforts of this leader from announcing the gospel to the world.

As Catholics we are anointed in Confirmation to bring Christ to others – first to our own home, and also to our neighborhoods, offices or places of work, and even in our leisure places with our friends.

Sometimes we bury our God-given talent because we are fearful or lazy, and as a result we do nothing in life about our Catholic faith. Our Lord will respond to such a person at the end of the world, "You wicked, lazy servant!...Take the talent from him...[a]nd throw this useless servant into the darkness outside...." (Matt. 25:26-30) Each of us has been given an allotment of time in which we fulfill God's Will on earth. Let us use the talents of body and soul given to us by God for His greater honor and glory while we can. We will not be sorry.

I Am the Lord, Your God

Moses became a special friend of God because, despite his human limitations, he obeyed God's requests and wishes. God asked Moses to return to the Pharaoh of Egypt and tell him to release the Jewish people from their slavery that they might return to their Promised Land. Although Moses received only a staff from God as his instrument, Moses obeyed God's request. In response, God accomplished the freedom of His people.

Then, in returning with his people, Moses was invited by God to meet Him at the top of Mount Sinai where God gave him Ten Commandments for his people. These same Ten Commandments are given to us today – basically a divine command to love God and to love our neighbor as ourselves. Unfortunately, the people of God were involved in their past bad habits when Moses returned from God.

In our day, the Ten Commandments are put aside by many and neglected by a people who prefer to obey their own sinful desires – who neglect prayer and see little or no evil in disobeying the Ten Commandments of God.

Apparently, many people – including our Catholic people – look upon God's law as suggestions and recommendations instead of commandments that are to be obeyed. Some of our Catholic people live as if they have never heard of God's commandments.

Someday there will be a personal reckoning and judgment when God will intervene in everyone's conscience and life to remind us that He truly exists and is serious about His commands. In His divine mercy, He will give us the chance and opportunity to return to Him in prayer and sorrow for our sinfulness.

Let us make up to God in sincere reconciliation and contrition. It is never too late – as long as we have breath in our body. Do not wait to return to God's friendship.

The Father Prunes His Faithful

A great mystery hidden in God is the need for human suffering. This mystery was made clear to His eternal Son, when God required Jesus to die in great pain on the cross. How can a good God allow His Son to suffer? And why does He continue to allow His loyal people to experience the same kind of suffering through cancer, heart attacks and other human ailments? Why does God allow suffering? We find our answer at the beginning of God's creation of man and woman.

God blessed Adam and Eve with everything they needed, but commanded them not to eat from the tree of knowledge of good and evil or they would surely die. (Gen. 2:17) When they disobeyed God, He cast them out from the Garden of Eden, in pain to bring forth children, and by the sweat of the brow to get bread to eat. (Gen. 3:16-19) We get a brief appreciation how offensive our sinfulness is to God.

Yet suffering has a significant value before God. In the Old Law, God saved His sinful people when they turned to Him in prayer and penance. At one point in history, God sent the prophet Jonah to warn the sinful Ninevites that God intended to destroy their city; when the king and all the people performed penance for their evil ways, God spared the city. (Jonah 3:10) God is pleased when we accept and offer our sufferings for our sinfulness or for the sins of others.

One wonderful and even heroic practice is to accept and offer our sufferings for the Holy Souls in purgatory who are unable to satisfy for their sins. In the Old Testament, Judas Maccabeus, a great Jewish general, after a battle sent two thousand silver coins to Jerusalem as an atonement for the dead soldiers that they might be freed from sin. (2 Macc. 12:43-46) Today, many Catholic people not only pray for souls in purgatory and offer up their daily sufferings but also offer daily Mass for them. In this later practice, through the Eucharistic action, Jesus offers Himself as a victim for our sins.

Just as the Father pruned His Son so that Heaven would be our eternal home, so too He prunes each of us so that we will produce a greater spiritual reward. It only hurts for a little while.

Tax Collectors and Prostitutes

In the parable of the two sons – one who refused to do his father's order but then did it; the other who said he would do it, but never did – we learn that God rewards those who fulfill His Will. When John the Baptist came, the religious leaders refused to believe him, but tax collectors and prostitutes did believe him. Consequently, Jesus reminds the Jewish leaders that the "tax collectors and prostitutes" – the despised people in His day – "are entering the kingdom of God before you." (Matt. 21:31)

In the average parish in the United States, very few Catholics come regularly to confession and only about fifty percent attend Mass every week. Even many Catholic youth, educated in Catholic schools and religious education, disappear from a regular practice of their Catholic faith as they enter college.

Perhaps part of the blame for this neglect lies in the architecture of new Catholic churches that remove or assign the Eucharistic tabernacle to a small room somewhere adjacent to the main church. In one Catholic seminary for years the Eucharistic Presence of Jesus was in a small room on the second floor. If the Lord of heaven and earth does not have a central and sacred place in His Church, it becomes only a large public hall. Sometimes it is difficult to find a crucifix in the new church building. In one new Catholic church, the Stations of the Cross were etched almost invisibly on the floor. Is Our Lord welcome in His own Church? It might be hard to prove in some Catholic churches. Then we wonder why the faith of our Catholic people is waning.

One new Catholic development that is a breath of fresh spiritual air is the growing number of Perpetual Adoration Chapels honoring Jesus in the Eucharist twenty-four hours each day. Prominently placed on a throne of honor is the Monstrance of Jesus in the Eucharistic Presence. Catholics from any parish are welcome day or night to join in prayer and adoration. It is an hour well spent.

Our Mission in Life

On December 29th, 1999, the Kennedy Center in New York City witnessed a packed house to honor a courageous blind singer and entertainer Stevie Wonder, who sang "We are the World United." The words and music were stirring; the applause for Stevie was well merited. Unfortunately, the title did not clarify what our world – and especially our nation – are united in.

Certainly, our world and our nation are not united in protecting human life, especially the unborn. In fact, our laws and practice locally and throughout the world promote and foster abortion of the unborn children, right up to the moment they are leaving the mother's womb.

Our presidential election in November 2000 provided our nation with a President who reverences human life from the womb to old age. Perhaps with God's grace our nation will return to a pro-life stance. Meantime, some of the Supreme Court Justices who opened the door to legalized abortion in 1973 by their Roe v. Wade decision have already appeared before the Eternal Supreme Court and now are experiencing the judgment of the Son of God. His judgment is final.

When Jesus sent out His Apostles and disciples, they were armed with the knowledge and conviction that God the Father had sent His Divine Son Jesus into the world to begin His human life in the womb of a young Jewish virgin, Mary of Nazareth, and then live out His life until

His death on the cross. When His time came for death, Jesus told His Apostles that He must suffer greatly and be killed and on the third day be raised. (Matt. 16:21) But they did not accept or understand these words. It was only after His bodily resurrection that His Apostles accepted and began to believe.

Now we are His apostles to the world. Have we accepted our Lord at His word and begun to live out our mission in life to follow Him to the cross – and eventually to heaven?

The Mercy of God

During the mid-1920's at age nineteen, young Helen Kowalska, the third child in a family of ten from a remote village in Poland, entered the Congregation of the Sisters of Our Lady of Mercy. The members of this order devoted themselves to caring for troubled young girls, but Sr. Maria Faustina (her professed name), because of her poor and uneducated background, had to serve as door porter and kitchen helper. Yet in 1931, this young sister was visited by Jesus Himself.

Sr. Faustina saw a vision of Jesus with rays of mercy streaming from the area of His heart. He told her to have an image painted to represent this vision and to sign it, "Jesus, I Trust in You!" Calling her the Apostle and Secretary of His mercy, He ordered her to begin writing a dairy so others would learn to trust in Him. In a series of revelations, He taught her that His mercy is unlimited and available even to the greatest sinners, and He revealed special ways for people to respond to His mercy. Until the time of her death from tuberculosis in 1938, Sr. Faustina willingly offered her personal sufferings in union with Him to atone for the sins of others.

By the time of Sr. Faustina's death, devotion to The Divine Mercy had already begun to spread throughout Eastern Europe. The process for the beatification of Sr. Faustina was begun in 1966. On March 7, 1992, Sr. Faustina was declared Venerable; on December 21, 1992, a healing through her intercession was declared a miracle; on April 18, 1993 (Mercy Sunday), she was solemnly beatified in Rome by Pope John Paul II; and on April 30, 2000 (Mercy Sunday), Pope John Paul II declared her a saint. She is now Saint Faustina Kowalska.

The message from Jesus is profoundly simple: God loves us, no matter how great our sins are. Jesus told Sr. Faustina specifically, many times over, how important it was for us to appeal to His Divine Mercy: "I cannot punish the greatest sinner if he appeals to My Mercy" and "The greater the sinner, the greater he has a right to My Mercy."

Jesus requested a special novena be said throughout the world so that He can dispense His Mercy. It must begin on Good Friday and end on the Second Sunday of Easter. Our Saviour also gave us His Divine Mercy Chaplet – a series of prayers that are said on Rosary beads. Both of these devotions can be prayed anywhere, anyplace, anytime. Pope John Paul II has given his strong support to Jesus' message and has stated emphatically that his pontificate is devoted to the Divine Mercy of God.

I believe in the Holy Spirit

The Advocate

"The Advocate, the holy Spirit that the Father will send in my name – he will teach you everything and remind you of all that [I] told you." (John 14:26)

It is sad that after twenty centuries most people are totally unaware that God is Father, Son and Holy Spirit – three Divine Persons who live and act as One God. Catholic people are baptized at birth with water "in the name of the Father, the Son and the Holy Spirit," Catholics bless themselves with the sign of the Trinity, and every prayer, Mass and blessing begins with these Three Divine Persons. Yet even our Catholic people find it difficult to explain the Blessed Trinity.

Probably the most difficult person to define is the Holy Spirit. Years ago, we used the Greek word for spirit and called him the "Holy Ghost." St. John's gospel refers to Him as our "Advocate" – one who pleads on our behalf and supports us. God the Father had sent His Son to redeem us; now the Father and Son send us the Holy Spirit to guide us in this life until we make it successfully back home to heaven.

It would be nice and helpful to us on earth if God would allow the Holy Spirit to appear visibly as He allowed His Son Jesus to appear and live with Joseph, Mary and the Apostles. But this is not in God's plan.

The Holy Spirit will remain for us as an invisible person of God who will inspire and instruct us throughout our lifetime. The more we communicate with Him through prayer, the better we will recognize His presence in our life. Maybe He will inspire an unexpected phone call or visit from a friend announcing some good or bad news. The Holy Spirit may direct the right person or persons into our life to challenge us to be more faithful to God. In whatever way the Holy Spirit relates to us, it will be for our own spiritual and moral benefit.

Just before Jesus was arrested, He promised that the Holy Spirit would come: "But when he comes, the Spirit of truth, he will guide you to all truth." (John 16:13) Let our hearts be open daily to the actions of the Holy Spirit.

Receive the Holy Spirit

Every Catholic parish in the world is privileged on Pentecost Sunday to welcome the Holy Spirit of God. He is much more than a king or president of a country who enters his palace or place of residence to begin His reign in our hearts.

Many parishes in the USA observe this feast day by inviting the bishop to confirm their young people – whereby these youngsters, generally in high school, pledge their commitment to the Catholic faith prior to their Confirmation. The bishop at the ceremony first prays that the Holy Spirit will come upon each candidate with gifts of wisdom, understanding, knowledge, counsel, piety, fortitude, and fear of the Lord. Then anointing the forehead with holy chrism, he says to each candidate: "Be sealed with the gift of the Holy Spirit." Then he says: "Peace be with you." With this simple sacred action, our Catholic faith reminds us that we have been confirmed and strengthened by the Spirit of God and now as young Catholic adults we commit ourselves to faithfully practice and spread our faith to others.

Unfortunately, there are Catholics and others who refuse the gifts of the Holy Spirit and live their lives apart from God and His Church. When we refuse the invitation of God's grace, we close our hearts to the Holy Spirit. Only we are able to open our hearts to God again. The beautiful painting showing the Lord knocking on the door as He holds a lighted lantern was criticized for lacking a doorknob on the door. The artist responded by explaining the door represented the human heart, which can be opened only from within.

As humans, we need to remember that God created us with the freedom to choose Him or reject Him. God confers His grace on us, but we make the free choice to accept or reject this grace. We literally choose our heaven or hell.

The Sin against the Holy Spirit

The scriptures speak of the sin against the Holy Spirit, which will not be forgiven. "And whoever speaks a word against the Son of Man will be forgiven; but whoever speaks against the holy Spirit will not be forgiven, either in this age or in the age to come." (Matt. 12:32) These words, at first, seem to contradict the Mercy of God, until we understand that if a person blasphemes the Holy Spirit, the eternal love of the Father and the Son, only that person can freely petition the Holy Spirit for forgiveness. But if he refuses the grace to be sorry, he will not be forgiven. He has freely closed his mind and heart to God. God the Holy Spirit knocks, but the unrepentant refuse to open – ever. Hence, there is no forgiveness.

Sometimes, over a period of years, and even an entire lifetime, some people live in rejection of God and His commandments and continue on to death – still in their state of rejection. Perhaps, no one has ever offered a prayer for their conversion back to God. One of the most famous conversion stories is the life of Saul, who persecuted the early Church and was present at the stoning of Stephen, a deacon-martyr. As Stephen was being stoned to death, he cried out: "Lord, do not hold this sin against them". (Acts 7:60) Later, Saul was blinded by a great light and heard a voice of Jesus calling to him. (Acts 9:4-5) Saul consequently was baptized as "Paul" and his sight was restored. His conversion has been attributed to the prayer of St. Stephen.

Our prayers for others are also very effective. "Pray for us sinners, now and at the hour of death" our Church teaches us in the "Hail Mary."

In addition to our prayers and penance for the conversion of people unreconciled with God and the Church, another salutary and merciful prayer is for the Holy Souls confined in the prison of purgatory. They too belong to the communion of saints and will certainly be grateful for our prayers of release to heaven. "May the souls of the faithful departed through the Mercy of God rest in peace. Amen". Maybe someone will pray for us someday.

Born Again of Water and the Spirit

In recent years, some preachers of the scriptures have emphasized that everyone needs to be "born again" if they wish to be saved. Perhaps they refer to the night meeting of the Pharisee, Nicodemus, a ruler of the Jews, with Jesus, at which time Jesus responded to the Pharisee's inquiry about Jesus' relationship with God: "Amen, amen, I say to you, no one can see the kingdom of God without being born from above." (John 3:3) Nicodemus asked Jesus how a person can be born again, and Jesus answered: "Amen, amen, I say to you, no one can enter the kingdom of God without being born of water and Spirit." (John 3:5)

Apparently these preachers only read the first response of Jesus and neglect the response about "water and Spirit," which is our Sacrament of Baptism.

Prior to the baptism of Jesus, John the Baptist said to the people at the Jordan River: "I am baptizing you with water, but one mightier than I is coming...He will baptize you with the holy Spirit and fire." (Luke 3:16)

After Jesus had been baptized and was praying, heaven opened and the Holy Spirit descended upon him in a form like a dove. (Luke 3: 21-22)

So born-again Catholics are baptized Catholics who celebrate the gifts of faith, hope and charity every day. They are Catholics who reverence and praise God when they wake in the morning, consciously reach out to their neighbors throughout each day in kindness and charity, and as they retire in the evening offer their thanks and gratitude for His guiding presence and assistance. Prayer and good works are the mark of a born-again Catholic. But everything grace-filled begins at the baptismal font.

That's the Spirit

A lady recently told me that she was "baptized in the Spirit" and as a result she is a Catholic today. In the past, people who have said those words were usually referring to an experience that happened to them. Our Catholic faith teaches us – in the words of Jesus to Nicodemus one evening – that we need to be born of water and Spirit if we wish to enter the kingdom of God. (John 3:5) In the mind and works of Jesus, baptism means water and the Holy Spirit. So "the baptism of the Holy Spirit" without water is not the sacrament about which Jesus was speaking to Nicodemus.

So what is the popular expression "baptism of the Spirit" all about? It is simply the daily continuing action of God the Holy Spirit upon our souls. In the Catholic catechism, we are taught that God prompts us daily with His power and love to grow away from sin and the devil and to seek and reach out to God and His ways.

Each moment of our day God constantly draws us to Himself. Most people, especially those who live in sin and spiritual darkness, are unaware of God's constant, daily presence. Like a mother and father who watch over their young children every moment lest they suffer harm, God watches over us always. As we come closer to God our Father and Creator, we are suddenly aware of His brilliant and beautiful presence within us. We can appreciate the experience of the future St. Paul on the road to Damascus. Blinded by God, he heard Jesus call: "Saul, Saul, why are you persecuting me?...I am Jesus...." (Acts 9:4-5) In the baptism of the Spirit, some people, like Saul, wake up to the constant presence of God, who remains with every one of His creatures and children daily. Some respond and some do not. The latter group at death go to either purgatory or hell.

Perhaps those numbers who respond daily to God go directly to heaven. We need to acknowledge "the baptism of the Spirit" or God's actual prompting grace as often as He comes. "Come, Holy Spirit, come daily."

Birthday of the Church

Everybody has a birthday – a day when we come from God and begin our life in this world. So too does the Catholic Church have a birthday, a day that is fifty days after Easter, called Pentecost Sunday. Jesus had risen on Easter Sunday and appeared to His Apostles and disciples over a 40-day period. Then on Ascension Thursday, with His task on earth completed, Jesus went back to heaven. But first He promised to send the Holy Spirit, the Third Person of the Holy Trinity, who would inspire and confirm His Church with His gifts and graces. For nine days, the Apostles and early Christians spent their days in prayer in anticipation of the coming of the Holy Spirit. It was the first Novena of prayer. Then, on the tenth day, the Holy Spirit descended on the early Church, as tongues of fire filled the Apostles and Christians with His gifts of wisdom, understanding, piety, knowledge, courage, counsel and fear of the Lord. These same gifts we receive in our Sacrament of Confirmation.

God the Father created each of us, God the Son redeemed us from sin, and now God the Holy Spirit sanctifies us and makes us holy – in preparation for heaven.

When we realize what God has done for us and to us, it is hard to believe that some are still not grateful to our good God. It must be disheartening to God when He looks upon the ingratitude of mankind. However, like a parent who has children that are loving and obedient, God truly appreciates those who remain faithful and loving. Our gratitude to God is best expressed in our life of daily prayer, sacrifice and good conduct toward one another. We ought to pray daily, "Come Holy Spirit, form us in the image of God."

Pentecost

We believe that Jesus Christ is the first advocate or spokesman for God the Father – His visible representative and intercessor for us here on earth. Jesus was sent by His Father to teach us how to live on earth through love of God and neighbor so that we would be welcomed home to heaven when we die. Now as His visible spokesman, Jesus Christ, returns to His Father, the Father now sends "another advocate" – the Holy Spirit of truth – as His invisible yet real spokesman to us on earth to be with us always. (John 14:16)

He began His Divine Presence in the world on the first Pentecost Sunday – coming down upon the Apostles in the upper room in Jerusalem nine days after Jesus ascended into heaven. "When the time for Pentecost was fulfilled, they were all in one place together. And suddenly there came from the sky a noise like a strong driving wind, and it filled the entire house in which they were. Then there appeared to them tongues as of fire, which parted and came to rest on each one of them. And they were all filled with the holy Spirit and began to speak in different tongues, as the Spirit enabled them to proclaim." (Acts 2:1-4)

This was the first day of the invisible presence of the Holy Spirit within the early Church. In fact, on this day of Pentecost, the Church of Jesus Christ was born and began its work on earth, resulting in the baptism of three thousand persons that day. (Acts 2:41)

Today, this same Advocate for God the Father, the Holy Spirit, watches over the Catholic Church to insure that the Vicar of Jesus, the Pope, teaches correctly the truths of Jesus Christ and guides the Church until the end of time. He also enters each baptized soul with God's grace and divine life and remains to eventually bring that soul back to the Father. He will only leave the soul if serious mortal sin becomes present. He will return with God's grace if the person in mortal sin repents, confesses and is absolved by the action of his priest. Otherwise, the Holy Spirit cannot return. We Catholics are truly blessed with the presence on earth of such a wonderful advocate from our Father. We should acknowledge Him often.

The World Needs Another Pentecost

Imagine a world that would accept a new Pentecost from God the Holy Spirit. Such an experience from God upon this world that has been trying very hard to live without God would certainly effect a mighty spiritual change in people. People bent on destroying life in all its stages from "the womb to old age" might make an "about-face" and see the beauty of God in everyone who comes from His loving hands. The powerful of the world might suddenly realize that all their power comes from their Almighty God who made them. As Jesus reminded Pilate, who thought he was all-powerful, "You would have no power over me if it had not been given to you from above." (John 19:11)

If the world were to experience the Holy Spirit at another Pentecost, we would imagine a rush from our Catholic people who have all but abandoned the Sacrament of Confession, since they would see their souls in the light of God's truth. The Eucharist would take on a whole new relationship with everyone. Perpetual Adoration would flourish. Families would be reunited in love and affection; neighbors and others would be at peace with each other.

If the first Pentecost of Jerusalem can ignite an entire town, what might happen if the entire world were visited by the Holy Spirit? What man is unable to accomplish, God is able and willing. Whether He will, depends on our prayers and obedience to His Will. This world needs the Holy Spirit. We should pray for another Pentecost.

To See Ourselves

Years ago people lived by the light of the candle, until Thomas Edison discovered the power of the electric light. Suddenly the world brightened so that people could see even more perfectly. Yet when the sun came out and shone through the windowpanes, we saw even better the microscopic particles floating almost invisibly in the air. Without the brilliance of God's created sun shining in our homes, our vision would never see the invisible world of dust and particles that we breathe daily into our lungs.

If we could transfer these thoughts to the spiritual world of our soul, we might understand the state of sin within us. Most of us examine our conscience with what might be compared to a spiritual candle. Although we may see the obvious sins and sinfulness, we are blind to the numerous slight offenses to God. We need the power of God's light and grace to illuminate all the corners of our soul so that we can see ourselves as God sees us. If that would happen, there would be no escape from the goodness or evil present. We would not be able to excuse ourselves lightly as if even small sins did not matter to God, especially if we are not sorry for them and make little effort to correct ourselves.

Other people, especially those with whom we live, notice our imperfections much more quickly than we are willing to admit to ourselves. But even if others fail to see within us, God does not. Someday He will turn on His brilliant light of the Holy Spirit within us, so that we too will see ourselves as God sees us. It would behoove us to clean up our act ahead of time. Monthly or frequent confession to a priest is God's gift. We should accept it while we still have time.

God the Holy Spirit – Our Inspiration in Life

Who is God the Holy Spirit? Perhaps we can use the example of an earthly father and his son. The father loves his son with a bond of love that varies from father to father. In God the Father and God the Son, that bond of love is a Divine Person, the Holy Spirit. More than a bond between them, rather God the Holy Spirit is a divine person who exists and comes to us in baptism, confession, Eucharist, confirmation, marriage, priesthood, anointing of the sick, and all our prayers and good works offered to God. And He comes from the Father and the Son.

The Holy Spirit is the divine channel of all graces from God. He appears at the baptism of Jesus as a dove and at Pentecost as tongues of fire. The sin against the Holy Spirit that cannot be forgiven, as mentioned in scripture, is our deliberate rejection of God through our refusal to be sorry for serious sin. A person who deliberately switches off his house lights at night will remain in darkness unless he freely returns to the switch and turns them on again. God the Holy Spirit is the light of grace in our soul. We need to return to Him with sorrow in our darkness of sin if we wish to return to His light. Otherwise the serious sinner will remain in darkness forever.

A wonderful companion and spouse of the Holy Spirit is our heavenly Mother, Mary, who desires to assist all her children to heaven. Our love of Mary and prayer to her will insure the release of God's graces and blessings through the Holy Spirit. She is our maternal advocate before God. "Turn then, most gracious advocate, thine eyes of mercy toward us," we say in prayer to Mary.

To God the Holy Spirit, whose feast of Pentecost we celebrate, we pray that He will inspire us and fill us with His love.

God Is Not the Problem

Sad to say, many people in the five continents of the world who believe in God do not accept Jesus as His Divine Son. The idea of a God-man is far removed from their beliefs. Consequently, Christianity is a belief that is unacceptable; and even for some, its practice by them is punishable with imprisonment or even death. In one country this past year, some young Christians were imprisoned because they explained their Christian faith in public.

Yet as Catholics we know and believe that God the Father proclaimed Jesus as His Son, first at His baptism by John the Baptist, and then again on Mount Tabor when Moses and Elijah appeared to Jesus. On both occasions God the Father called Jesus His beloved Son.

Despite 2,000 years of Christianity, the Catholic Church has managed to convince only a small portion of the world's inhabitants of the truth and wisdom of the gospel of Jesus Christ. It would seem that this apparent failure of the Church to win over to Jesus Christ the rest of the world is not going to change for the better without the divine intervention by God Himself. We truly need another Pentecost – an event whereby God would send His Holy Spirit – the third Divine Person of God – to enlighten our minds and change our wills to accept Jesus.

For this to occur, we need prayer to God. We need to ask Him to send His Holy Spirit. Without our insistent and daily prayer, God may pay little attention. But if we pray with persistence, He will answer. Jesus reminds us of the value of persistence in the parable of the man visited at midnight by a friend asking for three loaves of bread: "I tell you, if he does not get up to give him the loaves because of their friendship, he will get up to give him whatever he needs because of his persistence." (Luke 11:8)

We Catholics are so blessed with the divine and unchanging truths of God, as revealed by His Son, Jesus Christ, that we may tend to take them for granted and even sometimes ignore them. The rest of the world, had they been so blessed, might be much more attentive and grateful to God. Let us wake up a bit and begin to pray more.

Degrees of Love

One day after His Resurrection, Jesus challenged Peter three times: "Simon, son of John, do you love me?" (John 21:15-17) Three times Peter acknowledged that he loved Him, remembering that he had denied his suffering Master three times outside in the courtyard.

It is interesting to examine the Greek words for "love." The English translation of the word used by Jesus and Peter is simply translated as "love." But in Greek, the difference is significant. Jesus invited Peter to love Him with a supernatural love – the highest form of love; Peter answered with a word that means a natural love. It would be as if Jesus asked Peter if he loved Him enough that he would die for Him, and Peter responded with a word of simple affection. On the third request to Peter, Jesus descended to the level of Peter's love and asked him to love Him in an affectionate way. Since Peter at the time was not yet ready to lay down his life for Jesus, the Lord was content to receive even his natural love.

We as Christians are challenged by Jesus in the same manner. He says to us, "Do you love me enough to die for me?" Most Christians are not yet at that level of love. Many Catholics in the world find it hard to pray to God daily or attend Mass on a weekly basis. In the United States only half of Catholic parishioners come to Mass on a regular basis and even fewer come on holy days of obligation. In Europe the Mass attendance in most countries is very small. Consequently, our Lord's challenge to love Him goes unheeded.

The world has a great need for a new Pentecost – a new coming of the Holy Spirit who would infuse His graces in the hearts of people and bring them back to the need for the presence of God in their daily lives.

When Our Lady originally appeared to the three children of Fatima in May 1917, Lucia, the oldest, asked Mary why Francesco, the only boy, did not hear Her. Our Lady told her that Francesco needed to say many rosaries before he could hear her. We too need to increase our prayer life if we are to grow in our faith and appreciate Christ in our life. We need to learn to pray often.

The Holy Catholic Church

You Are Peter

In the movie *Shoes of the Fisherman*, the newly elected Pope from a Slavic country is challenged by a very liberal theologian regarding the Catholic faith. Finally, after a long debate, the theologian declares to the new Pope, "You are Peter."

This is what Jesus declares to Simon Peter in the region of Caesarea Philippi, when he says, "Blessed are you, Simon son of Jonah…And so I say to you, you are Peter, and upon this rock I will build my church…." (Matt. 16:17-18) In this commission of authority, Jesus changed Simon's name to Peter (which means "rock"). Consequently, successors of Peter have taken a new name upon assuming the papacy. Karol Wojtyla upon his election in 1978 as the 265th successor of St. Peter, took the name John Paul II in honor of John XXIII and Paul VI. Our Catholic faith acknowledges Pope John Paul II as the Vicar for Jesus Christ on earth. Although we believe that Jesus Christ is the head of the Church on earth, though invisible to us, He has appointed Pope John Paul II as His visible head and has declared through Peter, "Whatever you bind on earth shall be bound in heaven; and whatever you loose on earth shall be loosed in heaven." (Matt. 16:19)

Since the schism of the Orthodox Church in the 12th century and the Protestant revolution in the 16th century, members of the Orthodox and Protestant faiths have not accepted the Pope as their leader. Yet it is the hope and prayer of the Catholic Church that someday, with God's grace and the action of the Holy Spirit, everyone will acknowledge him. Jesus said on one occasion, "I have other sheep that do not belong to this fold. These also I must lead, and they will hear my voice, and there will be one flock, one shepherd." (John 10:16) Although the Catholic Church desires and prays for this unity, perhaps only God Himself can someday accomplish this feat.

In the meantime, we have an obligation as Catholics to honor, revere and obey the successor of Peter, the Pope, in all spiritual matters. Disrespect and disobedience cause doubts and unrest and certainly do not come from God.

The Official Summons

Most of us think of a summons as coming from a police officer or court judge. Usually such an action threatens our freedom or liberty. However, a summons from the Lord is a holy action that involves the common good. "He summoned the Twelve and began to send them out two by two and gave them authority over unclean spirits." (Mark 6:7) They were to be His representatives to the world. They went on their way to preach repentance. (Mark 6:12) The result of their efforts is the present Catholic Church, located in all the countries of the world, whose members today number nearly one billion.

When the Apostles and disciples of Jesus Christ eventually died, they left other bishops, priests and deacons to carry on Our Lord's summons to preach the gospel and baptize in the name of the Father, Son and Holy Spirit. Pope Linus and then Pope Anacletus were chosen to succeed St. Peter as the Vicar of Christ. Pope John Paul II is the 265th successor of Simon Peter. For almost 2,000 years, Jesus Christ has directed and guided His Catholic Church – despite trials and tribulations.

In recent years the Church suffered through the scandal of priests who misused and abused their priesthood through the molestation of children and young people. Although we believe that the Church is divine in her founder, Jesus Christ, and in her sacraments and commandments, she is human in her membership. In her membership, the Church can and does sin at times. It is important that the teachers of the Church admit her sinfulness and ask pardon from her Founder. When the woman, caught in adultery was brought before Jesus, He said to the scribes and Pharisees, "Let the one among you who is without sin be the first to throw a stone at her." (John 8:7) And to the woman, Jesus said, "[D]o not sin any more." (John 8:11) Jesus always forgives us if we are sorry, but He counsels us not to continue in our sins.

While scandal may occur among her membership, the Catholic Church as promised by her Founder, Jesus Christ, will continue until the end of the world. To Peter, the Apostle, Jesus proclaimed that the gates of the netherworld would not prevail against the Church. (Matt. 16:18) We are grateful for the promise and presence of Jesus.

God's Life of Grace

What the old Adam lost through his sin of disobedience, the new Adam, Jesus Christ, regained by His obedient death on the cross. Consequently, in obedience to Jesus, we are washed clean of sin at baptism and filled with God's life and light. If later as adults we reject God's commandments in a serious and deliberate way, we need only approach God's priest with sincere sorrow and amendment through the Sacrament of Confession, and we will receive a complete absolution of our sins. We are now restored once again to God's friendship.

Yet while the Sacrament of Baptism is still popular, the popularity of the Sacrament of Confession has declined to a murmur – at least for most people who call themselves "Catholic."

Years ago, people on a mission or retreat were introduced to a play whereby someone had been accused of being a "Catholic," but at the trial there was not enough evidence to convict him. Would there be enough evidence to convict us?

Every parish has a sizeable number of parishioners who have joined the parish but who only attend Mass and the sacraments at their convenience. These are Catholics by reputation or in name only.

When Jesus asked His future Vicar, Peter, whether he loved Him enough to die for Him, Simon Peter was unable to rise to that level of love. Yet Jesus accepted Simon Peter at his own human level of love. (John 21:15-17) I think that many Catholic people and other Christians who love God minimally are depending on a similar acceptance from God on the last day. Eventually, however, Peter did rise to the level of sacrificial love as he hung on a cross upside down and now is revered as a saint of the Church.

God's life of grace is ours for the asking. We are given an appointed time on earth to receive this Divine gift of God's life and should not wait until the last minute of our earthly life to accept and acquire this "wedding garment" of grace. We might delay too long. How will we respond to God's grace?

The Eucharist Is the Heart of Our Faith

When we examine ourselves, we discover that we possess a head, body, heart and soul – all of which have a purpose, and all of which have an important role to play in our life. A headless body would give no direction; a body without a soul becomes a corpse. Likewise, without a heart, we possess no love.

In the Church established by Jesus Christ, we need a Divine Leader for direction in life, a source of life producing the grace of the Holy Spirit, a body of people professing one faith and one creed. But without the presence of the Eucharist, our Mystical Body of Christ, the Church, would lack love.

The Eucharist is the center and source of love in the Church and in the world – providing us with the spiritual food of His Body and His life-giving Blood as our drink. Jesus in the Eucharist nourishes and feeds His Church with His Body and Blood. In the gospel of John, Jesus invites the Jewish people to eat His flesh and drink His blood in order to have life. "Whoever eats my flesh and drinks my blood has eternal life, and I will raise him on the last day." (John 6:54) Then one year later, on Holy Thursday at the Last Supper, Jesus instituted the Eucharist, giving His flesh and blood to the Apostles in the outward form of bread and wine.

The more we study the Eucharist and receive it regularly, we realize that this sacrifice/sacrament is the heart of our faith without which we lack charity and love. The Catholic who fails to attend Mass and receive Eucharist regularly soon loses his Catholic heart and falls away to laziness, indifference and sinfulness.

We Catholics, who are privileged to know, love and receive Jesus in the Eucharist daily or on Sunday, gradually develop a heart resembling the Sacred Heart of Jesus. He will invite us into His Sacred Heart to enjoy the divine joys and happiness present therein, and we will enjoy another special privilege of being invited into the Immaculate Heart of Mary, His mother. Then our joy will be complete. The two Hearts of Jesus and Mary will insure our happiness with God forever. Everyone is welcome.

The House on the Seashore

Popular places for families and single young people during the summer are the sandy beaches and seashores. Thousands of city people crowd the local sunny shores or drive to the lake areas in the mountains. More than a few meet their future spouse at this time. It is a time of relaxing from busy and demanding jobs during the rest of the year.

For Our Lord, such a place was Capernaum, a town or village at the northern point of the Sea of Galilee. Simon and Andrew, future Apostles, lived there with their families and fished the waters of the lake daily for their livelihood. The young Jesus loved to visit this fishing village – as was apparent by His frequent visits during His public life. Apparently the feeling of the villagers was mutual. "The crowds went looking for him, and when they came to him, they tried to prevent him from leaving them." (Luke 4:42) Unfortunately, this feeling of admiration and respect was not shared by the people in His own hometown of Nazareth, who "rose up, drove him out of the town, and led him to the brow of the hill on which their town had been built, to hurl him down headlong." (Luke 4:29) It is no wonder that Jesus remarked to them, "[N]o prophet is accepted in his own native place." (Luke 4:24)

Today Jesus, as He recalls His prophetic words, must smile through His tears over the present liturgical struggle over His Eucharistic Presence as He offers Himself to the Father daily through the action of His priests and then resides in the tabernacle or in a Eucharistic monstrance during the rest of the day and evening for adoration. And then we wonder at the lack of priestly vocations. Until all of our Catholic people together with our bishops, priests, deacons and religious men and women truly acknowledge Christ as their Eucharistic Lord, we will wait for vocations – and world peace. The people of Capernaum set a good example for all of us.

Going Fishing

The early Christians lived a life of daily fear under the Roman emperors, who enjoyed making sport of them in the public arena, whether at the hands of gladiators or the teeth of wild lions. Lest they be discovered as Christians, the believers identified each other through secret signs or codes. One such sign used was the figure of a fish, which in the Greek language spelled out letters abbreviating the name of Jesus Christ, Son of God, Saviour: I.X.TH.U.S. Many Eucharistic tabernacles today display this early Christian sign indicating the presence of Jesus within. Since many of the first Christians were fishermen, the symbol of a fish had a familiar significance. Jesus said to them, "Come after me, and I will make you fishers of men." (Mark 1:17)

When Jesus called Simon to be a fisher of men, Simon had been struggling all night to catch fish. But when Jesus came along and Simon obeyed His instructions to try one more time, suddenly the nets were filled with fish. (Luke 5:1-9) In life's struggles, very often we go our own way, failing to call upon the Lord for His guidance and assistance. Yet the presence of God and His Divine Son, Jesus, makes all the difference between success and failure. Simon Peter might have shown a stubborn nature at times, but he was not stupid. He recognized an outstanding happening with the presence of Jesus and said, "Depart from me, Lord, for I am a sinful man." (Luke 5:8)

Unfortunately, our present generation of Catholic Christians needs the blessing of more men like Peter, the fisherman–apostle, to recognize the presence of God in our daily lives and activities. Fortunately, we have a few, such as Pope John Paul II who is a true successor of Peter the Apostle, Mother Teresa of Calcutta of happy memory, as well as our own Father Nelson Baker who awaits the Church's judgment. But we need thousands more who will live their daily life aware of Christ's miraculous presence in their midst. St. Therese Martin of France – the "Little Flower" – used to remind herself that sanctity was simply doing ordinary things in an extraordinary way. Put God in charge of your life and everything works out His way. There is no better way – even in fishing.

The Body of Christ

Approximately 163 years before Christ, a Jewish general, Judas Maccabeus, rescued the Temple of Solomon in Jerusalem from foreigners and restored it to its original beauty. In celebration Judas and his followers "offered sacrifice according to the law on the new altar of holocausts that they had made." (1st Macc. 4:53) This is celebrated each year as "Hanukkah" or feast of Dedication. Two hundred thirty-three years later, in 70 A.D, the Roman armies destroyed the Jewish Temple again. What remains in Jerusalem today is the foundation of the building, which is referred to as the "Wailing Wall." Pope John Paul II visited this wall when he came to Jerusalem recently. Centuries after the destruction of the temple, a young man in Assisi, Italy felt called to rebuild a small church that was in need of repair, so he collected rocks and stones for the task. He claimed that God spoke to him and said, "Repair my Church." His name was John but he began a religious order called Franciscans and took the new name, Francis of Assisi. Eventually the Franciscan community grew and developed throughout the world.

What Francis soon began to understand was that God wanted Francis to repair His Church throughout the world – not the physical buildings but the spiritual structure made up of men, women and children. As Catholic people we sometimes fail to appreciate that together we make up the mystical Body of Christ of which Christ is the Head and we are the members. St. Paul reminds us, "For as in one body we have many parts, and all the parts do not have the same function, so we, though many, are one body in Christ and individually parts of one another." (Romans 12:4-5)

Like Francis of Assisi, we need to learn that the Church which Jesus established is not a physical structure but all of God's people joined together, with the grace of the Holy Spirit, and directed by Jesus Christ and His Vicar here on earth, the Pope. We too must come to appreciate this great gift of God's grace.

Our Great Treasure

Garage sales are no longer limited to a few neighborhoods. Today at certain times of the year there seems to be a plethora of garage sales. What is one person's junk from the attic, cellar, or garage becomes somebody else's treasure. Occasionally, a real masterpiece emerges, unbeknown to the owner.

On a spiritual level, we all need to examine our souls for the purpose of ridding our inner self of certain attachments to money, possessions and pride of life. With prayer and dependence on God, we will acquire and possess a spirit of poverty, less dependence on material things, and a greater generosity and humility. Maybe a future saint will begin to emerge from such an examination.

Virtue is really not that difficult to acquire and practice. With baptism, we already possess the virtues of faith, hope and charity.

Like athletes in every sport, it is necessary to practice, practice and practice some more. The spiritual life has the same needs – we need to practice faith to be faithful, to practice hope to be trusting and trustworthy, and to practice charity to be loving.

Our Catholic faith together with the Kingdom of God is like a treasure that some people are fortunate to possess and others are blessed to discover during their lifetime. It is a treasure for which we should thank Almighty God everyday – through our daily prayer life, frequent Mass, Holy Communion and confession. It is also a gift that we need to share with others by our work and example. Some Catholics are very reticent in speaking of their Catholic faith – to the extent that their co-workers have never known their great treasure. We need to proclaim our faith when opportunities are present.

In recent years, two families encouraged their fathers to be received into the Catholic Church through the rites of initiation. One was 90 years old; the other was 100. Both were received as full members of the Church. Others are waiting to be invited by you.

Lost Sheep

Recently, a local newspaper printed an interview with a very scholarly man, well-respected in his professional field, who was dying. He was quoted as saying that he did not believe in God and viewed his approaching death as the end of his existence.

Perhaps this man is representative of many in the world who do not believe in a personal God and have never had the joy and satisfaction of knowing our Triune God – Father, Son and Holy Spirit. How sad it is that some people live and die without knowing our marvelous and loving God. Who is to blame for this breakdown in our religious life – the parents who failed their children? Or are we to blame for not living our life as an apostle to others? Currently, our Catholic Church in the world is approaching one billion people, young and old. Imagine the influence that one billion Catholics would have on a non-believing world, if every Catholic lived the faith and tried to bring the faith to others by prayer and good deeds.

When Jesus commissioned His twelve Apostles, He instructed them to go to the lost sheep. (Matt. 10:6) Today these lost sheep might be among our many baptized Catholic people who for one reason or another have long since given up the practice of their Catholic faith. They may even have been our altar servers of old, Catholic school graduates, or young Catholic people who were never educated in the Catholic faith – who gradually through college or a marriage experience withdrew from their Catholic practices. They may only need an invitation to return to Jesus, the Good Shepherd.

One important quality necessary for a successful apostle is persistence in prayer for others. St. Monica, the mother of St. Augustine prayed and wept many tears for years for her son who led a very sinful life. He not only returned to the Catholic faith but eventually lived an outstanding life of holiness.

Jesus reminds all of those blessed with the faith that the Good Shepherd rejoices over finding the one sheep that strayed – for it is the Will of His Heavenly Father that not "one of these little ones be lost." (Matt. 18:14)

It is important that we reach out to others.

The Good Shepherd

Many tourists and pilgrims who visit the holy places of the Eastern world are surprised that the customs and habits of the people today still resemble the times of Jesus, Mary and Joseph, especially outside the cities. Shepherds and their flocks of sheep roam the countryside. Externally, the places of Our Lord seem to be untouched by the ages.

In the gospel of John, Jesus reveals that He is the Good Shepherd, who will lay down His life for us, His sheep. He speaks of other sheep that will follow Him and promises that "there will be one flock, one shepherd." (John 10:16)

Although our Lord's Catholic Church has survived three hundred years of Roman emperors, the constant uprising of various Christian sects, the twelfth century schism of the Eastern world from papal authority with the resulting formation of the Orthodox Church, and the establishment of Protestantism and the Anglican Church, She has yet to realize Our Lord's dream and promise of "one flock, one shepherd."

Our present vicar of Jesus Christ, Pope John Paul II, has worked tirelessly through his papacy toward this one goal – with a measure of success. The Orthodox Church leaders have welcomed him in his travels, and various Christian leaders have received him with respect and honor wherever he has gone. Many rulers of oppressive governments have welcomed him. Yet there are others who have been hesitant in their acceptance of him. But then, Jesus was not very popular with everyone in His day. On one occasion when he told the Jews that He and the Father are one, they picked up rocks to stone Him. (John 10:30-31)

The same is true of faithful followers of Jesus. They are not always welcome or appreciated everywhere. In fact, many are persecuted – sometimes by well-meaning people. It is the price you pay, if you wish to be a real friend of the Lord. Is it too much?

Humble Beginnings

Pilgrims or tourists visiting the Land of Jesus will enjoy the delightful Sea of Galilee where the Apostles spent most of their time fishing the waters. In fact, it was at the Sea of Galilee where Jesus called some of His Apostles. As He was walking by the Sea, Jesus saw two fishermen who were brothers, Simon and Andrew, casting a net into the water. Jesus said to them: "Come after me, and I will make you fishers of men." (Matt. 4:19)

The amazing thing about the Catholic Church is that it began with a small group of fishermen, a tax collector and a few ordinary men, and they accomplished so much. All the Apostles except two were put to death for their faith in Jesus Christ. Only the presence of God the Holy Spirit, who came down upon them on Pentecost Sunday, will explain the development of the Church from a small community of Jews and Greeks to a worldwide organization totaling almost one billion people. It certainly took a lot of fishing under the influence of the Holy Spirit to accomplish that number.

In our every day life, which we dedicate to God, we will also accomplish great things for God. We might begin in our own family – first setting the example by praying the family rosary together for various intentions. Then we might invite the neighboring family or families to join – each taking a mystery. As a family, you might try to attend Sunday Mass together – and even invite a friend. Maybe there will be an opportunity to help the poor or less fortunate in and outside your community. Any of these ways and others will assist the spread of the Catholic faith.

In all our apostolic initiatives, we need only invoke the Holy Spirit to inspire each of our particular works. It is the presence of God the Holy Spirit who can accomplish great results. Come Holy Spirit!

The Jewish Priesthood

In today's society the Jewish priesthood is non-existent, as it has been for almost 2000 years. Today we address the Jewish leader as "Rabbi," which means "teacher." When and why did the Jewish priesthood disappear?

The scriptures describe a priesthood established by God from the times of Moses to Jesus Christ – a period of nearly1300 years. In establishing the priesthood, God said to Moses: "Thus shall the priesthood be theirs by perpetual law, and thus shall you ordain Aaron and his sons." (Ex. 29:9)

This priesthood of Aaron continued throughout the years of the Old Testament even to the time of Jesus Christ. We read that Jesus was arrested and led away to Caiaphas, the high priest. (Matt. 26:57) Also, the chief priests and the Pharisees gathered before Pilate and requested a guard for His tomb. (Matt. 27:62-66) The Jewish priests were very present at the time of Christ.

After the ascension of Jesus, as the early Church continued to grow, the Jewish priesthood continued to exist. On the occasion of the cure of the man crippled from birth, whom Peter cured "in the name of Jesus Christ," the high priest and others questioned Peter and John about the miracle. (Acts 4:5-7) So it is evident that the Jewish priesthood continued after Jesus returned to His Father. Perhaps the destruction of the Jewish Temple in Jerusalem by the Romans in 70 A.D. is significant in the disappearance of the Jewish priesthood.

As Catholics, we are aware that our Divine Leader, Jesus Christ, established a new and perpetual priesthood at the Last Supper, the Thursday night before His death. At this supper, Jesus established the unbloody sacrifice of His body and blood at the first Eucharist and commissioned His Apostles as priests to continue His sacrifice. The Catholic priesthood began that evening and has continued throughout almost 2000 years to the present day.

As the Jewish priesthood of Aaron disappeared, the Catholic priesthood of Jesus Christ appeared and has served the entire world throughout the Christian era. God continues today to assist the world through His Eternal Priest-Son, Jesus, and through those who receive His Sacrament of Holy Orders. We need to be grateful for the service of His priesthood.

Orthodox and Christian Churches

Catholics who have not studied the history of the Church through the centuries may not be aware of the presence of the Orthodox Church in many countries in the world. The schism, or split, from the Catholic Church took place in the twelfth century when Archbishop Michael Cerularius disagreed with the Pope on the relation of the Blessed Trinity and the authority of the Pope. He separated from the Catholic Church, and the entire Eastern part of the church followed the bishop and has remained separated. Those bishops, priests and laity who returned back to the Church afterward are referred to as "Uniates" or "united with the Pope."

Today we have Greek Orthodox Churches and Greek Catholic Churches. In Lackawanna, there is a Serbian Orthodox Church on Abbott Road and a Greek Catholic Church on Ridge Road. Whether it is Greek, Syrian, (Egyptian) Coptic Orthodox or Catholic, the liturgy or manner of offering the Eucharist varies considerably from our (Latin) Western liturgy. In these churches, young men studying for the priesthood may marry and still be priests. However, when their wives die, the priests do not remarry.

After World War II, a number of married Catholic or Orthodox priests came to America and presently some serve in the Diocese of Buffalo.

It is the sincere prayer of the entire Catholic Church that through God's grace the Orthodox churches will soon rejoin with the Catholic Church and work as one church under the authority of the Pope. This will only happen with prayer, charity and reconciliation. We invite everyone to pray for this great event to happen.

Public vs. Private Revelation

From the time of Abraham, our gracious God chose to remain hidden from our bodily eyes and only revealed himself gradually through the time of the Old Testament. Finally, he revealed himself in the person of his Divine Son, Jesus Christ. Jesus is the full revelation of God the Father. When Philip asks Jesus to see the Father, Jesus responds: "Whoever has seen me has seen the Father." (John 14:9) The time from the conception of Jesus to the death of the last Apostle, John, is referred to as Public Revelation. What we know definitively about God and his wishes and commands for us comes during this New Testament time.

We need to know nothing further to gain our salvation. If this is our belief, then what is the need for Private Revelation, which has occurred since the time of the New Testament? What is the value of the many Church-approved appearances of Jesus and Mary at such places as Guadalupe, Knock, Lourdes, Fatima, and many other places down through the centuries? We are not obliged by the Church to respond to private revelation since Jesus has already revealed what we need to know and practice. Also there is nothing new revealed through private revelation. So why should we pay attention to these Church-approved appearances of Jesus and Mary?

First of all, if we are practicing our Catholic faith fully as we should, we do not need the reminders from Jesus and Mary to pray, do penance, treat our neighbor as ourselves, attend Mass and the sacraments regularly, respect life in all its stages, etc. But this is not the case with many today, in a world that prays little, performs little penance, resents one's neighbors, disregards Mass and the sacraments regularly, aborts life in the womb, etc. Out of love for their children in the world, God has sent his Son, Jesus, and his mother, Mary, back to earth during these centuries to remind us of our unfaithfulness to God and exhort us to return to God. Failure to respond to God's pleas is our individual choice. Since God respects the free will with which he created us, he does not compel us to love him. But he continues to try through his beloved messengers to speak to our hearts.

In the Old Testament, the people who refused to listen to the prophets were consumed by God's punishments, such as at Sodom and Gomorrah, site of the Dead Sea today. He is the same God, yet patient now because of his Son's redemptive action on the cross.

If Jesus and Mary believe their visits and their message to us are important to our spiritual welfare, should we not respond to them by listening?

Sacramentals

The Catholic faith teaches us about the seven sacraments and their importance in our life. But what are sacramentals and how do they assist us?

Sacramentals are sacred actions and things that help us recall and relive the life of Jesus. For example, the fourteen Stations of the Cross are a meditation on the Passion, Death and Resurrection of Jesus, which encourage us to live our life in imitation of Our Lord. The rosary, which consists of over 200 prayers, is a meditation on the entire life of Jesus, from His conception to His ascension into heaven. The use of holy water at home or in the church recalls our promise to be faithful to God, which our godparents made for us at the time of baptism. The various blessings upon religious articles, such as scapulars and medals, are an invitation to God to be present to us during life especially in time of need. The blessed crucifix in our homes and churches, a reminder that Jesus died for us and now awaits our return to Him, is a sign for us to live our life in harmony with Him.

Parish Support: A Real Necessity

Usually Catholics join a parish to receive some form of spiritual or educational service. Why do they need to contribute financial support? First of all, parishes that support a Catholic school require substantial monies to pay teachers' salaries and physical building expenses. Most Catholic parents could not, or would not, support financially a school on their own. Necessarily, then, the school needs the financial support of all the parishioners. This has been true since Catholic schools were first begun.

Secondly, other parish services such as religious instructions, weddings, funerals, and baptisms, require facilities and paid personnel. If people desire service, whether public or religious, they have to be willing to pay not only for the service but for the physical facility used. Most

Catholic people willingly support their parish. The minority who do not will always be with us. Most Catholic people are givers but there will always be people who only take and never give. They expect salvation to be free of responsibility. Thankfully these are in the minority. Our Catholic parishes continue with the faithful who are responsible and who do their best to financially support their church.

The Authority of the Catholic Church

Today many Catholics refuse to obey the Church in matters of belief and morality. Must Catholics always obey the Church's authority or may they do as they please?

When God the Father sent His Divine Son, Jesus, to the world, He instructed Him to confer authority to lead the Church in spiritual matters. Jesus said to His leaders, "Whoever listens to you listens to me. Whoever rejects you rejects me. And whoever rejects me rejects the one who sent me." (Luke 10:16) For two thousand years the Church, under the successor of Peter, the Apostle, has taught the faith of Jesus and lived out the mystery of His death and resurrection from the dead.

Those who call themselves Catholic are obligated to obey the Holy Father and his bishops throughout the world in matters of belief and morality. Some people scoff at obeying the Church because it does not comply with their way of life. Nonetheless the Church reminds the people that obedience to the commandments is essential to the Catholic faith. We may not agree with God's decision to give authority to the Church, but our denial will not change the action of God.

People cannot truly possess God unless they accept His authority – an authority He shares with His Church.

Mass Readings: The Word of the Lord

During the Scripture Readings at Mass, we hear the lector announce at the end of the reading: "The Word of the Lord." How did these readings and gospels become the Word of the Lord?

The books of the Bible were written by various people over a period of about 1500 years, beginning with Moses and other early writers and ending with John the Apostle. They represent the long story of God's relationship with His people on earth. The Jewish people preserved the books of the Old Testament and revered them as God's Word to them.

After Jesus ascended into heaven, some of His Apostles and disciples wrote the New Testament books. In the year 398 the Catholic Church collected all the books of the Bible and declared that 72 of them were written under the inspiration of God the Holy Spirit. This means that although they were written by human beings, God influenced them to write down what He intends for us to know – so God is the real author of the books of the Bible. The words written by His disciples on earth are truly His Word to us. That is why we can proclaim after each Scripture reading: "The Word of the Lord."

What Is a Parishioner?

Many Catholics belong to a Catholic parish and are called parishioners. What does this mean?

A parishioner is a person who, as a single person or as a member of a family, belongs by choice to a particular parish community known as a parish church. He or she accepts the responsibility of belonging to a community, like a family that prays and works together for the spiritual good of themselves and other people. Some parishioners become actively involved in the duties and works of the parish such as assisting the parish liturgy, the Religious Education Program, the men's and women's societies, the Catholic school program and other church related activities. Others remain passive and simply attend Mass on Sundays and Holy Days. However, all accept the serious obligation of financially supporting the works of the parish. Without this financial support, the parish community would suffer in its works and activities.

There are some who call themselves parishioners but who, in reality, are only occasional visitors to the parish liturgy. These are people who remain most of their lives on the outside fringe of the Catholic parish. They use the parish community for their convenience, much like people use a restaurant for convenience sake. It would be more proper to call these people parish visitors instead of parishioners. Fortunately, parish visitors remain in the minority in a parish community. A true parishioner of the parish is a responsible, caring and relational Catholic who assists the entire community in the work of the Lord.

Change Is Difficult

During Advent 2002, Bishop Mansell joined the bishops of the United States in implementing some changes in the celebration of the liturgy on Sundays and weekdays. Most priests and parishioners complied with the new instructions but, as usual, there were some who did not accept the changes. The Church experienced a similar but greater emotional explosion among its priests and members after the Second Vatican Council in 1964, but that was forty years ago and the Church is still here and operating as usual. Despite minor changes through the years, the Catholic Church remains faithful to her Founder, Jesus Christ.

Jesus encountered resistance to change from the Jewish people, especially the Jewish leadership. Over the years from the time of Moses and the Ten Commandments, practices had been added to the original Law of Moses, making it more difficult for the people to observe the law. Hence, some tensions existed between the Jewish leaders and the people. The Pharisees tried to discredit Jesus all through His public life by accusing Him of not following some of their traditions in the law.

During His life on earth, Jesus as a devoted Jew followed the Law of Moses. But now the traditions and practices of God's covenant with them would yield to the new covenant that God would make with the new people of God through the blood of his Son, Jesus Christ. The old Levite priesthood from Aaron would be succeeded by the priesthood of Jesus Christ, now passed on to His Apostles at the Last Supper. Great change occurred at the time of Christ. It required more than compliance with traditions. It required dying.

Sacrament of Baptism

As we celebrate the feast of the Baptism of Jesus in January each year, we appreciate the importance our Saviour gave to our own baptism. Jesus told Nicodemus that in order to enter the kingdom of God we must be born of water and Spirit. (John 3:5)

It is the Sacrament of Baptism given to us by Jesus that confers new birth – the birth of God's grace within us. Certainly we should regularly renew our commitment to our baptismal vows by living our daily life in conformity with His commandments and the holy gospel. The blessed water at the entrance of our parish church or, in some families, in our homes, reminds us of our baptismal promises and of our need to offer thanks for the gift of our baptism. A regular prayer for our baptismal sponsor, perhaps an aunt or uncle, is another way to show our gratitude for this gift.

At Easter time the Church invites us to renew our baptismal promises to live a life modeled after that of Jesus. The Sacrament of Baptism begins our journey of holiness in this world, which eventually ends in eternal joy in heaven. Let us be grateful for this great gift.

Anointing of the Sick

St. James says in his letter: "Is anyone among you sick? He should summon the presbyters of the church, and they should pray over him and anoint [him] with oil in the name of the Lord, and the prayer of faith will save the sick person, and the Lord will raise him up. If he has committed any sins, he will be forgiven." (James 5:14-15)

When many of us were growing up, we learned the importance of the last rites of the Church for people facing death. What we did not learn then was that these sacraments are very healing for the body and soul even while we are reasonably healthy.

Today the Church refers to these rites as the Sacrament of Anointing of the Sick and encourages all of us who have some physical sickness to receive this healing sacrament regularly. Some parishes invite everyone with a physical ailment to come for an annual Mass to receive Anointing of the Sick. We would encourage anyone entering the hospital for surgery to come to the parish church for this anointing sacrament prior to his or her hospital stay.

This most beneficial sacrament is available anytime for those who have need. A personal request or simple phone call is all that is necessary. Many times people will remain after morning or Sunday Mass for this special anointing. It is worth a visit!

Catholic Bible

A serious spiritual weakness among our Catholic people is a woeful lack of the scriptures in our family life. If Catholic families possess a Catholic Bible, chances are that it occupies a dusty place on the bookshelf or in the bottom drawer of a cabinet. Yet the Bible is the inspired Word of God, meant to permeate our spiritual life. At least Hollywood, with all its faults and failings, has made available to the world such biblical events as the Ten Commandments, Sodom and Gomorrah, Joseph and His Brothers and other moneymaking pictures.

Catholic parents, responsible for the religious and spiritual upbringing of their families, shortchange themselves and their children by refusing to read with them daily the Word of God – as present in the books of the Old and New Testament. Even fifteen minutes of scripture a day with their families would lessen the punishment that parents will face from God someday – for their family neglect of His Word. No amount of time parents spend driving their children to games of hockey, soccer, football, dancing or baseball will substitute for the lack or neglect of God's Word in the life of the family.

The best way to begin the return to God's Word is to dust off the Catholic Bible and put it in a place of honor in the kitchen or living room so it is available for fifteen minutes, either before, during or after the evening meal.

Try it – you may like it. You will see that each day Christ will be reborn in your home.

Reverence and Respect

It is interesting to watch people coming into church as they express their reverence and respect for God's house. Notice them as they make the sign of the cross with holy water at the entrance. Watch as they bow or genuflect as they enter the church pew. Do they realize that they enter the presence of God as He lives in the tabernacle? Now visualize the same people when they die and enter the presence of God in heaven. He is the same God who lives in the parish church. Will we treat God in heaven as we treat Him here on earth? Our Catholic people need to show greater reverence and respect for God when we enter His earthly home.

We need to teach our children and be aware ourselves of the Holy Presence of God in the Holy Eucharist. We need to be more prayerful, more receptive to listen to Him in prayer, to be more thankful and grateful for this great gift of God's presence.

The people of the Old Testament would stand in great reverence and awe at the entrance of their tents while their leader, Moses, would approach and speak with God on the mountain.

Now God has come down from the mountain and lives daily in our church – welcoming everyone to come and speak with Him. Let us use every opportunity, while we are here on earth, to visit with Him in the Blessed Sacrament. Our Divine Friend on earth will be our Divine Friend in heaven forever.

The communion of Saints

Saints Are Needed Today

From the time of Jesus Christ to the present, every century has produced its saints – men, women and children who have lived extraordinary lives of holiness and charity. Some have given up their life for Christ and for the faith. Because of the World Wars, large numbers of people lost their lives – maintaining their Catholic faith. Father Maximilian Kolbe, a Franciscan priest imprisoned by the Nazi government in a concentration camp, offered himself in exchange for a prisoner who had been condemned to die. Father Kolbe died of starvation and poison – and eventually was canonized a saint in the Catholic Church. Recently in the Roman Coliseum where the early Christians were fed to lions and killed as a sport for the Roman citizenship, Pope John Paul II – in harmony with other faiths – praised the saints and martyrs of this century. Without naming anyone in particular, he praised the millions of saintly people who died in concentration camps at the hand of dictators and oppressors.

In our own diocese of Buffalo, we boast of our own servant of God, Father Nelson Baker, who built the beautiful Basilica of Our Lady of Victory in Lackawanna, New York. Father Baker, a convert to the Catholic faith, founded a large hospital, Infant Home, and an orphanage for children. Although he died in 1936, he is revered today as a servant of God.

As we examine our times today in our nation and throughout the world, we discover the great need for saintly people to counteract the pagan practices of abortion, pornography, infanticide and the disgraceful living together of our young and old people – without the blessing of a sacramental marriage.

God revealed to Abraham that He intended to destroy the cities of Sodom and Gomorrah unless he could find ten saintly people. As this did not happen, God destroyed the cities.

Who knows how many saintly people are needed in the United States and the world to hold back God's destructive hands. Certainly, we are not better than Sodom and Gomorrah, possibly worse. Saints can make a difference in God's mind and mercy. Why not become a saint?

Patron of Parish Priests

As we grow up, most of us look for heroes or outstanding people to imitate. Many young people look to the sports world for their favorite hockey, football or tennis star. Maybe others find their attraction in the music world. Even golf today has a tiger.

Probably the least desirable or attractive place to look for a favorite model to imitate would be in an out-of-the-way village in France called "Ars." But had anyone in the eighteenth century taken the time to look, they would have discovered a man called John Marie Vianney, who was the parish priest of Ars. The bishop who appointed him was not sure what to do with his new priest since he seemed to possess very little skill in education and learning. But he was holy and devout, so the bishop sent him as pastor of a rather inaccessible parish called Ars.

What the bishop did not count on was the great value and attraction that priestly holiness and goodness has upon people. Father John spent long hours in the confessional, as his fame as a confessor grew. So many people were coming from all over France and beyond, that the government had to build a railroad to Ars to accommodate the crowds. Father John preached on Sundays with the front doors of the church open so that the men in the saloon across the road would hear his words and return to church. He had a special devotion to the Mother of God; hence his middle name "Mary" or "Marie." On one occasion as he was crossing the yard from church, a woman with a pair of scissors tried to snip a part of his black cassock as a relic, and Father John spoke sharply: "Go, make your own relics!" It is also said that John Vianney had little sleep at night because of the constant harassment of the devil, who would try to prevent him from sleeping. Father John referred to the devil as the "dumb ass."

Today in the Catholic world, all parish priests look to St. John Marie Vianney, pastor of Ars, as their star and model in the priesthood. He never made a hockey goal, threw a winning basketball or scored a hole in one, but Father Vianney scored a lot more since he brought thousands of sinners back to God and enriched the lives of Catholic priests throughout the world. He is a great star and spiritual hero in this world and in heaven as well.

St. John Marie Vianney, pray for us.

Jesus Calls His Apostles

In these days of claimed apparitions and locutions from heaven, we also hear complaints that God and His heavenly world have never appeared or spoken to us. It is true that God is very selective in His appearances or apparitions to people while they are still living on earth. He seems to favor children and young people. Perhaps they have not yet offended Him seriously in their short lifetime. In any case, while God our Father may not reveal Himself to us as He really is, yet He does relate to all of us in the world through His prompting actual grace – every day. God reserves his sanctifying grace for those who are baptized with water or who make an act of pure love of Him. He increases His life in us with every prayer, sacrament and act of love. Consequently, we grow in His grace every day.

If, on the other hand, we choose to deliberately commit serious evil, we lose God's divine life/grace immediately and place ourselves on the road to hell.

So rather than abandoning us, each day He prompts us to continue to grow in His divine life or to turn back to Him through sincere sorrow for our serious sins. We make the choice, with His prompting grace (actual grace) encouraging us. We either choose heaven or choose hell. God always respects His gift of free will in us. He never forces free will – only invites. Mary, His Mother, freely chose her role as Mother.

With God the Father, Jesus is always calling us, inviting our mind and will to follow Him and His life throughout our days in this world. Some follow Him; many do not.

His call to be an apostle is to everyone. Some follow as priests and religious, others follow in the life of marriage, and others prefer to follow Him in the single life. Many others do not hear and go their own way. Ultimately, we answer to Him and receive our place with Him or without Him forever.

The Forgotten Apostle

After the bodily ascension of Jesus into heaven (which we celebrate on Ascension Thursday, a holy day of obligation), the eleven Apostles – together with Mary, mother of Jesus, and over 100 Christians – met in the upper room of the Last Supper in order to pray. At that time Peter and those present cast lots to select a replacement for Judas Iscariot who had died. The lot fell to Matthias, who was added as the twelfth Apostle. (Acts 1:26)

According to legend, Matthias preached in Judea and present-day Turkey and on the shores of the Caspian Sea, where he was martyred. Other than the legendary commentary, we know nothing about Matthias. This seems to be the fate in history concerning all the Apostles. They remain unknown, yet in heaven they will all occupy a very prominent place, promised by Jesus Christ. Yet the call to be an Apostle is a privileged grace, a call by God and an act of God.

Our call to the Christian life is also personal. At baptism, we are called by name. "John – Mary: I baptize you in the name of the Father and of the Son and of the Holy Spirit." We are to continue the mission of the Apostles and be witnesses to Christ today. Our faith in the resurrection and ascension of Jesus gives meaning to our lives. Like Matthias, we have been chosen "to go forth and bear fruit."

Although this world will not acknowledge our apostolic faith and deeds, heaven records everything we do. Only 25% of our world today acknowledges Jesus Christ, and many of these Christians fail to live up to the practice of the Christian faith. The world today needs faithful apostles who are willing to do God's Will.

There is a famous statue of Jesus without hands and arms that is inscribed: "I have no hands but yours." Life is short. We need to assist Christ today while we have the use of our own hands. Tomorrow is too late.

Juan Diego

His name would have been unknown had he not met a beautiful lady shortly after the Europeans' discovery of the Americas. Juan, a simple native Indian, was on his way through the Mexican mountain area called Tepeyac Hill when Mary the Mother of God appeared to him and asked him to have a chapel built in her honor. In simple obedience, Juan took her request to the Spanish bishop only to be told that the bishop needed a tangible sign that he might believe the Indian. It seemed to be a reasonable request.

Most of our world looks to God for tangible signs prior to belief. Thomas the Apostle, the parish priest of Lourdes, France, the peasant people of Fatima, and sometimes the parishioners and priests of our own parishes – all look for a tangible sign from God before they are willing to believe the voice of heaven. In the meantime, requests from our God need to wait until God proves Himself to us. Herod challenged Jesus to show him a sign or perform for him a miracle. Jesus refused Herod's demand and instead Jesus went to His death on the cross. We have been an incredulous people for a long time – and perhaps will only change when miracles occur. "My Lord and my God!" uttered Thomas, but only after the evidence was produced. (John 20:28)

In the wintertime on Tepeyac Hill, Mary arranged roses in the rough tilma of Juan Diego and, when presented to the bishop, there resulted a beautiful sign of God's power – the image of the pregnant Virgin Mary in all her loveliness imprinted upon his tilma.

With the presence of Mary in their land, the Indian nation soon converted to the Catholic faith in the millions. God's signs and miracles brought an abundant increase of His grace and divine life.

Where do we fit into the many miracles of God's grace that we have received in our lifetime? Are we daily living the commandments and sacraments of Jesus Christ? Do we attend Mass daily or even weekly?

Is the Sacrament of Confession a monthly practice? Do we acknowledge Jesus and Mary – with the angels and saints as vital to our spiritual life? Maybe we are too tired, disinterested and bored to grow in holiness.

Time is a precious gift, but eventually runs out.

John is His Name

Not everybody is proud of his name. Very often parents name their child at birth after a favorite uncle or aunt or even sometimes the name of a public personality. I remember a young seminarian named George who kept secret his middle name, Washington, because he feared a mocking from his peers. It may be that some people go by their initials or their middle name in an effort to hide their real name.

At the birth of John the Baptist, some relatives expected the boy to be named after his father, Zechariah. But God had already named him "John" and announced it through the angel Gabriel: "Your wife Elizabeth will bear you a son, and you shall name him John." (Luke 1:13) His name in Hebrew is translated "God has shown favor." John lived up to the beauty and dignity of his name and his mission in life. As he grew, he retired to the desert areas and lived a life of prayer and penance. John fulfilled the prophecy of Isaiah as the one crying in the desert to prepare the way of the Lord. (Luke 3:4) John the Baptist was the voice that prepared the way for Jesus, the Word of God. After he had baptized Jesus in the Jordan, John realized his work of preparation was finished and he completed his earthly task with the loss of his head, the price of a dance.

Whatever name we have in life, we are all blessed by God. As creator, God Our Father invites us all to follow John the Baptist and then His Son, Jesus, in this world so we will be ready to follow them to the next world.

If we are careless and indifferent to God and His commandments and sacraments in this life, the chances of entering heaven are slim. Unlike a lottery or contest, there is no second chance when we die in that stage. There is no coming back to make amends. We will have been a failure in life and in death. Is such a chance worth taking? I do not think so.

All Saints' Day

On November 1st each year, the Catholic Church honors her saints. Who are her saints – but everyone who lives in the state of God's grace. That takes in a lot of people, from the newly baptized child to the millions of elderly living in God's grace. All are saints of God, destined to live with God forever. There is one difference, however, between the saints still living on earth and those who have gone back to God. The difference is the freedom to sin seriously and reject God. Those saints still living here have that freedom, and hence could still lose their souls to hell. The saints in purgatory and heaven are confirmed in God's grace. They made their choice for God at death and now enjoy the knowledge that they are or will live with God forever. The saints in purgatory, however, still need to suffer for the sins they neglected to pay for on earth. But they know that they are on their way to heaven.

Since the canonized saints in heaven already have a special feast day selected by the Church during the year, such as the feasts of St. Francis on October 4th and of St. Patrick on March 17th, the Church sets aside November 1st as a general feast day for all the saints on earth. It is possible that one of us could earn a special feast day if we were to practice heroic virtue or to be martyred for our Catholic faith. But for most of us who are doing our best to live the life of Christ in this world, we'll have to be content with November 1st – the feast of All Saints – as our feast day.

But then, how do most Catholics spend their special feast day? On the feast of All Saints, there are no crowded Masses of people celebrating their feast day. In fact, unless the school children were ushered into the morning Mass, the church would be almost empty. Yet the feast of All Saints is one of the six holy days of obligation for all Catholics.

Apparently, our Catholic people no longer consider it a serious, mortal sin to miss Mass on a holy day of obligation. Some perhaps no longer see missing Mass on Sunday as a grave sin. Yet it is – unless we are prevented from going, through illness or for a serious reason.

Jesus had difficulty with the Jewish people who treated His Father's sabbath day as an ordinary day – even conducting business in the temple on the sabbath. Jesus drove these people out of His Father's house – thus inciting the Jewish leaders against Him.

When the Day of Judgment comes to us at death, our neglect and lack of respect for His Father's Eucharist and House will play a big part in our particular judgment. Jesus may say with justification: "Since you were too busy for me on earth, I am presently too busy for you. Come back another time." Do not underestimate the Lord.

St. Patrick's Day

Green – whether it is in dress or drink – seems to be the color for St. Patrick's Day. I am told that everywhere you go in Ireland you see green in abundance, so I'm sure that the Patron Saint of Ireland would agree with the color.

However, I do not think St. Patrick is very happy with his country today, where there is much fighting and hatred. Perhaps the great unrest is due to the political scene between Catholics and Protestants. Nonetheless, St. Patrick and the great past leaders of this Catholic country are praying for peace and forgiveness.

Unfortunately, in recent years, some bad leadership has promoted successfully the legal acceptance of divorce in Ireland, an evil that will only continue to promote division and disunity. This legal permissiveness will most certainly affect the positive religious growth of Ireland and will most certainly contribute to its eventual demise as a respected nation. "Ireland forever" and "Island of Saints" are expressions that will soon disappear as the evils continue in this once great country.

Let our prayer be for St. Patrick to ask Almighty God to once more rid Ireland of the snakes that have returned so that Ireland will once again be the green "Island of Saints." St. Patrick, pray for them!

Who Is Your Patron Saint?

It has been a tradition in the Catholic Church until recently that the newly born infant would always be baptized with a saint's name – like

Joseph, Ann, Thomas, Mary or Michael. Parents named their child after a saint so that the particular saint in heaven would watch over and guide the new child throughout life. Many parents have lost that religious thought and name their children after the latest flower or sunset. It is unfortunate for the child to have to grow up without a patron saint.

On April 3rd, the Catholic Church and I honor my patron saint, St. Richard of Chichester, England. Richard gave his share of his parents' estate to his brother, Robert, in the thirteenth century to study law and eventually to be ordained a priest. His prayer, adapted into a favorite song today, is to "know thee more clearly, to love thee more dearly, and follow thee more nearly, day by day."

When his appointment as bishop was opposed by the King of England, St. Richard spent his nights helping his people and his days evading the King's wrath. He lived his life as a bishop helping the poor and unfortunate of his Diocese of Chichester and was loved by all his people, especially the poor.

It is a joy to have St. Richard as a patron and model. Should not every Catholic child have a patron saint to admire and imitate? Catholic parents would do well to get back to the saints for their children. They intercede for them before the throne of heaven, if they are asked.

St. Richard, pray for us!

Doctors of the Church

On October 15th we celebrate the feast of St. Teresa of Avila, Spain, who was a virgin, a religious of Mt. Carmel, and a Doctor of the Church. On October 1st we also celebrate the feast of St. Therese of Lisieux, France, who was also a virgin, a religious of Mt. Carmel, and a now a Doctor of the Church, as declared recently by Pope John Paul II.

Our appreciation of the title "doctor" is usually associated with the medical or philosophical field. We see a doctor for our aches and pains. Or in our classrooms, a person who is a doctor of science or philosophy addresses the students. But the Latin word "docere" means "to teach." A Doctor of the Church is a teacher of religion. That is why a bishop has the initials after his name "D.D." – Doctor of Divinity, since he is the official teacher for the Church.

In the earlier centuries of the Church, some men were designated as Doctors of the Church, such as St. Jerome, St. Augustine, St. Ambrose and St. Thomas Aquinas. They defended the teachings of Jesus as given to the Apostles, and recorded their commentaries in many writings.

Some outstanding women have been designated as Doctors of the Church, such as the two St. Theresa's – the first who founded many Carmelite monasteries for women, the second who never left her Carmelite monastery yet was declared "Patroness of all Missioners." She taught her "little way" of holiness – that nothing is too small that cannot be done and offered to God. We refer to the first as "big" Teresa and to the second as "little" Theresa – which has nothing to do with physical size – only to the spiritual approach each had to holiness and spirituality.

As Catholics, we do not have to receive the title of "Doctor" to teach the Catholic faith. Through our baptism and confirmation we are endowed with the graces and virtues to communicate the beauty of our Catholic faith to others. We need only our own desire to do it, coupled with a love for God and neighbor. Some Catholic parents as well as the catechists in our religious education program are prime examples of our present "doctors" of the faith. They assist the Church in bringing a knowledge and love of God to our world. We need them and depend on them.

Joseph, The Husband and Father

I do not believe that most husbands and fathers really and truly understand their great value to their wives and children. Otherwise they would never want to leave them, even for work. Certainly they would never divorce or abandon them for someone or something else. They would rather look for daily opportunities to strengthen their family bond. Daily they would come home promptly to their families with a sense of joy and happiness. Is this too idealistic to hope for from our husbands and fathers of families? What else is his vocation as husband and father than to love his wife and children?

If ever a man loved his wife and child, it was Joseph, the carpenter of Nazareth. His every day was lived in harmony and attention to Mary, his wife, and to Jesus, his adopted son. Today, because of his faithful love,

Joseph occupies a very high place of honor in heaven as Patron of the Universal Church.

It has been said that "the best thing a father can do for his children is to love their mother." I believe it is also true that a father's love for his children will not only stabilize them in their growth here but will remain with them throughout life – here and in eternity. It does not seem difficult to do, yet so many fathers are stingy with their love.

If husbands and fathers today would pray to Joseph and emulate his daily devotion to his wife and family, they would not only earn the respect of this world but would enjoy a place in the next along side of Joseph, husband and father.

St. Joseph, Our Forgotten Patron

In recent years someone has sold the real estate world with the notion that a buried statue of St. Joseph (and upside down, at that) would be beneficial to the sale of a home. I will admit that over the centuries the Catholic world has all but forgotten the gallant and chaste husband of Mary and the foster-father of Jesus Christ. But burying his statue seems hardly the way to acknowledge him.

A humble brother of the Holy Cross, Andre Bessette, who died in 1937 at the Oratory of St. Joseph in Montreal built through his devotion to St. Joseph, had a different appreciation of his patron. Instead of burying his statue, Brother Andre would ask people to "go to Joseph in prayer and penance." Even though Brother Andre, born in 1845, was assigned to greet people at the front door of the religious house (he was also the local barber for the community), Brother Andre was given his own private office because of the great number of people whom St. Joseph helped. The present awesome Oratory of St. Joseph in Montreal remains a testimony of the great love and affection not only of a simple religious brother but also of the Eternal Father Himself.

Apart from Mary the Mother of God, St. Joseph stands closest to God among all the saints in heaven. From the moment that he obeyed the angel in his dream – "When Joseph awoke, he did as the angel of the Lord had commanded him and took his wife into his home." (Matt. 1:24) – Joseph began his lifelong mission as protector of Mary and her

Son, Jesus. For that obedience, God has blessed St. Joseph forever with His special love and grace.

If we ever need a friend in heaven, we have it in St. Joseph. We need only call upon him. "Jesus, Mary and Joseph, I give you my heart and my soul. Jesus, Mary and Joseph, assist me in my last agony. Jesus, Mary and Joseph, may I breathe forth my soul in peace with you."

St. Blase: Bishop and Martyr

Every year on February 3rd, great numbers of Catholic people flood our churches to receive the Blessing of St. Blase. The priest, imitating the saint by placing two candles under the chin, pronounces the blessing: "Through the intercession of St. Blase, bishop and martyr, may God deliver you from ailments of the throat and from every other evil." Although this Armenian bishop lived in the fourth century, his blessing continues to attract Catholic people so that they leave their homes for church on his feast day. The history of St. Blase is vague, but the legend persists that a young boy recovered from a fish bone lodged in his throat through the blessing of Bishop Blase.

Without demeaning the value of a sacramental blessing, our Catholic people seem to be drawn more to a blessing than to the great sacrament which is Jesus in the Eucharist. Daily our Blessed Lord in the Mass offers Himself to us as the greatest blessing given to this world. As we honor God the Father daily in the Eucharist, He in response honors and dignifies each of us with the Body and Blood of His Son, Jesus. Nothing in this world equals this tremendous divine gift.

So, as we travel to receive a blessing for the ailments of our bodies, we should look up to see the greatest blessing of all – Jesus in the Eucharist – who benefits both body and soul. I am confident St. Blase would recommend this Eucharistic practice very highly.

Mother Teresa – A Beautiful Person

Internal beauty is a gift from God and is available to everyone. It is His image and likeness that God confers at baptism and increases with every prayer and good work. External beauty can be deceptive since this gift of God is measured by what people see. "Beauty is in the eye of the beholder," says the poet. Physical beauty is lost through our aging process or our abuse of body through alcohol, drugs or self-indulgence of food and drink. Meanwhile, internal beauty continues to grow through our relationship with God. As we may lose our physical beauty, we can increase the beauty of our soul which is seen sometimes only by God and his angels.

Mother Teresa continued through her prayer life and care for the sick and the dying to increase in spiritual beauty reflecting always the image and likeness of God. Each of us is privileged to do the same. God shows no favoritism but inspires daily each of us to imitate Him through prayer, penance and good works. Little things done in His name – a phone call to a friend in need, a visit to the sick, a prayer for the Poor Souls, a meal for someone in need – all these please God to bless us with His divine beauty and friendship. It is not hard to do! Mother Teresa did it every day! So can we, if we care.

Our Lord's Grandparents

Although Jesus was blessed by God His Father with a wonderful mother, Mary, and a very holy stepfather, Joseph, a non-scriptural source of their day refers to Ann and Joachim as Mary's parents and hence Jesus' grandparents. If they were living at the time of the birth of Jesus, they must have played an important role in the early growth and life of their Divine grandson. How much Jesus as a boy and youth must have enjoyed the company of His grandparents, we cannot know at this time.

But grandparents can play an important part in the early life of their grandchildren. While our mother and father have the important task of providing for our physical, educational and spiritual well-being, sometimes their commitments allow little time with their children. Meantime, if grandparents are available, they fill a necessary void for their families. I am sure many families have good memories of the help to their family from the grandparents.

The only danger is when the grandparents take over and dictate to the grandchildren and parents how they should behave and live – sometimes contradicting rules which the parents have set up. Then grandparents become counter-productive and sometimes form a wedge between parents and their children. Hopefully, such a situation is rare.

What can be said of grandparents who take an interest in their grandchildren? First of all, grandparents benefit personally by experiencing the complete affection and love of their grandchildren. From infancy to adolescence their grandchildren bring many days and years of laughter and enjoyment to their aging grandparents who have an opportunity to watch them grow. Because grandchildren are basically open and honest, grandparents also have the opportunity to respond to their deepest questions and thoughts – also, their worries and anxieties. What some grandchildren might not say to their busy parents, they will confide to a caring or interested grandmother or grandfather.

We do not know if Jesus was blessed with living grandparents during His lifetime but, if He was so blessed, we can be sure that this human relationship enhanced His life and provided a companionship and friendship that assisted Him in His relationship with people throughout His life. Grandparents can be a real blessing.

Saints Are Real People

Saints are real people! Some people think of saints in heaven as extraordinary people. Is it possible for anyone to become a saint?

People who have a problem with saints fail to understand what the word means. Saints are people in the state of God's grace or divine life, a gift that begins at baptism. When people here in the world nourish their gift of grace through prayer and charitable deeds, they grow in God's grace – His image and likeness within us. They are saints in the world. If they lose God's grace and life through mortal or serious sin, they are invited to return to God in the Sacrament of Reconciliation or through a perfect act of sorrow for their sins.

A person in this world who dies in the state of grace and lives in God's friendship continues into eternity as a saint of God. If they still have some sin to make up for, these saints remain for a time in purgatory – until God is totally satisfied they have made up for their sinfulness. Otherwise these people will go immediately to heaven with God our Father and will shine with God's divine life and grace forever as saints of God. They may be your father, mother, brother, sister or any relatives or friends who live now as saints of God. A few are singled out by the Church and declared as saints but most remain unknown to us until we enter heaven ourselves. It is not hard to become and remain a saint, if we are willing.

Human Suffering

One of the most difficult mysteries of our daily life is our human suffering, whether physical, mental or psychological. Yet God never intended this type of life. It is rather the result of Adam's rejection of God. At creation, God told Adam not to eat from the tree in the middle of the garden. (Gen. 2:17) But Adam and Eve disobeyed, and human suffering began that day, not because of God's intention but because of man's rejection of God.

Today we are no better than Adam and Eve. Most people live their lives in freedom – doing as they please. They may follow some guidelines of conduct, but their guidelines are not from God. They vary as individuals vary. Then we wonder why God allows sufferings caused by the weather and elements, together with bodily and mental sufferings. Our daily living without God and His commandments and without prayer to God contributes to the suffering around us.

We need to make God the center of our life – allowing Him to guide us in all our activities. Prayer, like the air we breathe, needs to become our daily habit. Those who are wise will invite Mary and the saints into their prayer life, since they occupy a close relationship with God. Another group of saints – the souls in purgatory – are also a source of help, if only we ask them to help us.

Although suffering in this world will continue until sin disappears, we can – by a good prayer life with God – receive the graces and blessings to live with and accept our human suffering. God will never allow more suffering than we can handle. Even to His suffering Son, Jesus, on His way to death on the cross, God sent Simon of Cyrene, Veronica, and His own mother to console Him. He will not do less for us – if we pray.

All Souls' Day

When we pray for our families and friends who have died and have not yet gone to heaven, we call them the Holy Souls or Poor Souls in purgatory. Which is correct – are they holy or poor?

Actually, both expressions are correct. Souls in purgatory are friends of God since they died in the state of grace, even though they had not sufficiently paid for all their sins and offences. Hence they are Holy Souls. Yet, since they still await the beatific vision of God in heaven, we refer to them also as Poor Souls. Because of their lives on earth, they still await the riches and beauty of God's heaven.

With the saints in heaven, the Holy Souls pray for us here on earth, since they now know and understand the great need of constant prayer to God to obtain what we need. We can return the favor by remembering the Holy Souls in purgatory in all our prayers, Masses and charitable deeds.

In our Apostles' Creed we express our belief in the communion of saints – all who are united in heaven, purgatory and on earth through our relationship to Jesus Christ. The month of November is a special time to remember our families and loved ones who have died and who await their final reward and place in heaven. Catholics devoted to prayer for the Poor and Holy Souls are wise since they are building for themselves a spiritual resource for the future, friends who will be waiting in the next world in order to thank them for their concern.

Be generous with your Masses and prayers for others and God will respond generously in kind.

Many Dwelling Places

A mother once inquired: Do you think there will be room enough in heaven for everyone? Our Lord answers that question in the words of John's gospel. "Do not let your hearts be troubled. You have faith in God; have faith also in me. In my Father's house there are many dwelling places." (John 14:1) Then Our Lord reminds His Apostles that where He is going, they know the way. When Thomas responds that they do not know where Jesus is going so how can they know the way, Jesus tells them: "I am the way…." (John 14:6)

Jesus is the Way for everyone to follow back to heaven. Yet, although the Apostles and the Church have known this secret, most people today are born, live and die in ignorance of Jesus. Even some of our Christian and Catholic people seem to live apart from the Christian Catholic Way to heaven.

Fortunately, for the many who spend their time on earth with worldly pursuits of pleasure and even sinful enjoyments, Jesus offers an alternative to eternal hell, called "purgatory" by the Church. This will be a temporary place of suffering and pain – away from heaven. As in heaven and hell, there will be high and low places, depending on the particular judgment of each soul. Just as we celebrate a feast of All Saints on November 1st each year, we also celebrate a feast of the Holy or Poor Souls in purgatory on November 2nd. Since this day is a holy day but not of obligation to attend Mass, very few Catholic people or families ever attend Mass on November 2nd. Yet, if we end up in the next life in purgatory – as is likely for most of us – this feast will be our feast day. We will welcome and thank anyone who comes to Mass to pray for our release. If we do not teach our children the value of prayer for the poor, suffering souls in purgatory, there will be no one in the family to pray for us. Think about it. Example – not words – teaches others.

Purgatory

Many Catholic people who attend a wake for a deceased friend bring a Mass card for the deceased. Is this appreciated by the family? Our Catholic faith informs us that when we die we face the prospect of going to heaven, hell or purgatory. Those who go immediately to heaven or hell already are living a life deserving heaven or hell. Most people do not deserve to go to hell and yet are not worthy of heaven immediately. Hence they go to a place of waiting, called purgatory, where they still need to make reparation for their sins. One of the most beneficial actions done for the souls in purgatory is the Catholic Mass, which involves Jesus offering Himself for us to God the Father. The Mass is our finest prayer for the Poor Souls in purgatory. We need to put ourselves in the place of the Holy Souls and appreciate their dependence upon our prayers and Masses offered in their behalf. Someday these Holy Souls may be our only intercessors at the gate of heaven. Think about it!

Poor Souls in Purgatory Need Prayer

Attending a wake is an act of piety and mercy, and the loved ones left behind appreciate your visit very much. There is a need to grieve for their loved one, and the presence of friends and relatives assists that grief.

Yet there is an equally necessary and needed act of mercy at the wake – namely prayer for the departed loved one who has already attained heaven in the minds and words of friends at the wake. In reality, the soul of the deceased may have been assigned to a place in purgatory after the particular judgment. Who knows the spiritual neglect – even minor – of our souls during life and at our death?

The story is told of the priest eulogizing Pat, a husband, as he lay in his coffin, as a fine, wonderful man, until his wife Brigid, from the front pew of the church exclaimed, "Father, will you please open the coffin and see if we are talking about the same man?"

People may seem almost perfect from the outside, but each of us has faults and failings – and sins – that prevent us from entering immediately the all-pure chambers of God's heavenly presence. It may be a simple lack of forgiveness, which our pride refuses to release. Long-standing grudges or hurts continue to scar our soul. Lack of responsibility to our family, which has caused a loss of faith among children, is cause to delay our entrance.

When the children of Fatima – Lucia, Jacinta and Francesco – quizzed Our Blessed Mother one day about some of their young companions who had died, the Blessed Mary responded by saying: "Maria is with me in heaven and so is Carmina. But Rosa (an 18-year old) is in purgatory and will remain there until the end of the world." It is very difficult to imagine why a merciful God would allow a young girl to remain in purgatory until the end of the world unless nobody will or does pray for her. We might assume our parents, family and friends enter heaven immediately upon death, but we do not know for certain.

It would be a better deed on our part not to assume anything but rather offer Masses and prayers for them. If they are in heaven, the Masses and prayers are not wasted; they are used by God for someone else in need in purgatory. The scriptures remind us that it is a holy and wholesome thought to pray for the dead so that they may be released from their sins. (2 Macc. 12: 45)

When the day comes that we may be waiting in purgatory, we will be overjoyed to have someone remember us in prayer and daily Mass.

Where Have the Weeds Come From?

The official at the Department of Agriculture grew weary at the constant requests to suggest a remedy for the annual appearance of dandelions every springtime. Finally, to each request, he responded, "I suggest you learn to love them."

It is similar to Our Lord's command to love our enemies. He doesn't mean for us to love evil – but only the evildoer. At the very least, as Catholics, we are exhorted by our faith to pray for sinners. We say daily in honor of Mary, "Pray for us sinners now and at the hour of our death."

We need to admit to God that we all are sinners and need God's forgiveness every day.

If, however, we refuse God's grace to be forgiven and continue on in our sinfulness, then we risk the punishment for serious sins in hell and, for less serious sins, the temporary pains of purgatory.

In Genesis, the first book of the Old Testament, Abraham spoke to God, who revealed that He was about to destroy the cities of Sodom and Gomorrah because of their wickedness. Abraham persuaded God to spare the cities if He find at least ten just men living there, but God was not successful in finding even ten such men. (Gen. 18:32)

In this world today, God continues to find similar wickedness and sinful behavior among His people. Again, God looks for the just and faithful people who live in harmony with God's Will. They form a reason why God spares the rest from destruction. Light will always overcome the darkness. Goodness is stronger than evil. God will always prevail over the devil with all His fallen angels.

Despite many evil and wicked people in the world, every parish has its saints – men, women and children who live exemplary lives in harmony with God. These people assist one another in their needs, attend Mass and services of prayer, even daily, and raise their families to honor, obey and respect their parents and others who take the place of their parents. The devil tries to disrupt these good seeds but without result. They already live in the Holy Spirit. Because of the just and faithful people, I believe God blesses the world.

Relics

When my own wonderful mother went to the Lord, I requested only one of her possessions, a magnifying glass that she used to assist her diminishing eyesight. The reason I asked for this particular item was that it contained her fingerprints all over the glass. In effect, it contained a part of her that still remained behind when she died and reminded me daily of her life here on earth.

Our Catholic faith teaches us to honor and revere the saintly people who live out their life on earth trying always to do God's Will. How many people respected the late Mother Teresa of India and enjoy now her picture as a remembrance. Some may possess some personal gift from her. In honoring with respect a saint's possessions, we honor the life of virtue they lived and are encouraged to imitate them.

A first class relic is an essential part – like a particle of bone of a canonized saint. A second class relic would be something the saint wore or used. A third class relic would be something touched to the saint's possessions.

We honor the saints in heaven best by imitating their lives of observance of God's commandments and faithfulness to prayer, confession and the Holy Eucharist.

Relics are reminders to us of how we too should live out our lives in union with God.

Saints Are Seldom Popular

If you are a good friend of God, you may not be welcome in too many places. Holiness, while it has an attraction for some, is also like a repellant to others. Such people are considered "holy Joes" or "somewhat unbalanced" and hence should be avoided in modern social circles. One such person was Jesus Christ.

Herod, the King of Israel, was attracted to Jesus for the wrong reasons. He looked to Jesus for some magic trick or display of power. Jesus remained silent and would provide no sign in Herod's presence. Herod had made Jesus cry by ordering the head of John the Baptist to be brought to Herod's wife on a platter. Jesus had no time for Herod's like. Herod died soon after John. We know John was declared a great saint. We do not know where Herod ended up in eternity, but we might guess.

Jesus loved His Father's people, the Jews of His world, but many, especially the Pharisees – the legal ruling class – did not relate to Him. So He reminded them that His Father did not assist them in the past because of their lack of love and obedience to Him. And now they treated His Son in the same way.

Today the response to God's Son is the same as it was in His day. Many refuse to acknowledge Jesus other than as the son of Joseph. The people in Jesus' day also asked: "Isn't this the son of Joseph?" (Luke 4:22)

Many of our so-called Catholic people are not much better in acknowledging God's Son, Jesus, as He comes to us daily in the Eucharist. The daily and weekly presence of Jesus in the Eucharistic celebration is nothing important or special on the calendar of fifty percent of our Catholic people. Although baptized in the Catholic faith, these young and old people have abandoned their earlier practice of Sunday Mass. Jesus is important only at their convenience and in their time. In many cases, their daily work and pleasure occupy their time. Even prayer becomes a hardship. And then they die – and without the grace of the sacraments, where do they go? Only God knows. Meantime, sanctity eludes many. It is unfortunate. But once dead, they are unable to return – to do better. The opportunity for sanctity is now. Do not waste time.

Great Is Your Faith

Our Catholic Church teaches us that when we receive the Sacrament of Baptism – usually soon after birth – we receive not only God's gift of grace and new life but also the gifts of faith, hope and love. These gifts, nourished through prayer and good works, develop into habits of faithfulness, trustworthiness and love. They are divine gifts and habits, which ultimately bring us to heaven.

The Canaanite woman in Matthew's gospel (Matt. 15:21-28) was not so privileged, but she did possess a natural gift of faith, which Jesus recognized. She believed that Jesus could and would help her daughter, who was tormented by a demon. When Jesus challenged her, saying that He had been sent to the lost sheep of the house of Israel, she rose to the occasion and responded right back to Jesus that even the dogs eat the scraps from the master's table. Jesus replied, "O woman, great is your faith!" (Matt. 15:28)

It is very apparent that Jesus is pleased and impressed whenever He meets people who truly believe and trust in Him. Such people move the heart of Jesus to work miracles of grace. We do not need riches, honors or station in life to impress Jesus, only a faithful, trusting and loving heart.

Because our Catholic faith is so rich in blessings and grace, Catholic people may tend to believe they have a monopoly on holiness of life.

But I believe they will discover that God sees the hearts of everyone and plays no favorites. In the village of Medjugorje, which is 1% Muslim and 99% Croatian Catholic, it is reported that Mary, the Mother of God and Queen of peace, has been appearing since 1981. On one occasion Mary reportedly told the six young visionaries that the holiest person in the village was a Muslim woman. So holiness of life is attainable by everyone in the world.

When the Catholic Church investigates the holiness of some proposed for sainthood in the Church, she measures with the yardstick of faith, hope and charity. How well did the proposed candidate practice their gifts of faith, hope and love? On this measure does the Church proceed to examine the sanctity of the individual. Consequently we need to live intensely these three virtues. Other virtues and practices embellish our holiness, but our faith, hope and charity determine our sanctity. The greatest of these is charity.

The forgiveness of sins

We Are the Prodigal Son

Recently, a medical doctor, father of three college-age daughters, gave each one a personal trust fund to use for her college education and personal needs. As the college years continue into working years in the business field, it will be interesting for the father to know how well each daughter used her trust.

Our Lord spoke regarding our similar responsibility to God in the parable of the talents (a share of his possessions), where a man dispensed talents to his servants before leaving on a journey and, upon his return, required an accounting. He rewarded those who increased his earning, but punished the one who had buried his one talent, commanding that the wicked, lazy servant be thrown into the darkness outside. (Matt. 25:14-30)

When God sends each one of us into this world and entrusts us to our parents, He endows us with the wonderful gifts of our body, together with spiritual gifts of our soul – mind, free will, memory and intellect. He clothes us with all we need to be successful in life here and endows us with the grace to re-enter His home in heaven.

Appreciating this great generosity of our God, why then do so many people abuse and squander their physical and spiritual gifts like the Prodigal Son of the gospel? (Luke 15:11-32) Most of us can see ourselves in this story and can identify with the Prodigal Son. In fact, from the beginning of man's creation, we have acted out this parable. Adam and Eve were the first prodigals. Having been endowed by God with so many gifts of mind, body and soul, they chose to disobey their Creator. The history of the first Chosen people from Abraham to Jesus Christ is the story of the Prodigal Son. In the past two thousand years the new people of God have not done any better. Jesus questioned whether we would find faith on earth when the Son of Man comes. (Luke 18:8)

Each one of us needs to approach the Father sorry for our sins, like the Prodigal Son: "Father, I have sinned against heaven and against you…." (Luke 15:21) Especially during Lent, the opportunity to make amends with God in the Sacrament of Reconciliation is present to us. We should not neglect it.

We Need to Forgive

"To err is human, to forgive is divine." How true this saying is, yet how difficult it is to practice it in everyday life. Most of us commit many errors in our life, and expect others to forgive and understand our human ways. But still, we ourselves are so reluctant to forgive others who err or offend us.

A prime case of the need for forgiveness in the life of Our Lord occurred at the time of His passion and death when Judas betrayed Him in the garden and Peter denied Him three times in the courtyard. These two chosen Apostles had lived with Jesus and shared food and intimate conversation with Him, yet they both offended Him greatly in His time of need. Both were in need of forgiveness, but only one remained to be forgiven. Judas went off and hanged himself. (Matt. 27:3-5) Had Judas confessed his love of Jesus, there would have been granted immediate forgiveness. God is always waiting and willing to forgive us, if only we will open our hearts in love for Him.

We need to imitate God's willingness to forgive and reach out to anyone in need of forgiveness. It may be that we are not aware that we have offended others, but once we are, we need to extend our hand and heart in love and friendship. And if we are holding a "grudge" or animosity toward another, we need to apologize and be sorry. Our Lord reminds us that "Therefore, if you bring your gift to the altar, and there recall that your brother has anything against you, leave your gift there at the altar, go first and be reconciled with your brother, and then come and offer your gift." (Matt. 5:23-24) We will feel better, too.

Love Your Enemies

In the case of most of us, our enemy is someone who has disagreed with us and spoken or acted uncharitably against us without ever apologizing. Were we citizens of another land or country that does not recognize the human rights of individuals or acts without any sense of justice or even mercy against individuals or families, the word "enemy" might take on a more serious meaning. Deep-seated feelings of hatred which have existed for centuries – as exist between places such as Northern and Southern Ireland, Israel and Palestine, Serbia and Croatia, to name a few – are difficult to remedy and resolve. Yet Our Lord commands us to love our enemies and pray for those who persecute us. (Matt. 5:44)

Having said this, Our Lord then sets a good example from His cross: "Father, forgive them, they know not what they do." (Luke 23:34) Though humiliated, spit upon, scourged and crucified, Jesus takes time to forgive His enemies.

Some may object and say that His forgiveness was a result of His Divine Nature as God, who is all-merciful. Yet Jesus is also human and experiences the pain of being human – much like we do.

Still, forgiveness of injury and injustices is very difficult for most of us. Our pride has been shaken and our lack of humility holds us back from forgiveness. It is really the devil or Satan that enters the picture and convinces us to remain firm in our pride and hatred. Stories are told in almost every family of relatives and even brothers and sisters who have stopped talking with each other for many years over some grievance or hurt, usually involving estate monies or some inane family event. In some instances the offended party does not even remember why they are angry – yet continues to hold a grudge and will not agree to be reconciled.

Some people even leave this world unreconciled with their loved ones. How foolish they will appear before the judgment seat of the Lord, when they try to explain their silly behavior. Anger and pride are not worth the price.

Fraternal Correction

When parents find fault with us and correct us, we may not like the correction but we understand that the correction of children's behavior is part of the task given to parents. But when our brothers or sisters or friends find fault with our actions, generally we resent their words and strike back at them verbally. Sometimes an argument or fight results. We may even hold their criticism against them for years and may even stop talking to them. So it is a difficult task for most of us to offer fraternal correction to another person, especially to a friend.

In the Old Testament God sent the prophet Nathan to correct King David, who had caused the death of a husband so that he could marry the wife. Nathan used a story of a rich man who offended a poor man. When David heard Nathan's story, he judged that the rich man deserved death for his offense. Nathan then said to David, "You are the man!" (2 Sam. 12:7) As a result, David accepted the correction and repented of his crime. In this case God allowed David to realize his serious offense through a story and, consequently, David sought forgiveness from God.

Maybe we ought not approach someone who is offensive directly, but instead in prayer we might invite God to do the correcting or to assist us in knowing the best manner in which to correct another. Our personal example is very persuasive to others. People who have abandoned their prayer life might be more impressed by someone who never neglects prayer, whether in public or in private. In a public restaurant we need more people who are not ashamed or afraid to make the sign of the cross prior to grace before their meal. We need to teach our children that prayer in public is most acceptable and attractive to others and certainly to God. For those Catholics who have stopped going to Mass on Sunday, the Catholic neighbor next door who leaves his driveway every Sunday for Mass with his family is a wonderful example of fraternal correction. "Deeds speak louder than words."

A Prophet without Honor

During His public ministry, Jesus, upon His return to His hometown of Nazareth, encountered rejection from his neighbors. The people of His native country did not accord Him the proper respect, and so He was not able to perform any mighty deeds there. (Mark 6:3-5)

In our lifetime, most of us have been the recipient of rejection, even at the hands of our friends and family who fail to accept, or who misrepresent, our words and actions. At those times, we can appreciate the difficult feelings of Our Lord, who had never been guilty of wrongdoings and certainly never offended anyone deliberately. We ourselves might have brought such a trial upon ourselves by our words and actions. Nonetheless, it is a painful experience.

On the other hand, some of us may be guilty of treating others with disdain for whatever reason – especially members of our family. A time of death can be an occasion of quarreling over money and possessions in the person's will. As a result, we might refuse to speak to one another for years. Our words and actions at that time might create a chasm of bitterness among the family. Sometimes people go before the Lord without being reconciled with a friend or loved one. In the parable of the unforgiving servant, Jesus chastises the servant, indicating he should have had pity on his fellow servant as the master had pity on him. Then the master hands the unforgiving servant over to the torturers. Jesus says, "So will my heavenly Father do to you, unless each of you forgives his brother from his heart." (Matt. 18:35)

Our life is so relatively short in terms of years that we should use whatever time we have to create and sustain harmony and peace with others. We need to begin today. Peace be with you.

Confessional of the West

Pope John Paul II has called the small village of Medjugorje in Bosnia the confessional of the Western world due to the large crowds from all over the world who come to confession daily. The Franciscan priests who service St. James Church together with many visiting priests from countries of the world occupy the many confessionals every day. On Saturdays, the local Croatian villagers stand in long lines to confess their sins.

It is interesting to observe the large number of people who visit professional psychologists and psychiatrists for assistance to their mental and moral health, yet they have not visited the Divine Healer in the confessional.

Our Catholic faith teaches us that only God can forgive sins, since every deliberate sin violates one of God's Ten Commandments and hence displeases and offends our Eternal God. In addition, serious or mortal sins like murder, abortion, pornography, adultery, fornication and impurities place us in danger of hellfire forever. Minor or venial sins like uncharitableness, lying, cheating, detraction and lack of prayer place us in danger of purgatory for a long time. The solution to our healing of soul and forgiveness is the Sacrament of Reconciliation on a frequent basis.

While many Catholics attend Mass on Sunday, very few come for forgiveness for their many sins. Maybe our people believe that confession of sins does not apply to them. What a surprise awakening they will have when they meet their Immaculate Lord. "I say to you, you will not be released until you have paid the last penny." (Luke 12:59).

Leprosy

Among the most feared and dreaded diseases during our Lord's lifetime was the bodily condition of leprosy, since it physically disfigured the leprous person. The lepers were banned from the towns and villages and lived in the desert areas. When someone approached a leper, the leper would warn him: "I am unclean." Before a cured leper could live among people again, he would have to show himself to the Jewish priests for approval.

Today, the medical world has found the cure for leprosy or Hansen's disease as it is currently called. But even in the 18th century, lepers were sent to an island in the Pacific Ocean called Molokai. A French priest called Damien deVeuster ministered to them and eventually became one of them. The Church acknowledges him today as a servant of God.

In a spiritual sense, mortal sin is like leprosy since it disfigures the soul by destroying God's grace and beauty within the soul. Deliberate mortal sins such as homosexual acts, abortion or impurities of mind and body, attack the beautiful image of God within us and cause God to withdraw His divine life from us. We then appear like the leper – hideous and disdainful. But like Hansen's disease, there is a cure: a firm intention to return to God, followed by a sincere confession to a priest with the resolve not to sin again. Otherwise, the sinful condition not only remains but continues to worsen.

In the gospel of Luke (Luke 17:11-19), only one of the ten lepers returned to Jesus to offer thanks for his cure. We need to do the same for the many times that God cures and heals our leprous heart and soul.

Confession to a priest should become a regular habit – at least once a month – to maintain our spiritual health. God is a very merciful God but expects our positive and regular response to Him. Do not disappoint Him as did the other nine lepers.

Confession is Good for the Soul

Very few Catholics come to the Sacrament of Reconciliation anymore. Is this because they have not sinned during the week?

It is difficult to understand why Catholic people do not use the Sacrament of Reconciliation often. Some respond that they have not offended God seriously and do not think confession is necessary for less serious sin. Others who have need of forgiveness of serious sin may not be ready to give up their sinful ways. Other Catholic people say that they are not aware of any sin in their life and feel no need for Christ's forgiveness. However Christ's forgiving grace is meant to be food and spiritual medicine for everyone – whatever the state of their soul. Jesus invites us to "receive the Holy Spirit" as He imparts the power of forgiveness to His Apostles.

Reconciliation of the individual assists the entire parish community and Church. When individual Catholics are separated from God's life and grace, the entire parish is impaired and affected with weakness. Through the reconciliation of the individual, the entire Body of the Church is strengthened and grows healthy and strong.

Let us be generous in approaching Christ's forgiving grace often in the Sacrament of Reconciliation. You will better yourself and the entire parish community.

Indulgences – What Are They?

Over the years some prayers and Catholic devotions had partial and plenary indulgences attached to them. Do indulgences still exist and what do we understand by them?

The word "indulgence" comes from the Latin word for "forgiveness." When Jesus gave the Apostles power to forgive sins, that power included also forgiveness of the penalty, or punishment, attached to sin. In daily life, when fathers and mothers forgive their children of disobedience, they may also, if they wish, forgive them any punishment. So too the Church may forgive sinners the punishment due to sin. One way the Church forgives is through special prayers, like the rosary or the Stations of the Cross. The Church encourages us to say the rosary or make the Stations of the Cross by giving these devotions the power of forgiving the punishment due to sin. Hence, while the Sacrament of Confession remits the sin, certain devotions take away even the punishment due to those sins. Although it is a lesser power of the Church, it is very effective. Conditions for obtaining the indulgence of the Church includes going to Confession, Holy Communion and praying for the intentions of the Pope.

However, the present age which has given up the Sacrament of Reconciliation or Confession is not too interested in the lesser privilege of receiving forgiveness of punishment due to sin. It is unfortunate for us that we are living in such an age and time.

Always Be Prepared

The Boy Scouts of America adopted as their motto a phrase we can all imitate, "Semper Paratus" (Latin), "Always be prepared" (English). No doubt the Boy Scouts are concentrating on this life, but this motto could be adopted for the life to come.

The gospel of Matthew challenges us to be on guard. "So too, you also must be prepared, for at an hour you do not expect, the Son of Man will come." (Matt. 24:44) In our lifetime, long or short as it may be, God Our Father provides each of use with the necessary graces to obtain our heavenly reward. If we squander these daily graces through neglect of prayer and sacraments, we may find ourselves suddenly *without* – when we receive a sudden call from death.

Jesus reminds us to sell what we have and give to the poor if we desire treasure in heaven. (Matt. 19:21) It is always interesting to read about the richest people in the world – but necessarily, if they do not dispose of their God-given wealth, they will leave it to others who may not appreciate it either.

Wealth has never brought joy and happiness in itself – mostly grief and disappointment. Our Blessed Lord, the wealthiest person in grace and blessing in the world, eagerly shares His spiritual wealth by showering us, upon request. His Father also invites us to share in the abundant treasures of His heavenly home. This type of wealth will bring us unending joy and happiness. We need only ask "Our Father" to give us our daily bread. The treasures of God the Father are inexhaustible and are ours for the asking.

In our lifetime, God the Father has given us priceless treasure in His forgiveness in the Sacrament of Confession and in the nourishment of the Body and Blood of His Son, together with the flow of blessing from the waters of baptism and the oil of Confirmation.

We may not appreciate these treasures now in this life, but we will certainly acknowledge them in the next life. But it may be too late. We may be like the wicked servant in the parable who knew his master's wishes but did not attempt to fulfill them. (Matt. 24:48) Too bad.

Lent – 21st Century

The world, created by Almighty God, has just completed a century – one hundred years of relating or not relating to God. Will this new century of life be better or worse than the previous one hundred years? Early in the previous century, God gave us Pope Pius X, who encouraged daily Holy Communion even among the young people. God foresaw our problems of faith and general laxity toward religious values, so He sought to strengthen His world with His Son, in the Eucharist. With hate-filled leaders like Hitler and Stalin on the horizon, God sent His Mother in 1917 to warn us and encourage the popes and the world to dedicate the Church and their countries to Her Immaculate Heart for peace. She promised that God would bring peace if we would comply with her request. For the most part her request to bring peace was ignored or put off. Either the world and the Church were occupied with other demands, or we did not believe her. Possibly, communication was slow. As a result, however, the world and Church are looking for peace.

Our Lady, however, has not forgotten God's promise of peace, and reminds us that there is still time. Ash Wednesday, signaling the beginning of Lent in this new century, is an apt time to begin our return fully to the Lord. As we change our hearts from hatred to love, Jesus waits to bring peace to the world and to the Church. At Mass, prior to receiving Jesus in Holy Communion, He says through His priest: "Peace be with you!" We then offer it to others.

Unless we begin our Lent with peace and forgiveness, our Lenten prayers and fasts mean little to God. But a Lent begun in forgiveness will lead to peace in the world.

Lent – A Time of Penance

Lent is that time of year when our Catholic people look with special devotion to the cross of Jesus Christ – forty days of penance in preparation for Easter – the day of Christ's resurrection from the dead.

Most Catholics are sincere in their approach to this period of penance and preparation. We acknowledge our own sinfulness in relationship to Our Saviour and wish to make amends with Him. We really desire to show Him by our prayer life and charitable actions that we do appreciate His tremendous sacrifice on the cross for us. We start out well on Ash Wednesday, but most of us do not make it to Easter Sunday with our prayers and penance.

Yet we should never be discouraged by our meager Lenten efforts. I believe our Lord blesses every small effort we make and welcomes us to keep trying – no matter how many times we seem to fail.

One thing we should do, if we desire success, is to place ourselves in the care of His Father and invite God the Father to assist us in our efforts of prayer, penance and charitable good works. It will amaze us how everything will become easier.

I am convinced that God the Father does not expect a lot from each of us, only our daily willingness to try again and again. Happy Lent, everyone!

Ash Wednesday

It is amazing to see the large number of Catholics, young and old, coming to receive blessed ashes on Ash Wednesday. Traditionally, the church burns the palms, a symbol of glory from the previous Palm Sunday and with the ashes marks the forehead of Catholic people with the prayer, "Remember, man, that you are dust and to dust you shall return." In some instances, the ashes spill down upon the face and clothing and yet most practicing Catholics do not mind. They will come to church that day to receive their ashes.

In times past, many would come on Ash Wednesday only for the ashes. It would seem to be commendable to praise our people for their devotion to receiving ashes, but only if they keep their spiritual priorities in order. Catholics who would regard this blessing as being more important than the celebration of Mass or Eucharist have their spiritual priorities misplaced. However, if ashes are a meaningful expression of prayer, personal penance and sorrow for sin for Catholics who now intend to live a life in imitation of Jesus, then Ash Wednesday becomes an annual new spiritual start that is meaningful and productive.

It is interesting to note that the Church now officially welcomes the real cremains of a deceased person – the ashes from cremation into a special place in Church during the funeral Mass of Resurrection. Now that the former stigma associated with cremation no longer remains. The cremains of a Catholic person are blessed by the priest during Mass. It is only fitting that the body that served our soul throughout our lifetime would be honored by the Church at end of our earthly life, even though that body has returned to dust. "Remember, man, that you are dust and unto dust you shall return."

Lent – A Time of New Life

Important events in our life – a marriage, a new job, a sickness, a family death – encourage us to make new changes in the direction of our life pattern. In the light of important happenings in our life many people make changes for the better. They resolve to be a better person in relation to others, and especially to God and His Catholic Church. One such important Church event is Lent, which means springtime – a time of 40 days of preparation for the passion, death and resurrection of our Saviour, Jesus Christ. All Catholics, reflecting on the sacrifice of Jesus on the cross in reopening Heaven for us, are invited to follow Him in prayer, sacrifice and penance for the forty days of Lent. From the very beginning of His life on earth, Jesus has continually invited us to follow Him to the Cross so that we follow Him to heaven forever.

In times past, the days of Lent seemed to emphasize bodily fasting from food and drink, which is still commendable. But today's emphasis is directed more to spiritual fasting – namely, the penance of forgiving others who have offended us, the penance of releasing our material possessions and money to the less fortunate, the penance of attending Mass every day, the fastings from too much TV and entertainment so that more prayer will become meaningful.

When we make even one change for the better, we set out on the path to become like Christ. As we become more like Christ, the Son, then we become more attractive to the Father, who adopted us at our baptism as His son or daughter.

Lent is an important event in our spiritual life – an opportunity to be a success in this life and, in death, to realize a new life.

The Generosity of God

Mother Teresa of India was asked where she goes when she needs money; she said, "I go to God because He has lots of it."

I believe the saints of this world are saints because they are simple. In their daily lives they live their simplicity of soul and as a result they go right to the heart of the problem. In the case of worldly needs, they go to the source of all wealth – namely God Himself – who provides for them. When Moses needed food and drink for all his people in the vast desert, he called out to God Himself and God rained down bread from heaven (Ex.16:4). God can do anything He wishes. We need only ask Him with faith. As a result, God does not respond to the faithless.

In God's generosity He endows all of us with His Divine Life – called sanctifying grace – at the moment of our baptism. As we grow in prayer and good deeds, God continues through the Holy Spirit to increase His grace or divine life within us. As we receive His Sacraments of Confession, Eucharist and Confirmation, this flow of God's divine life continues to grow within us. As we accept the Sacraments of Marriage or Priesthood/Religious Life, we continue to grow in the image of God. As we continue in our life of faith, hope and love of God, we will likewise resemble God more and more. We can never outdo the generosity of God's love. The only problem with God's children is sin – serious sin which destroys God's grace and hence His image and likeness within us. We can allow a whole lifetime of good to be lost because of evil – a person, place, or thing that draws us away from God.

We should not refuse to come back to God's forgiveness.

Repair Broken Hearts

It is interesting to notice that people in love call each other "sweetheart" or "love." Sometimes they will use the word "honey" or "dear" in their conversation with each other. Then when their love for each other flickers and fades away like the light of a candle, their tone of words changes until all conversation ceases. It is unfortunate that people in love with each other allow their love to disappear and die.

Something like that happens with people in their relationship with God. In our early years we learn about our loving God who has placed us in this world to know, love and serve Him, that we might enjoy Him forever in heaven. As we grow up, our spiritual candle flickers and fades into benign neglect. Perhaps we have discovered the new gods of technology – the computer world with the Internet and e-mail – that now absorbs our waking hours. Perhaps we have entered a sinful relationship, forbidden by God and His Church. Maybe we have become too busy in our world of entertainment that does not allow time for our loving God.

Whatever our reason for neglecting our relationship with God, we have fallen out of love for Him. He is no longer our heart's attraction and concern.

St. Augustine, whose mother, St. Monica, prayed without ceasing for her son, finally woke up to God after years of sin and neglect. "Our hearts are restless until they rest in thee," exclaimed St. Augustine upon his return to prayer and Sacraments of Confession and Eucharist. The Pope at the time said of Augustine: "The son of so many tears will never be lost" – thanks to his mother.

How then do people out of love fall back into love? The process probably begins with a phone call of concern and apology. Like the Prodigal Son, we need to be humble enough to say we are sorry. If in our broken relationship with God our Father we express our willingness to return to Him, God will act like the father in the parable, running to meet us and embrace us. (Luke 15:20)

Our time with loved ones is short; we need to repair any broken hearts. Likewise, our time on earth is also short. We need to embrace His Sacred Heart. His mother, Mary, will help, if we invite her. Do not wait too long.

Divine Mercy Sunday

On February 22, 1931 Jesus appeared to a Polish nun, Sister Faustina, to invite her to spread His message of Divine Mercy. "Paint my image according to what you see, with the signature: 'Jesus, I Trust In You,'" He said. "I want this image to be solemnly blessed on the first Sunday after Easter; that Sunday is to be the Feast of Mercy," Jesus declared. "Whoever will go to confession and Holy Communion on that day will receive complete forgiveness of sin and all punishment," Jesus promised. (Diary of Faustina)

Pope John Paul II beatified Sister Faustina on April 18, 1993 and declared her a saint in the year 2000. It seems apparent from Our Lord's approved apparitions to Sister Faustina that God sees a great need to appeal to mankind to return to Him – not to be punished for their sins but to receive His Divine forgiveness and Mercy. No matter what we have done to offend God, He has a great desire to forgive us.

I believe that the day is not far off when our Catholic people will return in multitudes to the confessional. The Divine Mercy of God is slowly breaking through the wall of pride, stubbornness and indifference that encircles our Catholic people, preventing them from returning to reconciliation and forgiveness. It may happen that some will put off returning to God and die in their sins. But God is present to them in His great Mercy if only they will freely turn to Him. We have the freedom to choose either way.

There were two thieves crucified with Jesus. One of them reviled Jesus. The other asked Our Lord to remember him when He came into His kingdom. Jesus canonized the second one on the spot, assuring the thief that he would join Jesus that day in paradise. (Luke 23:43) One criminal said "No" to Jesus; the other said "Yes." Which one do we represent?

The resurrection of the body and life everlasting

Death Is a New Beginning

Years ago, the wake of a loved one was held at home with family and friends present to celebrate the passing to a new life. Although there was an element of sadness, the general mood was joy and happiness that our loved one had led a good life and now was enjoying an eternal reward. This was a result of our Catholic faith that assures us of the existence of our home in heaven and of our bodily resurrection at the end of this world.

Unfortunately, not all people share our belief and, as a result, live in dread of death – as if it were the end of life forever.

Jesus looked forward to His death on the cross because He knew it was the means of satisfying for the sins of the world and would lead to His own bodily resurrection – three days later on Easter Sunday. As Catholics, we share in the mystery of Jesus' death and resurrection.

However, sharing involves responsibility on our part to live our lives on earth in imitation of Jesus Christ. Although we may not live the life of a Mother Teresa of Calcutta, we need to be prayerful, penitential and generous toward others as best as we can. Jesus calls everyone to holiness and sanctity.

Palm Sunday opens the final days of Our Lord's life on earth. It is a good opportunity for everyone to set aside this week for prayer and participation in these holy days. A good confession would prepare us to invite the suffering Lord into our lives. Prayer at home with the rosary would give the entire family an opportunity to participate in these days.

As we await the celebration of Easter and the Risen Christ, we might as a family reach out to another family – even living at a distance. We might make some new friends.

Jesus knew He was destined to return to His Father in heaven, but He worked right up to the hour – at which time He said to His Apostles, after fixing their breakfast, that they should follow Him. (John 21:19) We will follow Him eventually, but in the meantime, let us work to get ready. No time is like the present.

Rejoice

Everybody enjoys a person with a smile – a happy person. Happiness is an indication that all is well with the world around us and the world that awaits us. The promises of Jesus for those who are faithful to Him and His Words should make all of us celebrate every day.

As Catholic people who celebrate the feast of Easter, the bodily resurrection of Our Blessed Savior, we need to smile and be happy that we are now free to enter heaven. In the meantime, we are free to live our lives in communion with our Risen Saviour, knowing that He has conquered death by His death on the cross and His resurrection from the dead. No longer are we confined after death to a place of darkness, as were the people of the Old Testament. The gates of heaven have been opened to us. Heaven, a life of eternal joy and peace, is our gift from God. The only condition God places on us is that we live our lives here in harmony with His commandments.

Unfortunately, not all Catholic people respond to Easter and its preceding days of Holy Thursday and Good Friday as the central and most important Catholic moment in history. Many Catholics, young and old, have never experienced the sacred action of the Holy Thursday celebration of the Passover dinner during which Jesus changes the unleavened bread and table wine into His Body and Blood and the priests of the Church wash the feet of the designated Apostles and then re-consecrate themselves to God and His priesthood. Nor have the majority of our Catholic people participated in the Good Friday memorial in honor of Jesus crucified – walking the Way of the Cross. How many of our Catholic people, young and old, can say that they have witnessed the blessing of the new fire and the candlelight celebration at the Easter Vigil during which the candidates and catechumens for baptism, confirmation and Eucharist are received as new members of the Church? Most Catholics who practice their faith are content simply to attend Easter Mass. It is sufficient for them. But they miss the graces and blessings of the important preparation days. It is good that Our Lord did not miss them. Otherwise, there would not have been an Easter Sunday. Thank you Lord.

It Is I Myself

On Easter Sunday the Apostles gathered together in fear and great anxiety, waiting in the upper room where they had celebrated the Last Supper. We can hardly blame the friends and companions of Jesus for their fears, since they had witnessed at a distance His bloody crucifixion and death on a cross.

Suddenly Jesus, now risen in His glorified body, stood in their midst. The Apostles were terrified, but Our Lord reassured them, "[I]t is I myself. Touch me and see…." (Luke 24:39) Then He ate a piece of baked fish to show them He was real and not a ghost.

While Jesus remains hidden to us today under the consecrated bread and wine of the Eucharistic celebration, He has occasionally revealed Himself visibly. Perhaps the most celebrated appearance occurred in 1673 to a Visitation nun, Sister Margaret Mary Alacoque in Paray-le-Monial, France. Jesus appeared to her over a two-year period, showing her His Heart. "My Divine Heart," He said to Sister Margaret Mary, "is so passionately fond of the human race." But Our Lord mourned the world's indifference, coldness and thanklessness and asked for a communion of reparation on the First Friday of each month. On one occasion, Sister said she saw Christ with His five wounds dazzling as five suns. This was the beginning of the nine First Friday devotions to the Sacred Heart of Jesus, which has continued to this day.

Our Catholic faith reminds us that we need not see Jesus to know and believe that He is present to us daily in the Eucharist. As members of the Catholic Church, we believe Jesus is risen and now awaits our return to Him after death. Then we will see Him immediately as our loving Saviour and forgiving Judge. It will be a great day, if we are ready.

Lazarus, Come Out

We all have favorite people in our lifetime – friends that we truly enjoy spending a day or two with and people we trust with our confidences and life stories. Jesus had such a trust in Martha and Mary and their brother Lazarus of the town of Bethany. In fact, Jesus spent an evening with them prior to His death on the cross, at which Mary anointed His feet with costly perfumed oil and dried them with her hair. (John 12:3-7) Mary and her family were special in the affections of Jesus.

Yet when Lazarus was stricken with a deadly illness, our Lord did not come to his rescue right away. He waited instead, until Lazarus died. Such a response from a best friend was bewildering to Martha and Mary. Martha complained to the Lord that if He had been there, Lazarus would not have died. In response, Jesus assured her that her brother would rise. Then Jesus commanded: "Lazarus, come out!" (John 11:43) To the amazement of all in the district of Bethany, Lazarus, dead for four days, arose from his tomb and continued to live again for many more years. The apparent delay of Jesus was deliberate. He wished to teach Martha and Mary and all of us that as Son of God He has power over death. For Jesus, death is merely a transition from this life of temporary hardships and pain to a new life of eternal joy and life with God.

Since none of us has experienced death as yet, it is only human that we have a natural fear of dying. Yet Jesus reassures us "I am the resurrection and the life; whoever believes in me, even if he dies, will live, and everyone who lives and believes in me will never die." (John 11:25-26) In these words, Jesus is speaking of eternal life – not life in this world as we know it. It is, rather, the eternal life of the soul that begins at our baptism – the image and likeness of God known as sanctifying grace. We nourish that eternal life of the soul through daily prayer, good deeds offered to God and the sacraments, especially the Eucharist and confession. The only real, permanent death in the eyes of God is mortal sin, if there is no repentance. Otherwise, we all live in the eternal life of God. Lazarus never lost his real life – God's friendship. Neither should we.

Our Soul Is Priceless

Is it not amazing how much we spend on our bodies in our lifetime, both in feeding and clothing these "vessels of clay?" As our bodies continue to age through the years, we consume endless vitamins and prescription medicines in order to extend the health and life of our bodies. But ultimately we need to leave them in death so that they can return without our soul back to the earth from which God made them.

On Ash Wednesday each year, the priest or parish minister marks our foreheads with ashes from the blessed palms and says: "Remember, man, that you are dust, and to dust you shall return." How fragile we humans are – that we return at death to the earth. Yet this is not true of the other part of us – our souls that live in and energize our bodies throughout our time on earth. The soul, created also by God is an immortal spirit that continues to live on – apart from the body. Since God created our souls to His image and likeness as an immortal spirit – like the created angels – we will continue to live, think, love and remember in our spirits after death. Since God is an uncreated spirit, we will communicate with Him and the angels on a spiritual level.

Our soul is our main possession. While the body assists the soul in good and in evil and will someday at the general judgment at the end of time return to the soul to participate in heaven or hell, the soul continues to live on after death. We say at the end of our Apostles' Creed: "I believe in the resurrection of the body and life everlasting. Amen."

Consequently, we need to wake up to the truth that the soul, like the body, needs attention through daily prayer to God, regular nourishment with the graces of the sacraments, especially confession, Holy Communion, and daily acts of love and kindness toward our family and neighbors. Unless we nourish our souls in this manner, we will remain cold and indifferent to God and others – and place ourselves in spiritual danger. We need to remain alert.

Grieving Is a Human Need

Losing a loved one in death – whether it be sudden or prolonged over years of suffering – is a traumatic event in any family. Whether we are close in affection or distant, the death of a relative or friend presents an element of grief for the living. The custom of a wake at home or in the funeral parlor allows the family and friends to share their grief together and to begin to accept the reality and finality of death. At the same time, the Christian family can appreciate the truth of the resurrection of their loved one into heaven. But in every instance our human grief is something we need to deal with.

In some cases, people withdraw in their grief and hide – leaving the world of reality behind them. Some, blaming God for allowing death, cease their prayer life, leave their religious obligations and enter their own man-made cocoon. This particular grieving over a loved one may extend for years.

It is unfortunate for a family who declines to have a wake. Even for one day, a wake is an opportunity for families to talk, recollect and relive the good memories of their loved one. Wakes assist the underlying grief of the family and allow a release of the mental anguish caused by death.

In the past, some have been scandalized by the old Irish wakes that lasted for days. They were times of celebration and partying – with a generous flow of liquids and foods. But they were also a time to release one's grief and accept the loss of the friend or loved one.

However we handle our grief, it remains a reality of our human nature. Some parishes have a "healing, grieving ministry" which meets to share "death and dying" experiences. They are only a phone call away.

What Belongs to God

At a point in time when God was creating the world, He decided to create man in His own divine image and likeness. (Gen. 1:27) Consequently, man became the image of God, reflecting God in every way, that is, until he sinned and shattered the divine image.

It was not until God sent His Son, Jesus, into the world to die for man's sins, that God restored and returned His divine image to all mankind. Now restored to God's family once again, man was invited to enter heaven after his life on earth. How can we ever adequately respond to God in gratitude for His generosity?

In the gospel story of the devious Pharisees and the Roman coin with the inscription of Caesar, the emperor, Jesus says we are to pay to Caesar what belongs to Caesar and to pay to God that which belongs to God. (Luke 20:25) Since the coin was struck with the face of the emperor, Jesus told them to return the coin to the emperor.

God is not interested in our money or earthly possessions, but He is interested in each one of us, made in His image and likeness. God says in effect: give your money to the emperors of the world; I am interested only in *you* – in every one of you who reflects my image and likeness. God, our Father, desires that all of His created children willingly return to Him so that He might lavish them with His love for all eternity.

However, if unlike a coin which has no life, we freely choose to shatter our divine image by rejecting God and His commandments, then by our sinful will we place ourselves in danger of an eternity in hell. One youngster defined hell by saying, "Hell is where God ain't, and that's what burns you up!" But our Catholic faith also reminds us that the absence of God to us in hell is accompanied by severe and eternal pain of soul and eventually body. It is equally true that we will enjoy not only the spiritual joys and happiness of heaven but also the complete health of our body – if we remain faithful to God to the end of our lives here.

We need to look at the coin of our soul and choose wisely. Prayer will help.

Using Our Talents

Some parents with small children in school express anxiety over their children's lack of ability to achieve high marks in school and consequently sometimes push their children to anxiety too. While those parents may be sincere in their interest for their children's development, they also put a lot of pressure on their children.

God blesses each one of us with certain gifts of mind and body and expects that we will use these gifts for the glory of God and the welfare of others and ourselves. Those blessed with gifts of musical talent or artistic talent please God when they become musicians and artists and exercise their talents.

But sad to say, there are people in the world who through laziness, excessive alcohol or drugs, waste their talents. I have been told that many so-called "street people" were successful people at one time. Then something happened in their lives and they retreated to the streets. In effect, they buried their talents. This is the one thing that Jesus advises against. Probably all of us waste our God-given gifts and talents at some point in life, due simply to neglect or lack of gratitude to God. Yet when the grace to amend our lives is given to us, we need to respond in sorrow and gratitude. As long as we are alive in this world, we can start again – with God's grace.

Remember that our place in heaven is not determined by the amount and degree of talents given to us by God but rather how well we use and develop the talents that God has bestowed upon us. That boy or girl in class who might have appeared slow and awkward might outshine all of us – especially in heaven.

Varia

My Sheep Hear My Voice

Pope John Paul II has designated an annual "World Day of prayer for vocations to the priesthood and religious life." This papal request may not seem important to some people, but at the present time the need for priests and religious men and women is very important to the life of the Catholic Church. With the growing retirement of older priests and the decline of young people showing an interest in a religious vocation, the bishops are faced with the growing problem of filling their parishes with fewer pastors and parochial vicars. Fifty years ago, many parishes were blessed with two or three priests; today these parishes have one priest. In rural areas today, one priest is assigned to two or three parishes.

Vocational Directors in the nation have tried a variety of methods and programs to attract young and old to consider a vocation to the priesthood or religious life with little success. It would seem that more and more directors look to prayer to God as the best method. But no one as yet has been able to accomplish this method of prayer for vocations successfully. How do we get our people to pray for vocations, especially since they seem to show little interest in the subject of vocations?

Years ago, in Ireland, most families prayed the rosary together, after which they prayed what they called "the trimmings of the rosary." These were special intentions of their daily life and work. One of the favorite "trimmings" of every family was "that young John or Andrew would become a priest." Apparently, the trimmings were very successful since Ireland has furnished priests throughout the world for years. In Florida, there is an abundance of Irish priests – respectfully referred to as "F.B.I.'s" – foreign-born Irish. The pastor of one parish has four priest brothers – all from Ireland. Unfortunately, the custom of the trimmings never made it to the United States. Even the practice of the family rosary is seldom heard of among our Catholic families. Perhaps that is one reason why vocations to the priesthood and religious life are on the decline. Fr. Patrick Peyton, who was called the Rosary Priest, often said: "The family that prays together, stays together." If family prayer returned, maybe vocations would resume. It would be a good thing.

Vocation: Everybody Has One

I suppose it is natural for most of us to think of vocations as belonging only to priests and religious, since today the Church has such a great need for priests and religious. But the fact is that everybody has a vocation or calling to serve God – but maybe not as a priest or religious. Instead, the main calling of God to us is to the marriage state or single life.

Most young people are inspired by God to raise a family – as were our own parents. Others serve God as single teachers, nurses and social workers. All of these people in the world are following their vocation or calling from God.

It is true, however, that God also calls some to priesthood and religious life. Why then are there so few young people entering the seminaries and religious houses? The answer may be that many who are called by God at various times in their lives choose to ignore or to refuse God's invitation.

Our Lord gave us the parable of the word of God – the good seed from heaven – falling upon hard ground, or among weeds and rocks, and dying. Our lack of daily prayer, our involvement with pleasures, both pure and impure, our love for money and life, all tend to make us deaf to God's constant invitation to serve Him in a special way.

Can we blame God for a lack of servants of God, or are we to blame? In the Old Testament, God led His people to the Promised Land, but despite His wonders, His people chose to ignore Him for other worthless gods. We are doing the same thing today.

In the Old Testament, a rejected God let His people wander in the desert for forty years. Not one of them entered the Promised Land. Unless we respond to His voice today, we may suffer the same fate. He is calling us, but we choose not to respond.

Jerusalem

The Hebrew word "Jerusalem" is translated "city of peace." But if you read the newspapers, Jerusalem today is anything but a peaceful city. Three groups – Jews, Palestinian Arabs, and Christians – all lay claim to the city of Jerusalem. Crowds of young and old are fighting daily over their claim to ownership of the city.

The Jews claim ownership since the beautiful Temple of Solomon occupied a central importance until its destruction in 70 A.D. by the Roman armies. The Arabs claim that Mohammed ascended to heaven on the rock of the temple – called Dome of the Rock – in the Temple area. Christians lay claim since their Divine Leader, Jesus, was received as an infant in the Temple, preached to the people there and throughout the city, and finally was judged, crucified and ascended to heaven from Jerusalem.

There is very little real peace among these three groups of people. So it is difficult for the city to live up to its name – "city of peace." One suggestion was made recently to put "God" in charge of the city. Perhaps He could bring peace to all the disagreement and discord. At first, this seemed like a good idea, but it got lost amid the fighting and skirmishes in the streets.

Perhaps we, from a distance across the ocean, are too ready to criticize these disagreeing peoples, when we face very similar problems in our own country. Today in the U.S., Catholics, Protestants and Jews are at odds daily with each other over our schools, our worship especially in the marketplace, and our moral beliefs in society. Some claim from a letter of Thomas Jefferson that a wall of separation of church and State exists which extends to any public act of religion, like prayer to God. Unfortunately, our Justices of the Supreme Court have agreed with this theory. So in the U.S. of America, we hardly live in a city of peace and certainly not in the city of God. But we can still continue to pray – privately – that these things will change for the better some day. God bless America!

Prepare For Heaven

As the snows begin to appear in the North, many older retired people make their preparation to travel south to warmer climates. Leaving behind their heavy clothes and winter apparel, these snowbirds make their way by car, train or plane. One thing they need to take with them is their faith and their prayer life – otherwise they will travel spiritually naked.

No matter where we live or travel in this world, we always need to keep God in our vision. If we are to eventually reach heaven at the end of our life, we need to point our spiritual compass toward heaven. When John the Baptist spoke to his followers, he was like a voice crying in the desert to prepare the way of the Lord. (Matt. 3:3) His message of preparation was one of penance and repentance of sin. John's preaching eventually led to his death by beheading.

It is possible and more than probable that Catholics and others faithful to Jesus Christ will seemingly "lose their head" in the eyes of the world – a place where God and material possessions are at odds with each other, where spiritual values will be put down in favor of secular regulations.

At a public high school in June 2001, a senior girl who called herself a Catholic objected to prayer at her graduation ceremony and obtained an injunction from a federal judge forbidding prayer at the event. At the graduation ceremony, one senior boy – on his way up to the platform for his diploma – stopped abruptly and bowed his head in prayer before continuing to the platform. Another senior sneezed very loudly so that all could hear, to which the class in chorus called out "God Bless You." As the senior girl in question went up for her diploma, the class in chorus booed her.

It is a sad time – in a country that prides itself in life, liberty and the pursuit of happiness – that our young people must use subterfuge to honor their Creator at a public event.

God must laugh through His tears at such a country, much as He cried over Jerusalem, which had turned against Him. We need to pray and do penance for America.

Hang the Ten

Recently in the local newspaper there was a report of a Lockport man – a substitute teacher in the high school – who “wanted to have the kids grow up with some values.” Consequently, he lobbied the County Legislature, city councils and town, village and school boards to hang the Ten Commandments in schools and public buildings. Naturally, the New York Civil Liberties Union protested. What else is new! However, the man’s efforts to “hang the Commandments” met with approval, according to the newspaper, in the Niagara County legislature, the Lockport Common Council and several other town and village boards in the county. Would the God of Moses not have reached down from the heavens to embrace and encourage such a man? As for the Civil Liberties people, I dare say, the God of Moses would have very little time for them. I am not sure how much good the posting of the Ten Commandments would do. But in this world – with the killing of the unborn, the horrible abuse present among people, the open pornography in the media and in general, and the daily violations of God’s commandments – the posting of God’s laws would be a welcomed sight.

The words “Honor your father and mother” might have influenced the son who shot his parents and then went out to celebrate the evening. Perhaps the knowledge of “Thou shall not kill” might have had a good effect upon the child who shot another child. How many people, young and old, would have second thoughts if the words “Thou shall not commit adultery” were impressed in their daily lives?

We are a nation that has lost its soul. We have caved in to the sinful ways and culture of the Sodom’s and Gomorrah’s of the Old Testament. God promised Abraham that He would spare the city of Sodom if He could find ten just men. But God could not find even ten. Consequently, He destroyed the city of Sodom and all its inhabitants by fire.

Such a fate could await a nation or country today that has turned its back on God and His divine laws. It’s not too late to come back to God. But many may not.

Store the Right Treasures

Most Americans, but not all, can find all kinds of treasures for others in rooms and closets of their homes, in the hidden but valuable stocks and bonds and in their well stocked bank accounts. Some may cry poormouth, but another look and investigation will reveal how rich and wealthy we all are with this world's goods.

In Luke's gospel (Luke 12:13-21), our Lord exhorts us to guard against greed and store up the treasures of God's grace and eternal life, becoming rich in the things that matter to God.

Yet for the rich and the comfortable, this exhortation of Jesus is not easily accepted and is accomplished by only a few. Many older American families who remember the depression era of the 1930's are reluctant to trust the banks; they hide their monies, fearful of losing any. Younger families with children save some of their monies, investing some in their children's education – yet spending liberally now on cars, homes and enjoyable pursuits. For many young single people, giving a small portion of monies to the Church and other religious organizations is not a priority until they need the religious services of sacraments, Catholic school and parish assistance. Occasionally at death, there are a few people who, remembering their parish benefits, will leave a sizable amount of their estate to the Church and related charities.

It is always interesting to note how family members of a deceased relative respond to the Legal Will of the deceased. If someone is favored over the other by the Will, it may cause a dissension that lasts for years. Some relatives are upset that they received less or nothing at all. But in most cases, the deceased family members leave their possessions to the family members who cared for them during their lifetime.

If Catholic people would follow the instruction of Jesus, they would release their monies and possessions to those who are less fortunate during their lifetime and concentrate on acquiring the spiritual treasures and blessings of the Lord. Jesus reminds us on another occasion: "Do not store up for yourselves treasures on earth, where moth and decay destroy, and thieves break in and steal. But store up treasures in heaven, where neither moth nor decay destroys, nor thieves break in and steal. For where your treasure is, there also will your heart be." (Matt.6:19-21) Become wise in the Lord.

Put God in Charge

One of the first rules a wise traveler learns is to travel with very little baggage – just enough to take care of the immediate needs. A carry-on case is sufficient and allows the traveler to be free to move quickly.

Our Lord takes us one step further when He speaks of His requirement for being His disciple. Jesus addresses the crowds: "[E]veryone of you who does not renounce all his possessions cannot be my disciple." (Luke 14:33)

Earlier, when Jesus commissioned His Apostles, He told them not to take money, a sack, a second tunic, sandals or a walking stick. (Matt. 10:9-10) Jesus did not wish to burden His Apostles with unnecessary baggage that might hold them back or hinder the proclamation of the Good News.

We are reminded of the rich young man who asked Jesus what he must do to obtain eternal life. Jesus told him to keep the commandments. The young man responded that he had observed all these things from his childhood. When he asked Jesus what he still lacked, Jesus replied: "If you wish to be perfect, go, sell what you have and give to [the] poor, and you will have treasure in heaven. Then come, follow me." (Matt. 19:21) At that, the young man went away saddened because he had many possessions. (Matt. 19:22)

Divesting ourselves of our earthly possessions is a difficult task, especially when we are not used to being generous. There are some Catholic people who have signed over annuities and stocks to the Church to be paid upon death. One wealthy Catholic woman left one million plus dollars for her parish Catholic school in the South.

A very simple procedure would be to put God Himself in charge of your family and your finances. Then just follow His directions. You may be surprised how well God provides for your family and your possessions.

Love For The Poor

Many times there is a great variance in daily practice and life between our life and the words of Jesus. In the gospel of St. Luke (Luke 14:13), Jesus tells us that when we hold a banquet, we should invite the poor, the crippled, the lame and the blind. The closest resemblance to this admonition may be found in the many so-called "soup kitchens" in the city, where a daily meal is served for the less fortunate. I do not know of any individual Catholic families in suburbia that reach out in meals to the less fortunate or physically impaired. Throughout suburbia there is a growing number of adult homes for the impaired people who live in the community, but I am not aware that their neighbors – Catholic or otherwise – invite them to their homes, even for a meal. In fact, there are people in suburbia who protest and try to stop such adult homes from coming into their neighborhood. In more recent years, there are Catholic and non-Catholic people who work in conjunction with the Catholic Charities program for the immigrant families arriving from Africa and Europe – helping them to become settled in their new home in America. Certainly this charitable assistance is noteworthy and pleasing to God.

But the average Catholic family is too busy taking care and providing for their own family to become involved in this Gospel message to the less fortunate. Perhaps an occasional contribution at Church for the missions or Catholic Charities satisfies families that they are doing enough for the poor. Only Jesus really knows how generous we have been and how generous we could have been to the less fortunate.

Jesus Himself spent His entire life of 33 years reaching out and assisting the poor, the blind, the lame and the castaways of society. He would touch and embrace them with love as He cured them of their infirmities. If we were to follow His example, we would never pass by someone less fortunate without helping him. In so doing, we would be helping Jesus Himself.

Money And God

It is amazing what money and the lure of money do to people. In the case of family inheritance, money and its acquisition can separate and divide families quicker than anything else. To be disinherited by a husband or wife or by a father or mother causes pain and anger that sometimes lasts a lifetime. It is sad that we Catholic people allow something so insignificant as money to overcome us so much.

The newest media attraction, "Who Wants to be a Millionaire" with Regis Philbin, is a prime example of people's attraction to acquiring money. The show is so produced that it allows a contestant who hopes to win a million dollars to stop at anytime with the money already won, but the lure of the million dollars propels the person to continue to guess wrong and lose the large amount and then has to settle for a much smaller amount. The person's greed for money becomes his downfall on the program.

Our Lord in St. Luke's gospel reminds all of us: "No servant can serve two masters...You cannot serve God and mammon." (Luke 16:13) When money and acquiring wealth becomes our obsession in life, we gradually have less time for God and our religious obligations. As prayer to God becomes less important, so too does our regular attendance at Mass and the sacraments. We become like the rich man who dined sumptuously each day. (Luke 16:19) When he died, he cried out to Abraham to send Lazarus with relief from his torments, but Abraham told him that there was a great chasm to prevent anyone from crossing over. (Luke 16:26)

With God's grace, everyone is able to enter heaven. But the wise rich person does well to share his riches with God's poor while he has time.

It is better for all of us to acquire and invest our riches in heaven. One of our best investments is our prayers and Masses for the Poor Souls in purgatory who, in thanksgiving, will pray for us on our way to our final judgment and beg God's mercy for us before Jesus, our Eternal Judge. It is nice to have friends in heaven.

The Nation That Prays Together

In the months after September 11, 2001, Americans continue to suffer the effects of the terrible and horrifying destruction of thousands of American lives at the hands of suicidal terrorists. This unbelievable tragedy, however, has awakened the consciences and hearts of all of our American people. The American flag flies proudly at homes and businesses everywhere; our churches are crowded with people who feel the need to pray to God for understanding and sympathy for the dead. God is very much alive in the land of the free and home of the brave. Heroes in the uniforms of firemen, nurses, volunteers and even a priest appear in great numbers. Father Patrick Peyton, the priest who championed the family rosary, used to claim, "The family that prays together, stays together." Today, he might also say, "The nation that prays together, stays together."

Suddenly what began as a terrible tragedy is slowly becoming a silent blessing for our nation. God has returned to America – though He never left – and people everywhere are alive in Him. The pettiness and jealousies of our society seem insignificant in the light of the present devastation. Our President and national leadership are united to strengthen our country and bring a sense of peace, based on justice. America is slowly returning to the ideals and moral principles of our founding fathers.

The feast of the Holy Family celebrates the family life of Jesus, Mary and Joseph when Jesus was only twelve years old and was found teaching in the Temple. "Did you not know that I must be in my Father's house?" Jesus responds to his mother's anxious question. (Luke 2:48) This obedience to His Father eventually culminated in the painful offering and death on the cross in satisfaction for the sins of mankind. Yet Jesus rose from the dead on Easter Sunday and now invites everyone in the world to follow Him to the cross and to heaven. In the liturgy on New Year's Day, we celebrate World Peace – a goal of all nations. We must pray to God our Father for this great gift. "The world that prays together, stays together." Prayer to God is our key to peace – everywhere.

Peace Be with You

The very first word our Risen Lord spoke to His Apostles and to His followers upon His resurrection from the dead was "peace." Before and after Jesus (B.C. and A.D.), the world has tried to find peace without much success. Seldom has any country or any person looked in the right direction. There is only one person that can truly bring lasting peace, and that person is Jesus, the Prince of Peace. But hardly anyone will admit to that truth. So everyone wanders aimlessly trying to obtain peace and, as a result, fails.

It has been observed by many over the past twentieth century that we have witnessed more wars and destruction than during the previous nineteen centuries. Yet it was early in the last century in 1917 when God sent His Mother to a small village in Portugal called Fatima, where she appeared to three small Portuguese children, Lucy, Francesco and Jacinta. She revealed to the children that God desired that the world consecrate itself to Her Immaculate Heart and observe First Saturdays in Her honor. She showed them a vision of hell and told them that more souls go to hell because of sins of the flesh than for any other reason.

Mary said that she would return and ask that the Pope, in union with the bishops of the world, consecrate Russia to Her Immaculate Heart. She said that if the Holy Father would comply, then God would bring peace to the world. If not, she said that Russia would scatter her errors throughout the whole world. The final part of Mary's message – which Pope John Paul II recently revealed to the world – concerned the death of a pope. We need to pray for our Holy Father.

We know that it took 67 years before the Pope complied with Mary's request. Meantime, the world struggled through World War II, the Korean War, the war in Vietnam, and numerous wars and conflicts throughout the world.

Our Lady predicted that the Pope would delay her request but, eventually after tribulations and chastisements, God would bring an era of peace to the world. We have to speculate how peaceful the world would have been earlier, had our Holy Father responded immediately to Our Lady's request. Do we all not respond to God in the same way? Tomorrow or next year is time enough to repent and confess, we think.

Go to Your Room

Many people who live busy lives occupying most of the hours of the day look for a quiet remote place where they can relax and find some moments of rest and peace. Wherever that place is, it becomes a hide-away for a short time. Our Lord reminds us, "But when you pray, go to your inner room, close the door, and pray to your Father in secret. And your Father who sees in secret will repay you." (Matt. 6:6)

This "inner room" of Our Lord has no walls, furniture or air. It is the "inner room" of our soul – a place within each of us, where we can be alone with ourselves and with God – if we invite Him. Sometimes the busyness of our daily life disallows these silent times – but we need to schedule them if we are to meet with God. When Elijah, the prophet, went up Mount Horeb, the Lord came to him and told him that He would be passing by. At first a strong and heavy wind rushed through the mountains, but the Lord was not in the wind. After the wind, there was an earthquake, but the Lord was not in the earthquake. After the earth-quake, there was fire, but the Lord was not in the fire. Finally there was a quiet voice, the voice of the Lord. (I Kings 19:11-13) Our Lord came in a tiny whisper. He does the same today. In the quiet of our soul, the Lord makes His visit to us.

Some parishes are fortunate to have Perpetual Adoration of the Blessed Sacrament, whereby people may come for a period of time, perhaps one hour, and spend that time alone with their Eucharistic God. Whether in the early morning, afternoon, or evening, the Eucharistic Lord remains exposed for adoration 24 hours a day all year round. There we meet our God face to face. It is a great privilege. It will only be in heaven itself that we will again enjoy the very presence of God.

Meantime, let us "go to our inner room" often and visit with our Father. He is always waiting with open arms.

Fishers of Men

Every successful businessperson appreciates a windfall in his or her business ventures. Bill Gates, the world's richest man, started with a simple computer and, today, because of the immense appeal of computers throughout the world, he is a billionaire many times over.

So too did the simple fishermen along the Sea of Galilee, who would spend nights fishing with little success, discover a secret. One day, after His Resurrection, Jesus told them to cast the net over the right side of the boat. When the fishermen obeyed Him, they were hardly able to pull it in because of the number of fish – 153 large fish. (John 21:5-6)

Some of us go through life depending on our own efforts and talents, only to be disappointed with our results. Then a few people learn the secret of true life and invite the Lord God to take charge of their ventures. Things can only change for the better. Just as Peter and the Apostles learned that Jesus made the difference between success and failure in fishing, so too we will learn that God's presence makes the difference in our lives.

Naturally, God is more interested in our spiritual success rather than our material achievements. Though many people base their success in life on their bank accounts, Jesus recommends that we seek treasure in heaven instead. To the rich young man, Jesus challenged him to sell what he had and give to the poor. (Matt. 19:21)

I believe one of the best and easiest ways to obtain treasure in heaven is through daily prayer for the Holy Souls suffering in purgatory. As a soul is released to heaven by God because of our daily prayer, the blessed soul I believe will return the favor of praying for us not only while we are still on earth but especially as we approach the judgment seat of God. These blessed souls will be favorable witnesses for us before God. If ever we needed friends, we will need them at that time of our particular judgment. Do not miss this great opportunity for prayer. You will be very surprised and pleased with the results.

Thankfulness Is Becoming a Lost Art

The nine lepers cured by Jesus are not the only ungrateful people in the world. Everyone gifted by God with physical and spiritual health qualifies – since so few people think enough of their Divine Provider to thank Him daily in word and action.

Even our gratitude to one another is lacking in many families – namely our gratitude to our fathers who spend most of their lives trying to provide us with food, shelter and education; our gratitude to our mothers simply for the nine months of pain and sacrifice awaiting our births and then another twenty years waiting upon our needs. Probably few Catholic people have thought to express thanks to the priests who baptized them and gave them First Holy Communion, or even to the bishop who confirmed them.

I personally remember daily in prayer a particular postman and bakery lady who were generous and kind. Children especially, I think, are grateful for kindness that comes unexpectedly from parents and friends. We need to be more like children in our appreciation of God's many gifts to us.

Thanksgiving is an important day in the life of our nation since it provides everyone with an opportunity for thanking God for our nation of freedom, something many nations do not have. But one day alone should not be our only day of thanks to God and to one another.

Jesus, through His Church, provides Catholics with a daily opportunity of offering thanks to the Father in the Eucharistic celebration. In every Catholic church daily, we are privileged to offer the sacrifice of the Mass – in gratitude to God for all He does for us.

May we always remember to give thanks to our great God – Father, Son and Holy Spirit.

Practice Makes Perfect

The sports world provides us with some wonderful displays of developing perfection, whether it involves a baseball player hitting over sixty home runs in a season, a football player who exceeds over 100 yards of running during every game, or a golfer who breaks all the records of golf at every tournament. These people and others in the sports world attract the attention of hundreds of thousands of fans. The results of these efforts of sports stars seem to the ordinary sports fan to be attainable until they themselves try to accomplish them. Suddenly we awaken to the truth that many years of practice and failure are represented in the stars' present accomplishments. Perfection in the sports world or in any phase of life requires lots of time, effort and practice.

These same qualities are equally true in the spiritual life. Yet Jesus encourages all of us: "So be perfect, just as your heavenly Father is perfect." (Matt. 5:48)

Years ago, Catholics were presented with three steps of perfection: the purgative, illuminative and unitive ways. Probably, most of us are still in the first step – the Purgative Way – battling with our sinfulness daily.

Usually a day seldom passes that we do not speak or act uncharitably, find fault with everyone else, and in general, offend God through our sinfulness.

There are some who have stepped up to the Illuminative Way – whereby sin no longer has any hold on us. We basically enjoy a very good relationship with God and our neighbor. Daily prayer is a normal part of our life's activity.

A person in the Unitive Way, united to God, needs no formal prayer – they simply love God totally and see Him present in all His creatures and creation.

Perhaps at some times in our lives we experience for a short time three ways of spiritual perfection, even though we remain in our human struggles toward our goal. The two important helps in our journey are daily prayer to God, especially Mary's rosary, and the daily Eucharist. St. Therese of Lisieux, the Little Flower of Jesus, discovered a third help in her vocation – namely love: love of God and love of neighbor.

Wherever we are in our spiritual journey toward God and heaven, we need to persevere. Even if we fail at times, like our sports stars, we need to continue on toward perfection.

The Widow's Mite

The widow's mite that Jesus refers to in Mark 12:41-44 was the smallest coin circulating in Jerusalem at the time. Nobody knows exactly which coins were give by the widow, but they were from a series of tiny bronze coins struck by the Maccabean kings. Perhaps we could compare them to our penny.

Our Lord compliments the charitable contribution of the widow who gave to the Temple of God from all that she possessed – even though it was a small amount. Our Lord in this instance was not criticizing or disdaining the larger gifts of the rich and famous. Rather, He was praising the sacrifice of the widow, who gave from her poverty.

In the Old Testament, God required that a tenth of a person's property or possession be given to His Temple for the priests' welfare. Known as "tithing," this practice was observed throughout the Mosaic period and continued to the time of Christ. (Matt. 23:23)

Some Catholic people continue to observe God's law of tithing – giving a tenth of their income to their parish church and charity. In a Midwestern parish of 2,500 families, almost all the parishioners tithe, resulting in an average total of $75,000 every week. This money is used to support all of the students' tuition in the Catholic elementary and high school and supports a parish medical clinic for the community. In addition, the parish has Perpetual Adoration of the Eucharist and sponsors a number of young men for the priesthood. Certainly, God has blessed the generosity of those parishioners.

Imitating the generosity of the widow in the Gospel, there are some poor people who, while unable to contribute financially to their parish, provide the equivalent of a tithe of time and assistance through their volunteer service as religious education teachers, lectors, Eucharistic ministers, organists, choir members, sacristans, secretarial staff, and a variety of other services.

Our Lord in His observation of the widow does not comment on the amount of the gift so much as the heart of the giver: "[S]he, from her poverty, has contributed all she had, her whole livelihood." (Mark 12:44) Will the Lord speak as well of us? It is possible.

Patience Is a Virtue

Driving your car on the Thruway can be a very threatening thing for many people, especially at the rush hour in the morning or evening. While I do not know of any instant cures for people in a hurry, there is the virtue of patience that may help some. The word "patience" comes from the Latin word "patientia," which means to suffer. When people cut you off in traffic or involve you in a fender-bender, a certain anxiety and suffering occurs. It is perhaps the human trait to respond in kind, by imitating the hurried driver. Accidents can occur as a result.

When we transfer our attention to the church parking lot Sunday before, after or between Masses, we discover that the same rules of conduct apply. We need to be patient with people and with ourselves. The rosary beads in our fingers may assist some to relax. Also the realization that children and infants are involved in many cars may bring a greater caution to others. One solution might be to arrive early for Mass and make prayerful preparation; another might be to spend some minutes of thanksgiving after Mass, aware of God's presence in us. In either case, we would avoid the rush at the time of Mass.

Prayer seems to be a good friend of patience and might prevent an accident or two. Besides, the Lord would enjoy your prayer. Think about it.

Pray with Your Heart

Prayer is nothing but conversation with God. It is easy. Yet so many people do not know how to pray.

Since we are both spiritual and physical in our makeup, we should use both our mind and body when we speak to God. Although the mind and heart are more important to prayer, our bodies are most useful. We can pray sitting, kneeling or walking – whatever suits our heart. But most necessary is our open heart and clear mind. When God speaks with us, He needs our full attention of mind and heart. We need to clear out distractions of our daily work and duties and open our heart to what He will say to us. Some people hear but do not really listen to God's Word. We must be like a mother who is listening to her child's tiny voice even from the other room. She is attentive to every breath or cry of her child. She listens, so as to assist her child in need. God listens to us and we need to listen to Him always and every day. He is always speaking to each one of us every day. We need to open our heart and mind to Him, if we are to know what He is saying.

When we were in religious instruction, we learned that this divine prompting is known as actual grace, the constant voice of God prompting us to do good and avoid evil. When we respond to that grace positively, we grow in God's image and likeness. It's not hard to do and we will find it very rewarding.

Prayer and Fasting

Can prayer and fasting influence Almighty God to intercede and resolve our problems? We read in the Old and New Testament how pleased God was with the prayer, fasting and almsgiving of His people. One of the most noteworthy was the command of God to the prophet Jonah to advise the people of Nineveh to fast and do penance; otherwise they would be destroyed. Because of their positive response, the people were spared. The people of Sodom and Gomorrah would not respond to Lot, God's messenger, and were totally destroyed by salting fire. Presently the Dead Sea reminds us of their sinfulness and refusal to respond to God.

We are reminded by St. Paul that fasting has more to do with acts of kindness and charity than it does with food and drink abstinence. God is more interested in a charitable heart than an empty stomach. In prayer God is more attracted by our heart than our mouth. We need to pray more from our hearts. Almsgiving has nothing to do with our income tax report. We need to assist the poor and be deprived financially without any hope of a return, except from God.

Prayer, fasting and almsgiving are strong weapons to dispel punishment and promote peace and God's friendship.

How Powerful Is the Rosary

In October 1571, the peoples of Spain and Portugal were waiting with great fear and expectation as the huge Turkish forces sailed toward their shores. Because the Spanish and Portuguese armies were far inferior, everyone expected that their countries and eventually all of Europe would be occupied by Muslims, thus threatening the Catholic faith of Europe.

During that approaching threat, Pope Pius V from Rome called on all Catholics in Europe to pray the rosary daily without ceasing. The people responded, and as the Turkish ships approached the shore, a great wind came up suddenly and drove the entire navy out into the ocean and they never returned. In response, Pope Pius V declared that day of Christian victory, October 9th, as the feast of the Holy Rosary.

As Catholic people, we are blessed to have that particular spiritual weapon – the rosary. The full rosary consists of a series of Hail Mary's, Our Father's and Glory Be's, and 15 meditations on the joyful, sorrowful and glorious mysteries of our faith. Recently Pope John Paul II introduced five luminous mysteries or events which reveal the public life of Jesus. Even one-fourth of the rosary is pleasing to God and His Mother.

St. Louis De Montfort in France tells of the great power of the rosary in his booklet "The Secret of the Rosary" (Page 63). He reveals that one day a very devout and penitential woman went to St. Dominic for confession and was given as a penance one rosary to say and advised, if possible, to say it every day. She excused herself, however, saying that she had her regular spiritual exercise and had no taste for the rosary. Later, in prayer, she had a vision of herself appearing before the Supreme Judge. St. Michael placed all her prayers and penances on one side of the scales and all her sins and imperfections on the other side. The tray of her good works was greatly outweighed by her sins and imperfections. When she cried and implored the help of the Blessed Mother, Mary took her one rosary and placed it on the tray of her good works. This one rosary was so heavy that it outweighed all her sins and imperfections. Imagine then the worth of a daily rosary. Mary's rosary, even five decades, is a very powerful weapon against the devil and all evil – and a great means of Christian perfection. Listen to St. Louis Mary De Montfort. He knows.

Prejudice Is an Ugly Disease

Adolph Hitler held a hatred for one race of people. In power, he sought to erase them from the face of the earth. Joseph Stalin in his lust for earthly power used his energies to destroy people whom he hated and distrusted. Northern and Southern Ireland, North Korea and South Korea, North and South Vietnam – so-called cultured people – have vented their anger and fear toward each other because of their differences over the past years. In recent years, Serbians and Croats, like the Jews and Palestinians, have clashed with each other over their differences. Who's right and who's wrong does not really matter since nothing permanently belongs to them – it all belongs to God, eventually. So why are they fighting and what are they fighting for? Nobody really knows or understands.

Much of a person's problem areas begin early in life with what has become known as prejudice – a word that means to "pre-judge." For reasons of family and neighborhood education and upbringing we learn early in our life to classify certain people with the same tag or emblem. If some Irish friend drinks too much whiskey, we might assume that all Irish drink too much – which is a false prejudice. Perhaps in our growth development we listen to pre-judgment of our parents and friends about other nationalities and cultures and falsely assume pre-judgments about all. What is apparently true about one person does not apply to the entire nation of people.

Very often Catholic people receive a bad rap from the prejudice of many. The modern media is a case in point. It is refreshing at times when the modern media writes and speaks without prejudice about the Catholic faith and the Church.

The expression in the press of "the Hail Mary pass" and "the Immaculate Reception" on the occasion of a football score parallels the earlier reference many years ago of "hocus pocus" for magical events – a clear prejudicial reference to the Latin consecration prayers of the Mass.

A good solution to our prejudice is an honest respect for every person – accepting that person for what he is before God – someone made in His image and likeness, yet with faults and failings. Only God is perfect. The rest of us need God's grace to improve.

Temptation

Years ago it was popular to place a St. Christopher medal on the dashboard of a car in the hope of travel protection. The magnetic power of the medal would keep it in place. But in cars today, there is hardly any metal to attract St. Christopher.

Jesus is our Divine metal, so to speak, drawing us back to God. We are daily being drawn away from God through the world's attractions. This is how the devil tempts each one of us – away from God and toward himself.

The devil even tempted Jesus – first through his hunger, then through vanity in the world, and then through pride. But each time Jesus responded "No" to these temptations. We need to respond in the same way. But we, in our weakness, need the help and presence of Jesus and Mary to succeed. With Him, we can do all things.

While the devil can try to attract and seduce us, he cannot prevail over our free will. We can always freely reject temptation. All the saints were tempted in their lifetime, but they knew enough to turn to God for help in persevering in goodness and holiness. Even St. Augustine would pray "O Lord, help me in my unbelief." We all need to pray daily to God.

Some Catholic people erroneously consider temptations sinful and wish to confess them, especially temptations of impurity; but they are not sinful unless we deliberately take sinful delight in them. If we immediately begin to pray and call on God, Mary and the saints for help, these temptations remain only temptations and are a means to receiving God's grace, by rejecting them.

Some might wonder why God allows the devil to tempt us, but unless we are tried, how can we show our free choice for God during our life?

Who Will Take Responsibility?

Our seven Supreme Court justices who voted in 1973 to approve abortion in the Roe/Wade decision will not accept responsibility for April 20, 1999 in Littleton, Colorado. Our former Chief Executive in the White House, President Clinton, who signed his approval for the abortions of all infants in the womb, even those who are already leaving the womb, does not accept any responsibility for school violence. Principals, teachers and even religious leaders who are caught up with the pro-choice/pro-abortion movement, together with all those in America who sponsor and approve our cultures of death, shy away from any responsibility. The media, especially the film and video industry, admits no wrong for promoting violence. Meantime, fifteen people at the Colorado high school are dead from gunshot, and many others remain injured.

This reminds us of the old story about the three persons: everybody, somebody and nobody. Everybody was aware, somebody assisted, but nobody took responsibility.

Our Holy Father, Pope John Paul II, speaks constantly of the culture of death that our world has created through our approval and practice of abortion, pornography and euthanasia. But so far the world is not listening or acting to make a change of direction toward a culture promoting life. Consequently, the "Littletons in Colorado" will continue everywhere in our country and throughout the world. A change is needed. Since this world will not provide an answer, we must depend on Almighty God. Families need to reestablish daily prayer to God in their home life. Only He knows the answer, which He will provide if we ask daily and as a nation. He needs to be back in our government, our schools, and our homes. "God Bless America and the world" needs to become more than words – if violence is to change to peace.

The Power of God and Prayer

In 1973 the U.S. Supreme Court handed down a decision that legalized the abortion or killing of unborn infants in the womb. Even though recently the woman involved in the decision has recanted and joined the pro-life ranks, the court decision continues to be the law of the land.

Since the Court's ruling, it is estimated that over 35 million infants in the womb have been destroyed by medical means or devices. Financially, this murderous procedure has been very profitable for the medical profession involved. Psychologically, it has been very destructive for the mothers and fathers of the unborn infants.

It has been predicted that a nation that kills its children will eventually come to its own destruction. This demise of a nation will affect everyone, whether they favor a pro-life or pro-death mentality. Everyone in the nation will come under punishment since most Americans show little interest or fail to do anything to correct the situation.

Our Catholic people, together with other pro-life people who were asleep in 1973, have awakened to the horror of abortion and have rallied to reverse this abortion trend in the U.S. Their pro-life efforts over these years have witnessed a crusade for life which has partially stemmed the pro-abortion movement, but which still has a long way to go before bringing about a change of heart. Human efforts are not enough. We need to look at the divine efforts of God.

In the Old Testament, in the Book of Judges, when Gideon went to battle against the enemies of Israel, God reminded him that he had too many soldiers. When, in obedience to God, he reduced his rank to three hundred men, God led them by His strong arm and vanquished all of the enemies. God can and will do the same today, but only if we ask Him. With powerful prayer to God and trust in Him, Gideon successfully won the day in battle, despite the overwhelming odds. God only needs our trusting hearts to vanish our enemies and to win over those still searching for the good and holy.

The most powerful action we can take to put an end to abortion and reverse the "death mentality" culture developed in our country by the pro-choice forces is daily prayer to God and Our Blessed Mother. As has been shown throughout the history of the Church, prayer will bring change for the better. This is not to demean all the other efforts of the pro-life movement! But the real answer is prayer – and from everyone. God, if asked enough, will bring the change from death to life. Even one "Our Father" and one "Hail Mary" can bring victory over sin. "Better to light one candle than to curse the darkness." Begin today!

Turnabout Is Fair Play

"Cartoonists are poised to bush-whack the new president" – so the newspaper proudly proclaimed a few months ago. The thought and purpose of the cartoonist's article was based on his professional belief that leaders of our free society were open game to ridicule and mockery, just because cartoonists and others live in a free and critical society. He did not mention that there were any restrictions or rules in his free and unfettered "profession" – if that word is applicable to cartoonists. Political cartoonists seem to enjoy a freedom in character drawing without limit – whatever is their fancy of that particular day.

Certainly, our leadership is not without sin or imperfection, and some humor and honest description of behavior is good for everybody – but distortion and unfair humor at the expense of someone in the limelight is uncalled for. Nobody appreciates being "made fun of" – at least not in the public press.

It would be interesting if someone who is "fair game" in the press and who had the skill of a cartoonist were to draw some public cartoons for the public media of cartoonists in their everyday life at home and in their offices. Imagine the critical cartoonist portrayed with all his faults and failings – with the wife or the editor standing by. Would that meet with their approval?

After all, everybody is only kidding. Right?

The Blessings of a Catholic School

When Catholic people gather for a social or party, the conversation will very often revolve about their early Catholic school experiences with their teaching sister or nun. Seldom is there praise for the teacher; more often they recall some punishment meted out to them from the nuns. My reaction to their appeal for some self-pity is quiet amusement. It would seem that discipline was totally absent in their home or that they never merited correction of any kind.

The word "discipline" means "to learn" – to learn the truths that our Father in heaven has revealed to us to appreciate. Our Catholic schools are, and have been, schools of learning and discipline. Although our schools presently lack the plentiful presence of nuns or religious sisters, they have very dedicated lay men and women who enjoy the task of teaching and disciplining our Catholic students in the love and knowledge of God and His Church. Every student is the temple of the Holy Spirit and requires a special attention and instruction, so as to be formed as a meaningful citizen in the world and a future citizen in the life of heaven. Without the larger recompense, as provided in public education, our Catholic teachers continue to assist the Catholic education of each student.

Catholic parents today have to make additional financial sacrifices since very little is provided from the public sector. Nonetheless, the spiritual growth as well as the material well-being is important. Public education could learn a lot from Catholic education. Both public and Catholic education should be partners for the benefit of the students. Both would benefit.

Plan Your Summer

Summer is vacation time for many families. Perhaps it means more leisure time at home but, for some, summer includes travel.

When we travel, necessarily we plan a destination like Disney World. If we go by car, we need the AAA trip maps so that we can avoid the road construction and arrive in the shortest and safest way. If we go by air or train, we travel the safest and most economical way. We are happy to arrive at our destination and return safely.

If this is our method in this world, why do we not use it for travel to the next world – heaven? First we need to plan to go to heaven since arriving there does not happen by accident. As most of us hardly know the way, we need direction from God's leader, the Catholic Church, established by Jesus while on earth. Then we need to use the travel means and method designed by Jesus to travel in the right direction, principally the Ten Commandments, the seven sacraments, daily prayer, penance and charitable good deeds. In addition, Jesus has provided invisible guides to assist us in the form of protecting angels, Mary and the saints. All we need do is to ask their help.

It seems simple enough. Why do people make it so hard to attain? With God's help and direction, we will arrive at our heavenly destination with ease. His yoke is easy and His burden is light. (Matt. 11:30)

Do Whatever He Tells You

Can anyone fathom a completely obedient world – even a single obedient nation – one that listens to and obeys God's instruction and Word to the fullest? First of all, in such a world, every citizen, young and old, would live strictly according to God's commandments. There would be no need for a police department, since there would be no crime. Everybody would love God and neighbor and would freely live in harmony with each other. This type of living might best be described as "heaven on earth." With God in command, only blessings would result.

Something like this happened on earth in the town of Nazareth 2000 years ago when a young couple entered the covenant of Jewish marriage. "Joseph, son of David, do not be afraid to take Mary your wife into your home…She will bear a son and you are to name him Jesus…." (Matt. 1:20-21)

Now if we could multiply and imitate the life of Joseph, Mary and Jesus in our parishes and cities, we too might attain a taste of "heaven and earth."

I personally remember two couples – one in Hamburg and another in East Aurora – that reminded me of Joseph and Mary. So it is not an impossible life. Yet it does require obedience to God and His laws of love. When I entered the homes of these couples, I sensed immediately the presence of God – even the environment and atmosphere within the home spoke of God. A crucifix greeted you at the front door. They were not ashamed to promote the presence of God's Son on the cross as a sign of their Catholic faith. Many Catholic families keep the crucifix in their bedrooms – if they have a crucifix at all. They seem to hide their Catholic faith for fear of criticism. God has promised us that everyone who acknowledges Him before others He will acknowledge before the Father. (Matt. 10:32) And the contrary is also true.

Mary always affirmed her Son. She lived her affirmation and consecration every day of her life. Mary always stood by Her Son – right to the cross. So can we, if we will try.

Freedom

A lot of people talk about freedom, but few really appreciate its meaning. True freedom has responsibilities and boundaries to observe. Our civil laws allow us to drive a car as long as we observe the laws of safe driving and are aware of others on the road. We are not free to disregard signals, stop signs and speed limits – otherwise we may lose our freedom to drive.

The same rules apply to the moral laws given to us by God. We are blessed by God with the freedom of life, liberty and the pursuit of happiness. But freedom does not give us a license to kill, steal, cheat or malign others. We will lose our freedom and, if convicted, we will be confined in prison. There is no freedom in prison. In God's world, if we abuse our freedom through serious sin, we are eventually confined in the prison of purgatory for a time, or in hell forever.

Unfortunately, in some serious instances, our civil laws protect the criminals. Abortionists and their associates kill the unborn children, and our civil laws protect them with very little objection or protest from the majority of Catholics. Their kind of freedom, protected by the Supreme Court, pretends to give the abortionists the right to kill and to give the pregnant mother the freedom to choose to kill her infant in the womb. They call themselves by the name of "Pro-Choice," as if they may freely choose to kill their unborn infant, without any responsibility to the child or to society.

Fortunately, this so-called freedom without responsibility, like all distorted "freedom," will not stand up before the judgment seat of God, who still continues to govern His world and soon will judge every individual He has placed on this earth. "I believe in Jesus…He ascended into heaven, sits at the right hand of the Father; from thence He shall come to judge the living and the dead" – we pray daily, in our Apostles' Creed.

We are free to love God and His people, but we are not free to violate God's commands. Adam and Eve learned that lesson when God drove them from the Garden of Eden. Up to the point of their deliberate sin and rejection of God, they were free. But they chose otherwise and became prisoners of sin.

Are we not doing the same thing in America by our deliberate rejection of God – by our abortions, pornography, greed, materialism, and hatred of others – even family members?

We need to seek true freedom by returning to God, His commandments and sacraments. Only Jesus will make us free again.

Practice What You Preach

When the tiny woman in the white religious garb entered the exalted and venerable assembly of the United Nations a few years ago, the nations' representatives could barely see her because of her size. But once aware of her presence, everyone immediately stood up, without exception, to greet and honor her. Her name was Mother Teresa from Calcutta, India. They all recognized someone who loved and cared for the poor and the despised ones of the world. She literally lived the poverty and charity that she openly promoted in her speech.

In His words to the scribes and Pharisees of His day, Jesus chastises them for their plethora of words and instruction to their people and for the lack in their own personal conduct. He observes: "For they preach but they do not practice." (Matt. 23:3)

This counsel of Jesus is a reminder to all of those appointed over others and who influence others by their office: priests, parents and public officials. Priests, who ought to be men of prayer, must set the prayerful example for their parishioners; parents need to watch their words and actions before their listening and observing children; public officials need to practice honest service for those whom they represent. When these authority figures neglect to set the good example for others, the entire society suffers.

If we understand properly the true meaning of sanctity as honesty, purity and truthfulness toward God and our neighbor, we would value the need for saints and holy people in our world. A world that encourages immorality, pornography, abusive behavior and even abortion of the unborn is sick and is in need of healing and forgiveness. Only our prayerful request to God can bring the necessary cure for our sinfulness and restore our world to sanctity and goodness. In past times, God called forth outstanding men and women to be our witnesses for holiness. We need some today.

Do God's Will

In a southern U.S. city live twin sisters, both widowed, who spend many waking hours knitting afghans and hats for the orphan families in Afghanistan and Bosnia. They estimate that they have made about two thousand hats and two hundred afghans. The yarn is all donated by interested people. The twins live on Social Security, but they believe that this work is their apostolate for the less-fortunate, and they are more than pleased to do it.

In Luke's gospel (Luke 5:27), Matthew thought his task in life was collecting taxes. But God had greater assignments for him. Instead, Matthew was called by Jesus to collect His Divine words into a beautiful gospel for the world to appreciate God's Son. Of the four gospels, Matthew's is the longest and most detailed. Although as a tax collector he was considered to be a sinner, Matthew rose above this public denunciation to follow Christ. As a result, he died as a saint of the Church.

Sometime in our lifetime, each one of us has to rise above the public opinion and judgment of the world in which we live. Whether we are young or old, whether we are at home, in school, or in the business world, our peers find reason to judge our actions and put us down. Wise is the person who does not allow either flattery for our successes or criticism for our failures to influence our manner of living. With a "thank you" and a "God bless" to our friends and adversaries, we need to continue doing those things that please God.

If Mother Teresa of India had halted her work of charity at the first critical remark, the world would have lost a great apostle of India. Even St. Peter balked at the prospect of dying for Christ until he met Jesus on the Appian Way. St. Peter turned back and was crucified upside down.

God has given every person an apostolate to perform in conformity with His Will as well as the grace to achieve it. Motherhood and fatherhood are certainly among the highest apostolates – to raise a family in harmony with God. Mary and Joseph are prime examples for all to imitate. We need only to pray to God to know His Will for us and then accept His grace to follow Him.

What Does A Blessing Do

"Please bless me Father, for I have sinned," the penitent prays at the beginning of the Sacrament of Reconciliation. The same penitent dips his or her hand into the holy water basin at the entrance of the church and blesses himself or herself "in the name of the Father, and of the Son and of the Holy Spirit." What is a blessing but a prayer of petition to God to be present to us, protect us and forgive us from our weaknesses and frailties?

From the time of Abraham, whom God blessed through the words of the high priest, Melchizedek (Gen. 14:19), to the present Catholic priest at the Mass of the Blessing of Candles on February 2 – "God Our Father…bless these candles and make them holy. May we who carry them, praise your glory and come to the light that shines forever." – Almighty God has desired to live with and be recognized by His creatures. Hence He will bless everyone and everything in the world and will invite all back to His warm embrace.

But He has seen fit to give us free will. He needs to be invited by us. "Please bless me, Father" is our opening invitation for God, our heavenly Father, to enter our daily life.

"Bless us, O Lord, and these thy gifts which we are about to receive from your goodness through Christ, Our Lord," we say in blessing at meal time.

On February 3rd, the feast of St. Blase, we invite God to bless our throats from all disease and affliction. Hundreds of times during each day we are free to ask God's blessing upon our daily activities from the time in the morning that we ask God to watch over and protect our children and families to the hour at night when we as parents mark our children on the forehead, "I bless you in the name of the Father, and of the Son, and of the Holy Spirit."

Just as God watched over Abraham, our spiritual father, so He watches over all His offspring down through the centuries. Today, together with the Jewish and Arab nations, we as Catholics look to Abraham as our spiritual father and invite God our Heavenly Father for His blessing of peace upon all peoples of the world.

Peace

When Mother Teresa, who founded the Missionary Sisters to the Poor in India, stood before the assembled representatives at the United Nations several years ago, they asked her a simple question: "Mother, what is the distinguishing quality of your Catholic faith – marking it different from other faiths?" Mother Teresa, from her small four-foot stature, replied in one simple word after a long pause: "Peace."

At every Mass, the priest says, "The peace of the Lord be with you," and we Catholic people respond to one another, "Peace be with you." But what are we saying when we say "Peace"? Where does peace come from – but from God. What does it mean – but the goodness of God.

A beautiful hymn says, "Where there is charity, there is love; and where there is love, there is God." We might add, "And where there is God, there is peace." In order to possess "peace" of mind and soul, God must occupy our entire being. We need to invite Him into our minds, hearts, and souls, since He will come if we freely invite Him. "Come Holy Sprit, fill the hearts of your faithful, enkindle in us the fire of your divine love." Like the sunshine that fills a room, God's grace will fill our hearts – and we will have peace.

Today the families of the world need this gift of peace in the face of all the turmoil and quarrelling among nations – and only God can gift the world with peace. If everyone could only turn toward God in daily prayer – "Lord, send your peace upon this sinful and disturbed world" – peace would come. It would not be a false peace from some signed proclamation, but a genuine joy and happiness of living in God's Will.

Mother Teresa and her religious sisters possess very little of this world's gifts, but they do enjoy the peace of God that comes from charity to "the poorest of the poor" on the streets of India and the world, and the love that returns to them from God.

So the next time the priest at Mass says, "The peace of the Lord be with you," do something with it. Bring peace and charity to someone in need; do not just say the words. Otherwise, the Lord's peace will return to Him – without nourishing anyone or anything.

Peace!

Jews and Gentiles

As Catholic people who are not born Jewish, we need to be very thankful to a prominent member of the Jewish leadership for our Catholic faith, Saul of Tarsus. Saul held the garments of St. Stephen and gave his approval as the people stoned Stephen to death. But Stephen prayed for his persecutors and consequently Saul later was suddenly converted to Jesus and was baptized as Paul. St. Paul then traveled the coasts and cities of Asia Minor bringing the faith of Jesus Christ to the non-Jewish people, the Gentiles. Meantime, St. Peter, the leader of the Apostles, confined his attention to the Jewish world.

It is interesting that today very few Catholics have a Jewish heritage – as if the faith of Jesus was lost to the Jewish race. Most Catholic people find their ancient heritage in the non-Jewish world. Yet Jesus, his parents, his Apostles and the early Christians were Jewish. Some Catholic scripture scholars believe that the Jewish nation will accept the Catholic faith before the end of this world.

Certainly, God's Son, Jesus Christ, who remains a member of the Jewish race together with his mother, Mary, and foster father, Joseph, has a special love for his natural heritage, the Jewish race. However, until all these things come to be, we, as people who have inherited a wonderful faith and religion, remain indebted to two great men, St. Peter and St. Paul, who remained faithful to Jesus Christ through life and death. Should we do less for our Catholic faith?

We Need Encouragement

On June 11th our Catholic world celebrates the feast of St. Barnabas, a name that means "son of encouragement." The Apostles gave him this name because he was a great source of encouragement to St. Paul, both at the beginning and end of his ministry.

We all need encouragement and support from other people, especially from our family and friends, and we need to provide it for others. How little time does it take to phone a friend and compliment him for his efforts in doing a particular good? Does it take much time to write a letter of encouragement to someone who may be discouraged? The word "courage" comes from the word "heart." Many people spend their lives taking the "heart" out of people, while only a few are putting the "heart" back in.

The Sacred Heart of Jesus and the Immaculate Heart of Mary, whom we honor especially during May and June, symbolize the great love they show daily for all of us. Yet we hardly respond to their love. Through our daily prayer life and faithfulness to the commandments, let us petition them for the courage to live our lives in harmony with their intentions. We can encourage our families and friends to do the same. Let our daily prayer be: "Pure Heart of Mary, be my love; Pure Heart of Jesus, be my salvation."

Our Mountain

Directly across the sea from Rome, Italy, near the country of Croatia, is the small village of Medjugorje, surrounded by very tall mountains. It is there that six young people of the village claim that Mary, the Mother of God, has visited them daily since June 24, 1981. No one sees her except the six boys and girls. She is called by the Croatian title of "Gospa," Our Lady of Peace. Her message to the world is that God exists and desires the return of all of His children back to Him. She began her initial appearance on the side of a mountain and then invited the children to ascend the mountain for daily visits. The villagers have followed the six visionaries daily up the mountain – despite the sharp rocks and steep path – in order to be with the visionaries in their daily visit with "Gospa." Since 1981 millions of people from the countries of the world have visited the village of Medjugorje and have climbed Apparition Hill and Cross Mountain. They pray the rosary and make the Stations of the Cross as they climb.

It would seem that as God invited Abraham to climb the mountain with his son, Isaac, for a sacrifice, and Jesus invited Peter, James and John to climb Mount Tabor with Him to meet His Father, so God invites all of us to climb our own mountain of pain and sacrifice daily in order to eventually reach the Father.

Peter, James and John, together with the other nine Apostles, were willing but slow to believe in Jesus. They were like many of our Catholic people today. We want to believe in all the truths that Jesus has revealed from His Father, but our fallen human nature gets in the way. When our spiritual life is rosy and enjoyable, we find our Catholic faith easy to follow; but when pain, sickness and death enter our life, we sometimes balk and falter and look elsewhere for a more enjoyable faith experience. Our Lord never promised an easy way. He only promised a cross – yet He Himself will help us carry it.

Consecration

After the bishop ordains a man to priesthood through the imposition of his hands, he proceeds to bless with holy oil the fingers and palms of the newly ordained priest. As a result, the new priest is set aside as holy, or consecrated as a priest of God. No longer is he a layman, but a consecrated priest forever.

An act of consecration, however, is not reserved to priests or religious alone, but all may, by their own willingness, consecrate themselves to God forever. As a result, they commit themselves to God and promise to serve Him as lay people, whether married or single. Our parishes are filled with dedicated lay people who serve God and the Church in various ways.

Some people consecrate themselves every May and June to the Sacred and the Immaculate Hearts of Jesus and Mary. Others in recent times consecrate themselves to God the Father and pledge to live their Catholic life in harmony with God. Such people are naturally drawn to holiness with their close relationship with the Blessed Trinity. But still there are a large number of people who prefer not to become involved in the matter of piety or as some say "with religion."

Within recent years, Catholic married couples have formed "Teams of Mary" consisting of 5-6 couples that desire to grow together in goodness and holiness. They meet as a team monthly to share a modest dinner and discuss their common triumphs and failures in the spiritual life as husbands and wives. They also pray together and strive to grow together spiritually each month. It is interesting to observe their trust and love for one another. A team invites its own priest-counselor to each meeting. In one parish that invited 1,000 couples to join, only 7 couples accepted. In some cases, one of the married parties was unwilling – indicating perhaps a fear of growing spiritually or an unwillingness to try to change set ways of life. Whatever the reason, many are not drawn to be closer to God. They are content to be where they are – spiritually and religiously. Too bad! Sanctity is a great gift, as many will discover some day.

Prophet of the Most High

"As you are anointed priest, prophet and king, may you live always as a member of His body, sharing everlasting life," the Catholic priest proclaims as he anoints with holy oil the newly baptized baby. In Catholic life, we are fairly sure about priests and kings, but maybe our role as a prophet is not well understood.

In the Old Testament, God relied on His prophets to convey His messages to man. From the prophet Isaiah to John the Baptist, who was the last prophet of the Old Law and the first of the New Law of Christ, God communicated with His people. The prophet Jonah was sent by God to warn the people of Nineveh that their wickedness had brought about their destruction. (Jonah 1:2) The prophet Daniel was enabled by God to interpret the dreams of the great King Nebuchadnezzar. (Dan.

2:45) The prophets were not always believed and consequently suffered great rejection and even death. Yet they were spokesmen for God.

In the New Testament, apart from John the Baptist who announced Him as the Messiah and Lamb of God (John 1:29), the office of prophet is shared by all at the time of baptism. Every baptized Catholic receives the dignity of priest, prophet and king. In particular, this office of prophet is exercised in the Catholic priesthood. The priest preaches God's Word to us.

However, this does not dispense the Catholic layperson from the obligation to teach God's Word, both by speech and example. Parents need to convey to their children the truths of the Catholic faith. Catholic teachers in classrooms have a great opportunity to bring God and His commandments to their students. Even Catholic students among their peers need to exercise the prophetic duty.

Prophets today may not have a one-to-one relationship with God, but a regular practice of prayer and penance will improve that difficulty. Try it and find out.

Love One Another

In His last days on earth before His death, Jesus told His Apostles "I give you a new commandment: love one another." (John 13:34)

Since that moment, the entire world has struggled with that commandment. Just in this previous century, many nations have gone to war against their neighbors. Dictators have used their power in Germany, Italy, Russia, Cuba and other countries to impose their will upon the people – to the detriment of millions of their own citizens and of the neighboring countries. Loving one another has not been the governing motive of the world since the time of Christ.

Presently, the Jewish nation and the Arab Palestinian nation in the Holy Land are fighting intensely over Jerusalem, the City of Peace. Both of these people derive their origin in Abraham, yet they have very strong feelings of dislike and even hatred toward each other. Recently, their leaders met with our President at the White House without resolving their differences. Our own country has imposed an embargo for many years on Cuba because of the dictatorial government that denies its citizens freedom of speech and travel, together with other denials of human rights. As a result of the embargo on products into Cuba, the people of Cuba have suffered. Perhaps one of the worst cases of abuse of freedom is in China, where the people live under a very strict pagan dictatorship. Apart from a very small group of Chinese Catholics who practice their Catholic faith secretly and privately, most of the Chinese have no knowledge of Christ.

I think it is safe to say that there are people living in these countries who do love each other, despite the government. But, unfortunately, this commandment of Christ is not the standard of the government.

Even the United States – which defends its Constitution guaranteeing the right to life, liberty and the pursuit of happiness – legally permits abortion at any stage in the life of the unborn infant. There is no love in the murder of the unborn.

I do not know of any man or woman anywhere who can solve the world's lack of love. Only God and His Divine Son, Jesus, can accomplish this feat. We will wait and see.

Summer is a Good Excuse

As the weather becomes nice and warm, the Sunday Mass attendance seems to decrease. Perhaps some Catholic people can use weather as an excuse for not attending Sunday Mass. "It's too hot or it's too cold" seems to be a reason for staying at home. People who excuse themselves lightly may also find excuses for morality or immorality in their life as well. "It is only a small lie;" "I deserve to have this;" "God does not care;" "After all, we are in love." All these excuses add up to a life lived by our own rules.

It is difficult to deal with this excusing and lackadaisical attitude. The Church's response would be to encourage such people to wake up to the reality of God and the spiritual life of the soul before God wakes them up with sadness and pain. Some parents with children like that spend their life trying to impress them with moral and spiritual value in their later years, and some – to no avail.

No one can force another to live so as to enter heaven. We can only invite. Many times this invitation meets only with silence. But we cannot stop trying. The most attractive quality in a person is holiness. But many have yet to discover this.

Father Merrick

Very few eyes were dry during the wake and funeral Mass in May 1997 of our well-beloved Fr. Merrick Bednar. People from everywhere lined the aisles to pay their tribute to a priest who had lived fully for them in his priesthood and who could no longer be contained in this world. In his brief thirty-three years, he managed in his meticulous manner to assist thousands of people, young and old, to appreciate the value of living a life fully, even though in pain and suffering.

Fr. Merrick's source of assistance was in his prayer life and in his family life. Both carried him through trials and tribulations. He also allowed an occasional golf game or a ride in the latest new car to bolster his spirits.

We are all better people in every way for allowing Fr. Merrick into our lives, even for a short time. God bless Fr. Merrick, his mother, Peg, as well as his family: Michael, Michele, Mitch, Maggie, Mollie, Martial, Mark and Maura.

The Servant of All

One of the titles of Pope John Paul II is "Servus Servorum Dei" – the servant of the servants of God. Jesus emphasizes this title on Holy Thursday when, prior to celebrating the first Eucharist and the Sacrament of Holy Orders, He knelt and washed the feet of His Apostles and said to them, "If therefore, I, the master and teacher, have washed your feet, you ought to wash one another's feet. I have given you a model to follow…." (John 13:14-15)

However, in our American parlance, the word "servant" conveys the idea of a subjected person – even a slave as in the days of the Civil War.

People who migrated to America from Africa were often sold into slavery to the wealthy landowners and became slaves or servants of a particular household. President Abraham Lincoln eventually freed these people from slavery so that they could live apart responsibly.

The Church has returned to this Christian title by ordaining men to the order of "deacon," which means "servant." The word no longer connotes "slavery" but "Christian service" to others. Although there are other men who are ordained to the traditional diaconate who then continue to the priesthood, there is a growing number who as a celibate or married man choose to be permanent deacons servicing the Church. They continue also in their normal occupation whether single or married. Many parishes and institutions are blessed with the service of these permanent deacons.

Our Holy Father, Pope John Paul II, certainly merits the title, among others, of "Servant of the servants of God." Despite physical and spiritual handicaps of mind, body and soul, John Paul reaches out to the poorest of the poor – traveling to the farthest end of the globe to meet them and invite them to stand firm in the faith and even to return from a faith left behind years ago. Someday we may be referring to him as John Paul the Great. He merits the title. It is also possible for us.

Msgr. Richard T. Nugent
Biography

Msgr. Richard T. Nugent was born March 4, 1925, in Buffalo, New York and baptized Richard Thomas at St. Margaret Church in Buffalo. He was the second son of John E. and Dorette E. Millring Nugent. The family included Richard's three brothers – Rev. John E., Thomas, and Robert F. – and four sisters – Patricia A. Walsh, Noel Nancy Nugent, Dorette (Babe) Zilliox and Carol F. Gruber.

He attended school initially at St. Margaret School under the St. Joseph Sisters. After five years at the Little Seminary High School and College, Buffalo, he attended St. Bonaventure College and Seminary, graduating in 1945 and 1949 with B.A. and M.A. degrees.

Father Nugent was ordained to the priesthood by Bishop John F. O'Hara on June 4, 1949 at St. Joseph New Cathedral, along with 17 other seminarians.

His first priestly assignment was as the administrator of St. Mark Church in Rushford, NY, a small 50-parishioner parish near Rushford Lake. He spent the next summer as chaplain at the nearby Scouthaven Boy Scout Camp and was then appointed in 1950 as an assistant pastor of SS Peter and Paul Parish, Hamburg, NY. After four years, he was assigned as assistant pastor of Immaculate Conception, East Aurora, NY. In 1962 the bishop appointed Father Nugent as the Associate Director of Religious Education and of Religious Vocations. In 1965, he was named the Diocesan Director of Religious Vocations. In addition, in 1968 the bishop appointed Father Nugent as the Diocesan Director of Retreats and Associate Vicar of Religious. In June 1972, under Bishop McNulty, Father Nugent was made a Prelate of Honor. Finally, in 1974, he became pastor of St. Bernadette Parish, Orchard Park, NY, where he remains at the time of this book.

Msgr. Nugent was awarded the Junipero Serra Award in 1998 by the Buffalo Serra Club. In that same year, he received the Mother Colette Hilbert Award from Hilbert College in Hamburg, New York. In 2000, Msgr. Nugent was honored with the Curé of Ars Award by Christ the King Seminary, East Aurora, NY.